The Mendacious Colours of Democracy

The Mendacious Colours of Democracy

The Anatomy of Benevolent Lying

Alex Rubner

ia
imprint-academic.com

Copyright © Alex Rubner, 2006

The moral rights of the author have been asserted
No part of any contribution may be reproduced in any form
without permission, except for the quotation of brief passages
in criticism and discussion.

Published in the UK by Imprint Academic
PO Box 200, Exeter EX5 5YX, UK

Published in the USA by Imprint Academic
Philosophy Documentation Center
PO Box 7147, Charlottesville, VA 22906-7147, USA

ISBN 184540 049 6
9781845400491
A CIP catalogue record for this book is available from the
British Library and US Library of Congress

www.imprint-academic.com

Dedicated to Judith in loving memory.

Without her this book and other publications of mine would not have seen the light of day.

Also by Alex Rubner

Fringe Benefits
The Ensnared Shareholder
The Economics of Gambling
The Price of a Free Lunch
Three Sacred Cows of Economics
The Export Cult
The Might of the Multinationals

Contents

Acronyms and Abbreviations viii

Preface 1

Part A

Chapter I   The Nature of Mendacity 7
    The Saintly Perfectionists 7
    A Restrictive Definition. 11
    The Three Modes 17
    Mendacious Vocabularies 20

Chapter II   How and Why We Lie 29
    Eclectic Mainsprings 29
    Institutional Mendacities 40
    Some Writers Lie 45
    For Good and Bad Causes 52

Chapter III   The Convoluted Motives 87
    The Knots of Altruism 87
    The Consequential Effects 97
    Passive Lying 108
    Biblical Prophecies 122

Part B

Chapter IV   The Blotted Democracies 131
    From Pericles to Blair 131
    The Crosses Borne by Democratic Politicians 144
    The Whimsical Electorate 157

Chapter V   The Furtive Saviours 179
    Four Prescriptions 179
    External Disciplines 187
    Dishonesty To Do Good 200

Chapter VI   The Tools of Their Trade 209
    Après Nous le Déluge 209
    The Inflation Gadget 217
    Esoteric Contrivances 229
    The Attractions of Capital Goods 237
    Some Deplorable Obscurities 247
    One Plus One Is Not Always Two 256

Chapter VII   Two Vague Conclusions 267
    Democratic Governance 267
    The Truth About Lying 272
    The Hazards of Telling the Truth 278

Bibliography of Sources 281

Index 287

Acronyms and Abbreviations

BoE	Bank of England
CEO	Chief Executive Officer
CBI	Confederation of British Industry
DDR	Deutsche Demokratische Republik (Communist East Germany)
DM	Deutsche Mark
ECGD	Export Credits Guarantee Department
ERM	Exchange Rate Mechanism
ERNIE	Electronic Random Number Indicator Equipment
EU	European Union
FSA	Financial Services Authority
FT	*Financial Times*
GDP	Gross Domestic Product
GNP	Gross National Product
GESTAPO	Geheime Staatspolizei (Nazi domestic secret service)
HoC	House of Commons
IMF	International Monetary Fund
KGB	Russian Secret Service
LBC	Left Book Club
LDC	Less Developed Country
LSE	London School of Economics
MP	Member of Parliament
NCB	National Coal Board
Multi	Multinational Corporation
NHS	National Health Service
OECD	The Organisation for Economic Cooperation and Development
PC	Politically Correct
PFI	Private Finance Initiative
PR	Public Relations
PSBR	Public Sector Borrowing Requirement (deficit of state budget)
RPI	Retail Prices Index
SS	Schutzstaffel (Hitler's bodyguard)
UN	United Nations
VAT	Value Added Tax
WHO	World Health Organisation
WWI	1914–18 World War
WWII	1939–45 World War

Preface

Part A (chapters I to III) defines, elucidates and exemplifies mendacity.[1] Part B (chapters IV to VII) dwells on the blemishes of democracy and discusses why many well-meaning politicians in democratic countries deceive the electorate. I am arguing that the nature of representative democracy impels altruistically-motivated elected parliamentarians to feel entitled to lie to their voters. My compilation passes over the perfectionists (among whom are John Wesley, George Washington, St Augustine) who oppose lying in *all* circumstances — even 'to save the souls of the whole world'.

While telling-the-truth is generally deemed to be praiseworthy, it can sometimes have disagreeable consequences. The *Book of Judges* conveys a salubrious warning to the devotees of truth who ignore the possibility of perilous consequences. Samson, a judge in Israel for twenty years, entered upon a sexual liaison with Delilah. Conspiring with the Philistines, the temptress urged him to tell her the source of his strength. At first he gave a false clue and this lie saved his life. Twice more she begged him to disclose the truth and again he deceived her. Delilah pestered him until he wearily divulged that the secret lay in his unshorn locks of hair. This enabled the Philistines to capture and torture him. They gouged out his eyes and he became 'Eyeless in Gaza'.

People lie actively by writing, shouting, winking and in several other ways. I have debunked the notion that passive lying is always less depraved. Lloyd George's estranged wife was a passive liar when she sat next to him in a court, where her husband lied on oath about his adultery. Her mendacity consisted of not uttering a single word in public.

---

[1] To tell untruths to torturers, sadists, child molesters, etc. is, in my view, morally justified, but I still connote such declarations as lies, for lies they are.

Chancellor of the Exchequer Denis Healey was a passive liar when he juggled with figures to give the false impression that inflation was lower than it actually was. The authorities (justifiably) lied in 1942 when they told the relatives of British prisoners-of-war that their dear ones had died in captivity while they were in fact killed inadvertently by a submarine of the Royal Navy. The Ministry of Defence was guilty of (unjustifiable) passive lying when, between 1946 and 1996, it suppressed the true facts. A wealthy fellow-traveller, the publisher Victor Gollancz, remained an avid liar in defence of Stalinism even after he was convinced that the accused in the staged Moscow trials had been framed. Gollancz chose not to disseminate the truth but provided the (British) Communist Party with facilities to lie actively by promulgating the supposed guilt of the accused and acclaiming their death sentences.

This book does not accentuate the lies which serve to enrich liars materially but highlights non-pecuniary motives. While many of these are related to benevolent lying, readers are invited to be wary of altruistic declarations as these often furnish alibis for undeserving liars. Moralists focus mainly on the intent of liars while I also lay stress on the ensuing consequences. Accolades are therefore only bestowed on benevolent liars when both the intent and the sequels are commendable.

The performance of the Biblical Jonah, concerning his role in the Nineveh affair, is scrutinized. He is emulated today by a host of secular, putatively scientific, predictors who seek to mislead the public. Writing in academic journals, they boast proudly of their 'clever' mendacity. Simultaneously, they plead that, as their motive in spreading false forecasts is laudable, they should be given recognition as meritorious liars. Numerous actual, allegorical and hypothetical illustrations have been gathered to elucidate diverse aspects of mendacity. Although my thesis has a global drift, and I have cited examples from many parts of the world, most of the events which I describe occurred in the UK in the 1951–2005 period. Economics is the provenance of many of these incidents. This is so, in part, because of my professional background. Moreover, economic and related political endeavours lend themselves more readily to lying than other themes. Sanitary engineers, pilots and professors of Italian literature are no less prone to lie but have fewer openings to become proficient liars.

Those who fought in the nineteenth century for universal suffrage did not envisage that, having been achieved, it would bestow one day upon largely uninformed and capricious voters the right to participate *directly* in the actual process of political decision-making. Their intended function was merely to select the parliamentary representatives. But today's electorate is much more demanding. The voters insist that they are entitled to instruct MPs on what to say and how to cast their votes in the HoC. In Marquand's superb depiction: 'the spectators in the stands have begun to descend on to the field'. As a result, politicians in the Western world are no longer in a position to respond to legislative proposals in accordance with their considered views. Politicians must decisively test the opinions of the electorate even though the majority of the public are ill-suited to arrive, on many issues, at logical conclusions. As the electorate's attitudes cannot be ignored, prudent members of parliament frequently omit to tell the truth. In order to do good, politicians are often even compelled to be dishonest. They engage in benevolent lying for otherwise, because of the likely obstruction by stupid voters, they cannot advance the national interest as they see it. Hence they feel pressured to resort to esoteric obfuscation, 'ripping wheezes', fudging, sleights of hand. Errant politicians have thus made it possible for praiseworthy measures to be adopted thanks to fudging, the manipulation of facts, recourse to subterfuges and even the articulation of outright lies. By these means they have smoothed the path to the consummation of meritorious laws.

Politics is a noble, but also a dirty, business. To resolve the dilemma of democratic governance, various influential persons have proposed the emasculation of the elected legislature by transferring weighty decision-making powers to non-democratic domestic bodies and foreign institutions. Leaving aside such extreme measures, all MPs who want to achieve something concrete must be prepared to employ unpalatable tactics. Our forbears would be shocked if they learnt that nowadays — in their retirement — British senior civil servants, top economic advisers, members of parliament and a host of cabinet ministers have not hesitated to publish frank memoirs in which they boastfully disclose how they cheated their colleagues and the public. These revelations, among a host of other sources, have furnished authoritative material which helped me to sustain the case I am propounding.

PART A

Chapter I

The Nature of Mendacity

> The nicest people are not always the most effective politicians
> *Denis Healey*

The Saintly Perfectionists

I am naming those, who are opposed to lying in all situations, the perfectionists. John Wesley, St Augustine and Immanuel Kant are famous proponents. When we deal at a later stage with those who do approve of lying under given circumstances, we shall be investigating separately the intentions and the consequences of the liars. Such a task is not called for when examining the performances of the perfectionists because they act as they do in the belief that the repercussions of all lies are automatically always pernicious. As an old English proverb would have it: 'It is even a sin to lie against the devil.' The religious foundations for this kind of totalitarianism, which allows for no exceptions, are well documented. John Wesley stated that those who lie because they think it will generate beneficial results deserve damnation; to the God of Truth, benevolent lies are an abomination. He subscribed to that ancient axiom: 'I would not tell a wilful lie to save the souls of the whole world.' In his autobiography Gandhi gave the impression that he also adhered to this absolutist creed: 'For me, truth is the sovereign principle ... the passion for truth was innate in me ... I never resorted to untruth in my profession.' Christopher Dawson, professor of Roman Catholic Studies at Harvard and one of the (few) modern perfectionists, pronounced: 'as soon as men decide that all means are permitted to fight an evil, then their good becomes indistinguishable from the evil that they set out to destroy'.

St Augustine was a sinner in his youth before be became an extreme religious perfectionist; fortunately he spelt out his messages in written detail. He wrote to a Spanish colleague to praise him for his zeal in raging against heretics. However, he also reminded him how illogical it was to draw them out of hiding by employing lies. Why, he asked, are we hunting them down? It surely is either so that we may teach them the truth or, by convincing them of error, keep them from harming others: 'Therefore, how can I suitably proceed against lies by lying? Or should robbery be proceeded against by robbery, sacrilege by sacrilege, and adultery by adultery?' St Augustine argued that God in not just an enemy of 'unjust lies' but of all lies: 'He who says that there are some just lies must be regarded as saying that there are some just sins. What could be more absurd?' He propped his vehement condemnation of 'beneficial lies' by outlining two hypothetical situations. He instanced a seriously ill patient who inquired about the well-being of his son. If one told him the truth, to wit that he had died, and in consequence the anguished father also dies, people might clamour that the patient had been slain. While St Augustine conceded that he had been moved by such an accusation, he nevertheless refused to acknowledge that telling the truth could ever be described as homicide. He supported his case by formulating a sensitive proposition: 'If you reject the wish of a "shameless" woman to have sexual intercourse with you and as a result she dies of a broken heart, will then chastity also be homicide?' St Augustine beseeched the purveyors of benevolent lies: 'It is not true that we sometimes ought to lie. And what is not true we should never try to persuade anyone to believe.' This outstanding perfectionist did speak of the occasions on which he had once felt pressured to rehabilitate 'compensatory aims', i.e. good deeds executed by bad means. He announced proudly that he had always overcome such temptations because he would have no truck with those who enunciate that lies are ever just. He said that he behaved as he did because, as a matter of principle, his faith knew of no reason to concede the existence of 'any lie that is not a sin'. Though he never said so explicitly, one may safely infer from his writings that he considered his absolute refusal to lie as being more meritorious than any means to alleviate the suffering of others. St Augustine proclaimed that he refused to countenance any exceptions to his hard guideline. Yet, he laid down that, despite all he had argued on this subject, one may make deliberately false statements with the intent to deceive if these 'are licensed by divine command or inspiration'.

The quintessence of the reasoning by the following three perfectionists is mainly of a secular nature. Samuel Johnson opposed lying for both bad and good causes because he opined that once one starts to tell a lie, whatever its kind, one is never believed again even when telling the truth. He also refused to tolerate benevolent lying because lying in general tended to destroy the 'confidence of society, weakened the credit of intelligence and interrupted the security of life'. Johnson feared that a well-intentioned lie would, just like an evil lie, spread the disease and affect adversely the body politic. His biographer did not agree with him. James Boswell maintained that every servant with any degree of intelligence understands that announcing to visitors that his master is not at home is not an affirmation of a fact but a customary phrase to indicate that the master does not wish to be seen; therefore there can be no bad effect from such a lie. Johnson would have none of this; he was not prepared to allow his servants to say that he was not at home when this was untrue: 'a servant's strict regard for truth must be weakened by such a practice. A philosopher may know that it is merely a form of denial but few servants are such nice distinguishers. If I accustom a servant to lie for me, have I not reason to apprehend that he will tell many lies for himself?' I have not come across any other perfectionist who is so obsessed with the evil of lying that he advocated, as Johnson did, cruel punishments for mendacity. Since many liars are 'so insensible of right and wrong, they might properly be awakened to a sense of their crimes by denunciations of a whipping-post or a pillory'.

Critics of the Scottish-German philosopher Immanuel Kant attacked his extreme perfectionism because 'it would make any society impossible' as it was not practical always to tell only the truth; furthermore it, was perverse to tell the truth when this harmed others. The fanatical Kant responded that lies always harm somebody — if not a particular person then humanity in general: 'To be truthful in all declarations is a sacred and unconditionally commanding law of reason that admits no expediency whatsoever.' Kant not only sneered at what he called the 'supposed' right of altruists to lie but went beyond this. He was prepared to share the truth even with people who had no right to know the truth. Kant stated explicitly that he would not exonerate any kind of lies just because of their ensuing virtuous consequences: 'It is a formal duty to tell the truth to everyone, however great the disadvantage that may arise from it.' One infamous illustration produced many negative reactions from contemporary commentators; even today few discuss Kant's other contributions to philosophy without mentioning it. He declared proudly that if a man, who planned to kill a given person, came to his house and asked him whether the intended victim was there, he would reply faithfully 'yes' (if such was the case). He strove to display unashamedly his conviction that it was better for the intended murder to be carried out than that he, the honest philosopher, should willingly participate in the evil act of lying.

American infants are already told in their cradles about the saintly first president of the US. By the time they go to school they will have learnt by heart what little George had said: 'I cannot tell a lie, Pa; you know that I cannot tell a lie. I did cut it with my hatchet.' Some historians claim that no such event took place. This may be so but national-political legends exert a powerful didactic influence and one may therefore deal with this celebrated saying even if it is historically flawed. The boy did not elaborate (not even when he was an adult) what had motivated him to be a perfectionist; he certainly did not bring religion into it. I have been particularly struck by his repeating the word 'cannot'; it appears to suggest that young Washington suffered from a mental and/or physical impediment that prevented him from uttering a lie if and when he might opt to do so. Normal persons have the choice to tell the truth or to lie. If they withstand the temptation to lie and choose to tell the truth, which could be painful or costly, one may applaud them for their heroic morality. But in the case of little George his genes or some other factors, over which he had no control, were responsible for his incapacity to make such a choice — his famous utterance implies that he was so programmed as not to possess the internal power to utter an untruth. A person, blind from birth, can honestly assert that he has never seen the sun rise; this is an unfortunate fact of life which, however, does not make him a hero. If George *could* not lie, then he is hardly a model for those of us who are able to choose whether to lie or tell the truth. (St Augustine has related how he had been in positions where he was tempted to lie but managed to withstand the temptation). But whatever has occasioned George's behaviour pattern, an important feature was brought to light, one which in my view is not creditable for a president of the United States. Little George, the youthful perfectionist, wanted it to be known that his make-up was such that he could not lie; we are expected to sing a song of praise for an individual with such an upright character. I question his probity. Never to lie — not even to save your country? Not even to convert heathens to Christianity? Not even to promise justice at home and abroad?

By commencing this book with a few remarks on perfectionists may misleadingly indicate that this is due to their weighty importance. The opposite is the case. While I could not have avoided mentioning their existence, they are today a tribe of little quantitative significance. I wrote about them at the beginning to clear the decks. My thesis is exclusively concerned with non-perfectionists. Today there is almost unanimous agreement that lying is at times desirable and morally justified. There are of course sharp differences of opinion on how, and under what circumstances, mendacity may honourably be employed.

A Restrictive Definition

Voltaire announced solemnly: 'If you wish to converse with me, define your terms'. It is in fact highly unrewarding to embark on a book which commences with a detailed definition. I have done so at my peril by delineating the core of lying at the start before specific aspects of lying are laid out. My search for an elaborate working definition was forced upon me for otherwise I would have had to call for divine guidance as St Augustine did when he wrestled with the concept of time. He prayed: 'For so it is, O Lord my God, I measure it; but what it is that I measure I do not know.'

> A sane person is a liar[1] when he disseminates *significant* messages, factual information and forecasts that *he* considers to be false. Lying is the *plausible* and *purposeful* deception of others by acts of commission and omission.

People lie explicitly and implicitly, orally and in writing. They act a lie non-verbally by gestures and the tone of their voices. They feign grief and pain. They lay false trails. Davenport-Hines has unearthed a doctored picture of Dorothy and Harold Macmillan sitting close together on a bench. They were an estranged couple but the sad Conservative leader did not want the public to know it. In fact they were seated with some distance between them. To gain reassuring publicity, the middle of the photograph was cut out. Dorothy and Harold were presented to the electorate as a harmonious pair. Christina Michalos[2] has described how a royal photographer doctored the picture of the Earl of Wessex's wedding; he replaced Prince William's unhappy expression with an aesthetically pleasing smile.

Lying is a personal endeavour. Governments, parties, churches and corporations are never mendacious. Only individuals, acting alone or in concert with others, carry out the actual lying though the impact of lies is frequently enhanced if the disseminators play a prominent role in notable — and particularly in respected — organizations.

'Where there is error, may we bring truth' is a phrase in a renowned prayer by St. Francis of Assisi. Per se, it is a valid avowal though it has a precarious implication: it sustains the widespread disposition to describe all who utter inaccuracies as liars. With very few exceptions every lie is indeed a factually flawed assertion. But, in the methodology which I am employing, it does not follow that all errors and inaccuracies are automatically lies.

---

[1] Giannetti would have it that animals too are capable of lying and has furnished some amazing illustrations. A stratagem, said to be employed by certain primates to avoid the physical aggression of threatening males, is to pretend to be hurt by, for example, ostentatiously limping. When the potential aggressor is nearby, the monkey limps but as soon as he disappears from the scene, the monkey again walks normally; if the threatening creature returns, the monkey suffers a sudden 'relapse'. Though the temptation, to include such clever animals in my definition, was great, I have resisted it.

[2] 'When The Camera Does Lie', *The Times*, London, July 20 1999.

What about persons who inadvertently relate the truth while being convinced that they are setting forth an untruthful account? As their motive was to deceive, I classify them as paradoxical liars.

According to English law and most moral critics a successful plea of genuine ignorance[3] clears some communicators of untruths from the charge of lying. Such a defence obviously does not apply to individuals who are, and/or have proclaimed themselves to be, experts on specific subjects. But even such persons are not necessarily guilty of lying when they prognosticate about future happenings. The head of the German government, Helmut Kohl, declared in 1988 that he personally would not live to see the unification of Germany. He misled his listeners through his incompetence as a forecaster but this does not prove that he set out to deceive. His compatriot, Karl Marx, predicted with certainty the progressive impoverishment of the proletariat. He too should not be called a liar though his widely disseminated prediction did not come true. One may safely assume that he believed in the validity of his erroneous glimpses into the future.

Oscar Wilde asserted that the highest development of lying — to wit, something he heartily approved of — was 'Lying in Art'. He has been followed by many others who refer to sculptors, painters, writers of fiction as liars but, as well-intentioned liars they are deemed to deserve being praised and not castigated. According to my conceptual approach, artists are imaginative professionals who, unlike photographers, are not charged with the task of describing events or individuals in a factually correct fashion. They are

---

[3] Eysenck's pertinent, though probably now antiquated, example of ignorance: 'A large-scale study in the US was carried out on the relation between cancer in the womb and circumcision — the hypothesis being that wives of circumcised husbands are less likely to contract this disease because of greater hygiene practised by circumcised men. Many thousands of women were investigated and asked about their husbands' penile status; hundreds of hours were spent on computers, which transformed the data into digestible statistical fodder. When far-reaching conclusions were arrived at from these results, a psychologist asked quite innocently whether many of these women actually knew whether their husbands had been circumcised! After much ridicule had been heaped upon his head, a special investigation was organized to answer this question and it turned out to be "no". Quite a few had only the haziest notion of what circumcision meant — some thought it meant wholesale amputation. Many women had never seen their husbands in the nude and had no idea whether they had or had not been circumcised.'

not liars when they employ their talents to create 'inaccurate' replicas. As the public do not expect them to be truthful (in the orthodox sense), they cannot be said to be deceitful. Of course 'poetic and artistic licensees' should also escape scot-free.

An American general once denounced the Soviet Union: 'They lie intentionally, he said, unable to suppress his anger.' Margaret Thatcher would have it that 'You don't tell deliberate lies but sometimes you have to be evasive.' The words 'intentionally' and 'deliberate' are in this context tautological. By definition, all lies are told to deceive. There are unintentional errors — lies are never unintentional or non-deliberate.

A deception only qualifies as a lie when it is purposeful. The liar must have in mind a definite objective, e.g. to enrich himself, derive pleasure from self-aggrandizement, obtain spiritual satisfaction from promoting a cause dear to him, etc. In the absence of a definite reason for seeking to deceive others, the individuals who spread inaccurate information may justly be denounced for their ignoble deeds but they are not liars. In the following example the perpetrators were guilty of laziness but not of planning to deceive. In his autobiography Douglas Jay recalled the dismay that he encountered after joining *The Economist* in 1933. He found that the journal's authoritative index of wholesale prices included data that were made up in the office. When the true figures could not be obtained in time for the printing deadline, the journalists made them up. Jay was too charitable to describe this furtive exercise as mendacious and suggested that the compilers of the index 'had been guessing the figures'.

My definition is only concerned with substantial lies. This excludes, inter alia, the simplification of technical messages prepared for non-experts and minor adjustments of statistics. (This is akin to the de minimis rule where judges pay no heed to petty inaccuracies or minor unlawful acts). When Werfel wrote *The Forty Days of Musa Dagh*, he knew full well that the Armenian defenders had held out against the Turks no longer than 36 days. But to make his book more impressive, he chose a wrong figure. '40' is an often cited symbolic number in the Bible where, for example, it is related that Moses had stayed on Mount Sinai for forty days and Jesus had spent forty days in the wilderness. Though, conse-

The Nature of Mendacity

quently, his title was inaccurate, Werfel still does not deserve to be castigated as a liar.

Only significant falsehoods qualify as lies. This, therefore, excludes the wearing of Robin Hood garbs, bluffing during a game of poker, relating fairy tales to infants and other playful activities.[4]

To function effectively as a liar, the deceiver has to be credible and his falsehood must be plausible. In the following four examples the individuals, who spread mendacious messages, were not liars because their audiences surmised that they did not mean what they said.

(a) When the Speaker of the HoC is asked to reprimand an MP for using unparliamentary language, he often responds with: 'I did not hear this.' The Speaker, guilty of uttering this untruth, should nevertheless not be accused of lying as the HoC is very familiar with this formula which conveys to the offender that his reprehensible conduct was noted but not deemed to be so serious as to warrant a formal reproof.

(b) In Teheran's central bazaar a vendor swears 'on the life of my wife and seven children' that his last-mentioned proclaimed price is the 'final offer'. This is of course not an honest exclamation for he reckons that the potential buyers, surrounding his stall, are fully aware that he would be happy if the bargaining continued.

(c) My colleague is bound by convention to invite me to his daughter's wedding. He does not really want me to come and has no illusions about my inclination to be there. Under these circumstances I am not to be dubbed a liar when my reply refers to 'our distress that a previous commitment prevents my wife and I from having the pleasure to participate in the happy celebration'.

(d) On the eve of the first Gulf War, France was suspected of being a lukewarm member of the anti-Iraq alliance. When an associate of President Mitterand, Michel Vauzelle, arrived in Baghdad, the world speculated that France was negotiating unilaterally with Saddam Hussein. Vauzelle denied that he had a message from Mitterand for the Iraqi authorities.

---

[4] Bernice Kanner has pleaded that when mothers tell their children: 'you get sties in your eyes from peeing in the road' or 'if you don't wash behind your ears, potatoes will growth there', these are not really lies. She is right.

Laughingly, he insisted that he was in Baghdad as a tourist. This diplomatic falsehood should surely not be called a lie.[5]

How does my definition regard people who are bullied or even tortured and as a result feel impelled to make expediently false declarations? Many serious analysts maintain unyieldingly that lying can only be a 'voluntary' activity. My methodological stance treats all untruths, including those which are articulated under threats and/or tortures, as lies — provided the falsehoods verbalized by the victims are sufficiently plausible to have a desired impact on the tormentors. I surmise that torture is a mitigating feature which the heavenly archangels take into account when preparing their dossiers but, in my terrestrial elucidation of mendacity, lies are lies, whether induced by the perils of death or personal malevolence or altruism.

The credibility of those who disseminate lies varies with time. A mendacious trick that misleads one generation may be shrugged off by a succeeding, more sophisticated, one. The women, who first wore brassieres with built-in padding, were then specified to be liars. It was said that this novel invention was meant to deceive, particularly men, in that it made the proud owners appear to have larger and more shapely breasts than nature had provided them with. Initially, these artificial aids, giving brassiere-wearing women a voluptuous figure, were called 'gay deceivers'. But by the time tens of millions of women were wearing them, the cheating had ceased and the wearers no longer deserved to be described as liars as had been the fate of the pioneers. (Homosexual emancipation had also made it necessary to change the nomenclature: they are now called 'falsies'.)

Many distinguished luminaries in the social sciences uphold the seemingly attractive notion that individuals can lie to themselves. Thus Nietzsche has argued that the most frequently exposed lie is the one said to oneself. Self-deception is a self-contradictory, absurd incongruity for it does not entail the deception of others. An economist, who has concluded that the Albanian economy is booming but appears

---

[5] Gordon Brook-Shepherd relates how in 1938 the British ambassador Sir Neville Henderson was instructed to register a protest against Germany swallowing up Austria. Herman Goering, then acting head of the German government, countered this with an official explanation: Hitler had merely crossed the border into Austria 'to visit his mother's grave'.

The Nature of Mendacity

on the radio to say that Albania is afflicted by a deepening recession, is clearly a lying charlatan. But if he utters this falsehood standing in front of his bathroom mirror, he invites pity but should not be connoted a liar.[6]

To sum up: several attributes must prevail before an uttered falsehood is described as a lie. Two important features are (a) the belief of the disseminator that he is indeed spreading an untruth and (b) his intent to deceive. A group of borderline liars must at least be mentioned though I fear that a strict interpretation of my definition bans them from the club. Is it a perverse oxymoron when a person, imbued with the evil design to deceive, uses the ruse of telling the truth in order to convince his sceptical audience that in reality he is lying? His disclosures are aimed to make his listeners think that what he is communicating cannot be the truth because it would be out of character for him to let his adversaries know what is the truth. He conjectures that his audience would conclude that the opposite of what he is revealing is the truth. In 2002, on the eve of the second Gulf War, the top spokesmen of Saddam Hussein announced that Iraq did not at that point of time possess dangerous, mass-destructive weapons which could be used with immediate effect to halt the advance of any invading force. The astute dictator was convinced that these denials (and his own unsavoury past) would merely confirm, in the eyes of his enemies, that the opposite was the truth. That indeed proved correct. By telling the truth he sought to deceive and in that respect he succeeded. His premise proved accurate. Ought we to call him a liar?

The Three Modes

There is a deep conceptual gulf between those who lie for selfish, frequently material, objectives and those who lie for altruistic motives which is one of the main themes of this

---

[6] The sophisticated, though untypical, example, cited by Giannetti, is very enticing but I do not believe that it invalidates my generalization: 'To avoid arriving late at appointments, I put my alarm-clock forward by 30 minutes, so as to compensate for my natural lateness. The secret of this tactic is NOT TO REMEMBER. As long as I manage to forget that the information I am receiving is false, all is well. But, if I begin to remember the truth, every time I consult my clock, I begin to make the relevant "discount" and am back to square one.'

book. Liars make use of one of three techniques. Category A incorporates all the direct, undiluted forms of transparent deceptions. It includes the claimant who cheats the welfare state by collecting benefits for his five non-existent children. He is neither better nor worse than the scientist who publishes fraudulent research reports, allegedly based on meticulous interviewing, or the academic who displays 'findings' derived from experiments that were never carried out. Politicians and businessmen also belong to this category when, for nefarious reasons, they woo customers and voters by issuing spurious statistics. So is the commercial practice of certain Asian manufacturers who export goods to Europe with labels that denote (say) Austria as the country of origin.

Category B embraces oblique and sophisticated falsehoods which, intellectually, are more complex than the straight lies of category A. Hitler and others have opined that the bigger a lie, the more credible it is. This may indeed be so when fables are told to simpletons but otherwise it is not a valid generalization. To entice sceptical audiences to believe in the factual accuracy of subtle falsehoods, it matters greatly whether the liars can proficiently dress them up in plausible costumes. Tennyson realized the attraction of such a strategy which is why he warned that 'a lie which is half a truth is ever the worst of lies'. Throughout the ages this line of thinking has been taken up by moralists; several have proclaimed that 'a half-truth is a whole lie'. Astutely effective liars therefore insert some true features into a statement which, overall, is mendacious in substance. Thus a company's chairman, eager to find an excuse for the heavy losses suffered under his tutelage, may assert that these were brought about by the imposition of a new tax: the government is to blame. His explanation is indeed true — but only to a minor extent. 20% of the losses are indeed accounted for by the new tax but 80% are attributable to his incompetence — the chairman is a clever liar.

When government statisticians are ordered to set aside their calculations, which show that the RPI rose by 12% and told to announce instead that the increase was merely 2%, this represents straight lying by the politicians and the collaborating civil servants (category A). When, however, politicians 'cook' the index by subsidizing a few weighty items — thus making the fluctuations of the RPI unrepresentative of the general rise in inflation — the perpetrators are practising an entangled deception which belongs to category B. The statisticians should be granted absolution and the guilt for cheating the public must be borne by their political manipulators. The erstwhile president of Lockheed was guilty of an elegant, but wilful, deception by draping an untruth in sanctimonious language. This captain of industry was summoned to defend at a Congressional committee the bribes which Lockheed had paid to bolster its exports. He did not deny the soundly established facts but expressed his displeasure at the obnoxious word 'bribery' that had been used to describe what he termed an 'honest sales technique'. Congressmen were told that he would very much prefer it if they referred to the apposite expenditure as 'gifts', earmarked to engender 'a general climate of goodwill to foster our sales'.

The practice of dishonest traders who deceive buyers by means of forged certificates-of-origin was classified above as straight lying. A parallel, but in essence a category B deception, was carried out by a famous UK distributor of electronic products; the firm was found guilty by a court of 'passing off'. It operated with such original ingenuity as to earn for itself an outstanding place among the country's highbrow corporate liars. In the 1980s the British public deemed the quality of many Japanese consumer goods to be among the best in the world. This perception was exploited by the foxy managers of this chain store in a perverse fashion. They did not lie explicitly by attaching MADE IN JAPAN labels to the goods which they marketed. Instead, they chose to deceive their customers by selling the articles, produced outside Japan by non-Japanese companies, under the (specially created) brand name MATSUI and bedecking the articles with a logo that resembled the rising sun. Successfully, they thus sold goods manufactured in Singapore, Yugoslavia, Italy and other countries as Japanese products. To ensure that their implicitly mendacious message was also fully understood by even the most stupid customers, they advertised this merchandise under the slogan of 'Japanese Technology Made Perfect'.

Category C encompasses refined forms of passive lying that entail the suppression of the truth and/or the non-disclosure of relevant facts. (I disagree with the many who have gone on record to opine that these sins, if indeed they are to be denoted as sins, are less odious than the dissemination of positive lies.) The suppression of truth constitutes a lie if it harms people who are entitled to know the truth — the entitlement is determined by subjective value judgements. The current history school books of Japan and Germany do not glorify Emperor Hirohito or Adolf Hitler but many of them are composed by passive liars who either omit altogether, or have toned down considerably, the negative features which typified the pre-1946 policies of their respective countries. If the children are being deceived, it is not by what is in the school books but rather by what is missing.[7] The official encyclopaedia of the USSR used to be regularly revised in accordance with political criteria. When luminaries, who had been venerated in old editions, were crassly vilified in subsequent editions, this exemplified straight lying which typified Soviet culture. Much more sinister and effective was the contrived mendacity that consisted of omitting altogether from current editions the mention of former national heroes who had officially become enemies-of-the-people. Photos of (the dead) Lenin, surrounded by his old comrades, were doctored. The pictures of commissars, the memory of whose historical achievements was to be expunged from official publications because they had either been shot or exiled to Siberia, were just blotted out. This became known as airbrushing. More sophisticated still was the substitution of a picture of a current leader to replace the erased image of one of Lenin's disgraced comrades.

Mendacious Vocabularies

Euphemisms are employed by polite individuals who want to cloak an unpleasantness or avoid saying things that might embarrass others. Those who have an axe to grind describe murderers as either 'tormented killers' or 'freedom fighters'. Contraception is labelled 'family planning'. Keynes and his acolytes, so implied William Hutt, were Machiavellian liars. They advocated inflation which could, however, not be sold openly to the electorate: 'But an inspired insight enabled the

---

[7] In this respect, the Japanese were always more prone to suppress the truth than the Germans. But only in the twenty-first century did their Ministry of Education go so far as to approve a new history textbook which, despite protests from Korea and China, omitted altogether mention of any Japanese wartime atrocities.

Keynesians to perceive that, if called something else, for instance "the maintenance of effective demand", it became respectable'. Euphemistic gadgets are also employed to obfuscate the truth. In learned journals political scientists do not hesitate to treat mendacity as a professional attribute of democratic politicians. Yet the word 'lying' hardly ever appears in academic writings. The shy professors boycott this obnoxious term and consequently it is rarely listed in the indexes of their books. Undoubtedly, they recall the days when their nannies impressed upon them that even when a blatant lie is uttered, good children do not explicitly call the sinner a liar. Semantics is the branch of linguistics concerned with the meaning of words. If anyone has nothing better to do, he could collect all the different literary guises under which the English-language words 'liars' and 'lies' make their appearance. They would probably exceed two thousand, thereby reflecting the emotionally-loaded attitudes surrounding this subject. The lists below are only samples of the much larger numbers that could be garnered from literary storehouses but even my scanty contribution illustrates the sensitive nature of the theme we are investigating. Very few of the cited words constitute genuine (neutral) synonyms. The overwhelming majority have a tendentious function. Thus the sting of lying is made more painful and repugnant when those, who seek to demonstrate their deep abhorrence for a given piece of mendacity, choose an even more loathsome nounal substitute and/or select a repugnant and offensive adjectival qualification. Those who regard the word 'lying' as unsuitable — in particular when the mendacity is backed by benign motives — anaesthetize the horrors of the tabooed expression by opting for covert embellishments, i.e. ameliorating nouns and gracious adjectives. Hence, 'good' mendacity is apparelled in attractive garbs; 'bad' mendacity is dressed up so as to emerge even more obnoxious. Both kinds are represented in my lists.

An author, labouring on a book on the craft of disinformation, had planned to title it *The Lie Makers*. He was persuaded to publish it as *The Truth Twisters*. The preparation of false forecasts by shameless economists has been analysed by Chiang who mentions en passant that the business of contrived forecasts is to be censured on moral grounds. Yet he has not used the obvious taboo word. He employed a clever euphemism, 'artificial' forecasts, that was intended to leave no stain on the swindlers who set out to cheat their ingenuous audiences. The memoirs of the Chief Secretary of the Treasury Joel Barnett illustrate this politician's penchant for soft expressions. In his chapter, headed 'Fiddling the Figures', readers are told much about cheating and lying but, alas, these two striking words do not surface. He gives a good reason: 'I know that there were a variety of ways the figures could be "fiddled", and if purists dislike that world, "adjusted" would be an acceptable alternative.' In the Bible mild phrases frequently appear when blunt and direct expressions are called for. According to Luke it was at the Last Supper that Jesus told his apostle Peter: 'the cock will not crow tonight until you have three times over *denied* that you know me'. And so it came to pass. When Jesus was arrested and Peter followed at a distance, he was denounced thrice to the authorities as being one of Jesus's men. But he lied and disowned his Master three times, saying: 'I do not know him'.

In 1985 Robert Armstrong, representing the British government in an Australian court, made history by highlighting several suspicious euphemisms. Under cross-examination he denied lying but conceded that he might have 'misled' the court; on another occasion, he again rejected the charge that he had been guilty of lying but agreed that he had been merely 'misrepresenting the facts'. At one point in the proceedings, when the judge responded angrily to Armstrong's denial that his answers had been misleading replies, he conceded that his responses 'did not say all'. The judge jeered: 'we may have fallen into an exercise of semantics'. When the British government's senior civil servant was asked about a letter, which he admitted was composed by him, his reply was weird: 'It does not contain a lie ... it (gave) a misleading impression.' The judge demanded to know what is the difference 'between a misleading impression and a lie'. He was told that a 'lie is a straight untruth' which led the judge to mock unkindly: 'What is a misleading impression — a sort of unbent untruth?' Armstrong replied in a sensational fashion: 'It is perhaps being economical with the truth.' This phrase has since been immortalized. When Alan Clark, as a minister of the Crown, gave evidence to a commission of inquiry in London, where his testimony was challenged, he aped Armstrong by saying that he had been 'economical with the actualité'.

Parliaments in the English-speaking countries are deemed to be holy places where one may hint implicitly that a colleague was a liar but must not say so explicitly. Despite the salty outburst of a Texan Congressman, who once called Poindexter (the National Security Adviser) a 'lying son of a bitch', such language is usually not tolerated on Capitol Hill. In their perceptive study, Jane Mayer and Doyle McManus would have it that in Washington 'where deception is admired as an art, lie is perhaps the last dirty word'. In the HoC there are very severe conventions. When Duncan Sandys, a defence minister, exclaimed: 'that is a complete lie!', he was forced to recant which he did; he then maintained that what his opponent had said did not 'correspond with the truth'. All intelligent schoolboys in Britain know that Winston Churchill circumvented the ban on the forbidden word by calling attention to 'a terminological inexactitude'. There are of course also non-semantic alternatives. While one may not lie categorically in the HoC, it is not against the rules for ministers, who seek to avoid disclosing the truth, to answer awkward inquiries by 'sidestepping' the essence of the question. Matthew Parris, who has delved into the chronicles of the HoC between 1861 and 1992, came up with a bewildering variety of ungentlemanly expressions which were actually uttered. He has listed separately those which slipped through and those that the Speakers had ruled out of order. Among the disallowed profane words were 'bollocks', 'bugger', 'poached bullshit'. Allowed were 'you old windbag', 'does not give a fart', 'snivelling little git'. Parris contrasts this liberal, though inconsistent, scope for abusing one another to the draconian rules which prohibit members of the HoC from accusing their confreres of lying. He has enumerated thirty instances when the Speakers banned euphemisms. Among them were 'perverter of the truth', 'telling porkies', 'resorting to trickiness'. Those remarks, which escaped censure, included 'shameless lack of candour' and 'cooking the figures'.

Semantic Costumes of [the] Truth

absolute truth	everyday truths	not telling the truth
adjusting the truth	extravagant truth	not the literal truth
adulterating the truth	filtering the truth	not the real truth
aesthetic truth	flippant with the truth	not the whole truth
an improbable truth	full truth	objective truth
avoiding the truth	gigantic truth	perverter of the truth
battling with the truth	graceful untruth	plain truth
bending the truth	gracious untruth	playing with the truth
bereft of truth	half-truth	poetic truth
everyday truths	historical truth	precious truth
betraying the truth	horrible truth	profound truth
bogus truth	hushing up the truth	refined truth
calculated untruth	irrational truth	revised facts
cavalier with the truth	lack of truthfulness	sacrificing the truth
compound of untruths	less than the whole truth	sanitising the truth
concealing the truth	lurid truth	selective with the truth
decorating the truth	massaging the truth	shadings of the truth
departing from the truth	mincing the truth	stretching the truth
deviated from the truth	naked truth	the clouded truth
disagreeable truth	negligent with the truth	truth in masquerade
dismantling truthfulness	not exactly true	twilight of the truth
disrespect for the truth	not loyal to the truth	withholding the truth

Some Pertinent Phrases

advertisers lie as fast as a dog licks a dish	all relevant details were not disclosed
an accurate but selective answer	an officious lie is a benign lie
badly misrepresenting the facts	bending one's belief to convenience
beyond the confines of veracity	conning him into believing he had won
creative engineering in veracity	deliberately concealing from view
diverging from established facts	drawing a red herring across the trail
duplicitous assurances were given	embellishing lies by picturesque fantasy
factually unproven facts	found guilty of the act of imprecision
his memory distorted the truth	his memory exaggerated what happened
I am a man of unclean lips	It is not a lie but an untruth
leading us up the garden path	lied his way out of danger
lied out of both sides of his mouth	lied out of necessity
manipulating facts to fit the argument	not as honest as he ought to be
not conforming with reality	picking a figure out of the hat
pulling the wool over the readers' eyes	put on a false trail
she concocted a transparently false alibi	she tells enough white lies to ice a cake
speaking with a forked tongue	taking liberties with slanting
they improved their academic degrees	what a goodly outside falsehood hath!
with the best intentions, he did not tell the truth!	

The Literary Robes of Lies, Liars and Falsehoods

a born liar	a perfectly magnificent liar	abominable lies
a thumping lie	a worthy lie	accomplished lies
adjusting history	adjusting true results	agreed lies
an incomplete answer	bad lies	bare-faced lies
bear false witness	beautiful lies	beguiling the public
benign lies of politics	biased reporting	big falsehoods
big fat lies	big thumping lies	black lies
blameless lying	blatant lies	blatant fiddling
boundless liar	calculated mendacity	camouflaging
careful lies	charitable lies	cheating
clever wheezes	cock-and-bull stories	colossal lies
comfortable lies	complete set of distortions	compulsive liars
concoction	consecrated falsehoods	consistent lying
consummate lies	contemptuous falsehoods	convenient fiction
conventional lies	cooking intelligence	cooking up a story
counter-factual claims	creative accounting	creative lies
crucial dishonesty	culpable exaggeration	damnable lies
deadly lies	deceptions	deluding the listeners
departure from reality	depraved lies	despicable lying
dirty lies	disinformation	disingenuous advocacy
dissembling falsehoods	double-dealing	double falsehoods
downright lies	dressing up facts	duplicity

elaborate lies	embroidering the story	equivocating
excusable lying	extravagant with honesty	fabricator
false perspective	falsification	falsity
feigning	fabulist	factual misrepresentation
fibber	fictitious stories	foul lies
fudged figures	furtive circumlocution	gentle falsehoods
gerrymandering statistics	good lies	great lies
hairy lies	half-the-picture	harmless lies
holy falsehoods	hoaxes	horrible lies
humane lies	hysterical lying	imposture
imprecise accounting	improving the results	impudent lies
inauthenticity	inaccurate data	incomplete testimony
inexcusable lies	injurious falsehoods	insidious lies
inspired lies	instinctive liars	inventive lies
inveracity	inveterate liars	it's only a fiddle
just lies	justified false propaganda	lack of openness
lying like a trooper	lie like mad	lied through his teeth
lied my way out of danger	living a lie	lordly lies
ludicrous falsehoods	lying disposition	lying out of politeness
made-to-order evidence	magnanimous lies	make-believe
making up stories	manipulating the facts	masked falsehoods
massaging figures	meritorious lies	minor porky
misinformation	misleading descriptions	mischievous falsehoods
misrepresentation	mock candour	moral lies

naked lies	natural born liars	necessary lies
neurotic lies	noble lie	non-figures
not really correct	obscuring the real facts	odious lies
omitting vital details	open lies	outright lies
partial account	pack of lies	painless lies
palpable liar	pardonable lies	paternalistic falsehoods
pernicious lies	plausible mendacity	prevarication
prefabricated lies	premeditated lies	permissible lying
pious deceit	polished confessions	polite fiction
pretending postures	privileged lying	quibbling
real lies	reckless liars	righteous lies
romancer	sacred lies	sanitizing reality
saving lies	shameless lies	shamming
selective about the facts	sheer fabrication	sick lies
sincere lies	slanting real happenings	social lies
solid lying	somewhat dishonest	spin-doctoring
spurious stories	subterfuges	swindlers
swearing falsely	swinish lies	tactical errors
tall stories	tampering with honest data	tell porkies
tendentious compilations	terrible lies	thrown off the scent
tissue of lies	token figures	twisting the facts
twisted reporting	two-faced conduct	unadulterated falsehood
uncandid	underplay	ultimate lie
uncomfortable assertions	useful falsehoods	utilitarian lies
verbal rogues	well-intentioned lies	white lies
window-dressing	whoppers	wicked lies
	worthy falsehoods	

Chapter II

Why and How We Lie

> The truth is often a terrible weapon of aggression. It is possible to lie and even to murder for the truth.
> *Alfred Adler*

Eclectic Mainsprings

While individuals do often lie for a variety of non-material impulses — about their heroic deeds, charitable contributions, sexual conquests and a host of other pleasing matters — the quest to improve their material well-being is perhaps the single most prevalent motivation. For this purpose people set out to deceive relatives, friends, neighbours, bus conductors, insurance companies, employers, tax inspectors, doctors and officials of the welfare state; parents lie about their religious belief, occupation and address to get their offspring into desirable schools. By circulating mendacious messages, liars collect awards (to which they are not entitled) and/or seek to evade fiscal obligations. In his autobiography the publisher John Calder confessed an original, brutal instance of materially-motivated mendacity. When still a young, relatively impoverished, married man, his wife gave birth to a baby girl. She implored him: 'No one must know that this is a girl. Send your grandfather a telegram right away, saying it's a boy and you'll get your money.' As predicted, the old man was supremely happy that there was now a male Calder to carry on the name for another generation and duly enriched the infant. The deception worked for a short time. When his grandfather discovered the truth, he 'immediately set about disinheriting me'.

When business executives lie to defraud the tax authorities, shareholders and creditors, they often manage to do this without falling foul of the law. With the help of professional advisers, sophisticated business mendacity is not a crude affair as are most illegal applications for unemployment benefit; it is an elegant refinement of the truth. Depending on who they wish to cheat, business executives often understate or overstate the profit outlook of their enterprise. Thomas Aquinas denounced traders engaged in the (unsophisticated) crime of 'selling a lame horse as a fast one'. This stricture rarely applies to mendacious City magnates for these do not participate in the fraudulent sale of horses which are *obviously* lame. They also rarely resort to such vulgar distortions of company accounts as to report an inventory of 100 apples when there are only 50 apples. With the assistance of creative accounting — the euphemistic appellation for telling an untrue numerate story — they can dupe the ordinary citizens who credulously believe in the sanctity of certified company accounts and have little idea how the gentlemen of the City or Wall Street are in a position to manipulate profit-and-loss statements. The sinners sleep soundly as they fervently believe that outsiders lack the knowledge to expose them as liars. A US professor has caricatured such conduct by relating how an American corporation set about selecting one of the eight top accountancy giants. The president interviewed them, asking each what is the sum of 2 + 2. Seven of them replied that it was of course 4. The partnership that was chosen replied: 'what number did you have in mind?' The loyalties of directors and senior employees are often, but not always, potent enough to impel them to lie to serve the interests of the (private or public sector) bodies with which they are associated. In theory liars, found guilty of criminal commercial offences, are liable to be punished irrespective of whether they personally, or their institutions, had benefitted. In practice, however, juries and judges often treat more lightly culprits who can deliver proof that they, personally, had not lied to fill their own pockets .

Rich and/or famous people can earn money with lies if they sell their souls to advertising agencies which may call upon them to deceive their fellow citizens by posing as the putative consumers of given brands of soap, cars, perfume, tobacco, etc. These are often goods which in their personal life they would not touch with a barge pole. Famous people, especially writers in the hope of reciprocity, insincerely compose favourable book reviews. Several have actually in later life publicly admitted that it is the practice of certain publishers to arrange for eminent authors to give agreeable endorsements of books which they have not read.

When advertising agencies take space in newspapers to bring to public notice the picture of a new car model, together with details of price and performance, they are doing their job and telling the truth. But when they employ hidden tactics, particularly with sexual undertones and naked bodies, wherewith to publicize the merchandise of their clients, they become liars. They resemble the disreputable nightclubs which position truly attractive girls outside their doors to deceive passers-by to think that the girls inside the club are equally attractive. They rarely are.

Individuals lie in various ways to make themselves look good in the eyes of outsiders. The Romanian dictator Ceausescu let it be known that on his birthday he had received greetings from royal personages, such as the King of Spain and Queen Elizabeth — blatant falsehoods which, however, did the trick. Even the very poor find it often attractive to lie in order to bolster their vanity. Men and women are frequently flattered when questioned by market researchers and opinion pollsters. They set out to present themselves to the persons, who interrogate them, as being cultured, knowledgeable, righteous and moralistic persons. They lie. When the *Saturday Evening Post* asked its readers how many of them had been to the opera in the previous year, the number who replied in the affirmative exceeded considerably the actual total attendance at all the opera performances in the US. Adult males, surveyed by the BBC, have lied wildly about the kind of programmes which they were habitually viewing. They claimed to be glued to their sets in order to watch cerebral programmes while in fact they were fans of sports events and soap operas. Cyril Kersh has told an old but apposite story about *The News of the World,* the UK's Sunday paper with the largest circulation. Murders and sexual scandals had been its pre-war raison d'etre. To cloak its sordid reportages and gain some quasi-respectability, a few columns were regularly devoted to innocent matters such as 'missing persons', 'musical lyrics' and occasional features on politics. To test his hunch, that the UK's morals had changed, the post-war new editor arranged a readership survey. Understandably, the interviewers charged with eliciting the paper's most popular features were not told by respondents how much they liked the reportages on rape and buggery. Many replies mentioned 'we are very keen on the "missing people" column and the sport features' and similar untruths. The survey persuaded the editor to drop sex and bestialities. He lasted for two weeks in his job. At the start of the third week, a newly appointed editor turned the clock back. With the aid of the old formula, he boasted the sales which were ultimately to top 8.5 million copies.

It used to be thought that only lowly employees, working in companies which offered sickness benefits, exploited this by not coming to work because they mendaciously pretended to be ill. Lately the excuse of being ill — and in some cases even asserting to be in an advanced stage of a life-threatening malady — has been used successfully by several liars in the top echelons of large corporations. Thus in April 2004 the British press reported how a disgraced finance executive who, fearing he was about to be discharged, had persuaded his fellow directors that he was diagnosed to be afflicted with prostate cancer. This fabrication enabled him to hide his fraudulent activities from the staff and the authorities 'for an extra three years'.

People lie because of cowardice. Though promised anonymity by the interviewers, they tend not to give replies that clash with the views and beliefs and political allegiances of their peers and neighbours. This is even more so when men-in-the-street are invited to live political television shows where they are encouraged to ask questions and vote by raising their hands. Among the attendees are of course also individuals with extremist views on sensitive subjects but only infrequently do they 'dare' to show their true colours. Almost all attendees are generally keen to appear as socially progressive and unselfish creatures. Germany's pioneering psephologist, Elisabeth Nolle-Neumann has described this phenomenon as 'the spiral of silence'. She has argued cogently that many German voters, approached by opinion pollsters, tend to avoid expressing unorthodox/minority opinions because they fear isolation from the run-of-the-mill masses. This applies also to the UK where a cynical addendum is germane. When lying to pollsters, the liars are aware that they can never be penalized (or exposed) for making mendacious declarations. They may also comfort themselves with the knowledge that their false declarations can be atoned, once they are actually in the polling-booths. It was no secret that most of those who claimed to speak for the black community in the US viewed the casting of a vote for presidential candidate Ronald Reagan as an act akin to treachery. In consequence, on the basis of interviews with representative samples of black electors, opinion pollsters underestimated by something like one half the number of black people who would vote for Reagan. The pollsters came a cropper for many of the respondents had lied. These fears of the prevaricating black interviewees had of course nothing in common with the lying that millions living under brutal dictatorships have had to pursue. Their tactical falsehoods were articulated to make life bearable; the mendacious avowals of these liars made it possible for their children to receive a university education, a privilege often denied to those whose parents opted not to lie.

Some false underestimations deserve to be called lies. On the 70th anniversary of the Russian Revolution Gorbachev made history by denouncing Stalin's crimes. He declared that the Stalinist regime had killed 'thousands of lives'. Per se, this was true but in fact Gorbachev was a liar for, though he knew the true dimensions, he had chosen not to acknowledge that the Stalinist regime was responsible for the death of millions. Barry Cooper says of this underplaying that it was as if a German post-war politician had denounced Hitler for 'killing thousands of Jews'. The reverse, overestimation, is also a form of lying. The Oxford Dictionary describes romancing as an 'exaggerated or picturesque falsehood'.

Uttering falsehoods is a natural attribute of mythomaniacs. Some of them are not sane adults and must therefore be excluded from the club. The majority do qualify, especially those who manifest intellectual excellence in their professions. In this context Harold Laski, the famous professor of political science and one-time chairman of the Labour Party, is clearly a liar. On many occasions he masqueraded before his students and colleagues as one who was constantly contacted by influential men of power on both sides of the Atlantic. He used to regale his credulous student audiences with accounts of conversations that in fact did not take place. His academic colleagues, who wrote about Laski's peculiarity after his death, were reticent in their condemnations.[1] Harry Sacher probably summed it up best by explaining Laski's strange conduct as being due to a 'tincture of vanity'.

The vanity motivation must not be confused with another wide-spread engine of lying, which was defined by Oscar Wilde as 'lying that is absolutely beyond reproach . . . lying for its own sake'. Max Clifford was at the beginning of the twenty-first century the UK's most notorious PR practitioner who represented tarts and millionaires alike. He admitted unashamedly that he was happy to serve his clients by lying. But, apart from his professional devotion, he also had a personal vested interest in deceiving others. He proclaimed proudly that he loved lying 'because I enjoy it — it's great fun'.[2] The pleasure of lying is obtained by demonstrating one's skill in cheating, to wit breaking the law, in order to demonstrate that one is cleverer than the enforcers of the law. When very rich people hoodwink customs inspectors and thereby evade paying the appropriate duties, their motivation has nothing to do with the incidental material benefit gained: the lying is targeted to obtain a non-material gratification. St Augustine, in his *Confessions*, has written at length about his guilty past when he lied solely for the pleasure of lying: 'Many and many a time I lied to my tutor, my masters and my parents, and deceived them because I wanted to play games. And in the games I played with them I often cheated in order to come off the better, simply because of a vain desire to win had got the better of me.'

---

[1] The student Callaghan, later chancellor of the exchequer, wrote kindly of his patron: 'In later years I had to conclude that on occasion he was romancing, but at the time he made me feel I was indirectly in touch with the great world of politics where the real decisions were taken.' Professor Frankel also said it in a muted tone: 'Laski may at times have been too histrionic: even carried beyond the confines of veracity.' With hindsight Laski's writings, in which he praises Stalin's achievements, appear highly perverse. A few of his defenders have suggested that he reproduced mendacious reports because he had been duped. Professor A.J.P. Taylor reviewed a Laski biography and by implication debunked this alibi: 'Laski knew, none better, the difficulties of his policy; he did not need any disillusioned Communist, returned from Utopia, to tell him the evils of Moscow rule.' I believe that Taylor is right and this, I regret to say, makes Laski a very deplorable liar.

[2] Petronella Wyatt, 'The Archbishop calls on Max', *The Spectator*, May 16, 1998.

In the experience of Jules Kroll, head of a renowned US firm which specializes in white-collar crime, employees sometimes lie (as part of their fraudulent activities) not 'for an economic but for a psychic reward, to get back at someone, to gain revenge for having been passed over for a promotion ... Sometimes [the motivation] is based on the deep pocket theory. They tell themselves that this is a big company, they can afford it.'

To take one's seat in the HoC, the newly elected members must first take an oath of loyalty to the sovereign. How can republican MPs do this without being called traitors to the cause by their supporters? They indeed do take the oath as required but then inform those who ought to be informed that they had done so while simultaneously crossing their fingers, thus invalidating the oath. Is it a puerile game or lying or both?

The truth can be painful and embarrassing. Liars therefore often offer this as an excuse. John frequently went on business trips to Birmingham where he spent the evenings in the bed of his mistress. Returning home, he regaled his wife with fictitious stories of how he had spent his leisure hours. Theodoracopulos has gone on record in *The Spectator* to assert: 'I am not a liar, unlike most Greeks ... I only lie not to hurt and then it is more a case of withholding the truth. I would not tell an ugly woman she is ugly.' Roy Harrod lied passively about Keynes's gay life. He later defended himself, saying that he did so in order not to offend members of the Keynes family who were still alive when his book came out. To appear as PC, prominent figures in the West operate today a benevolent censorship which suppresses the truth that might offend members of racial, religious, sexual and national minorities.

Lying for the sake of expediency assumes diverse forms. Individuals who plead guilty to an offence they have not committed or plead guilty to a minor offence when originally charged with a major one — often do so because they cannot be bothered to appear in court and rebut the charges. A few journalists sent by Western newspapers to Stalinist Russia asked to be recalled as soon as they realized that they could not send meaningful dispatches. Others, however, sent lying accounts out of conviction or for material rewards. Quite a number — call them 'opportunistic liars' — were not prepared to deceive their readers by penning mendacious stories, and forewent writing honest stories which would displease the dictatorial regime and thus could bring about their deportation: they confined themselves to preparing nondescript, platitudinous reportages on non-dangerous subjects.

In 1916 Aidan Crawley's father was a chaplain on the Somme where desertions had induced the commanding officers to issue orders that an example should be made of anyone straying from his unit. One day the chaplain was sent for to comfort a young man who had been found guilty and was about to be shot. Having advanced with his platoon, he had lost his way. Though he found his way back to the British lines, he reached another unit that was half a mile from where his battalion was entrenched. The young soldier had not deserted and the delayed return to his own unit was due to the fog that covered the area. Witnesses were to testify that the other members of his platoon had only kept together because they were experienced soldiers while this was the boy's first sortie. The colonel agreed with the chaplain that the youngster be reprieved. The case was shunted up to the divisional echelon. There, they were not concerned with the merits of the affair but with discipline. If 'this boy were let off, it might lead to a rash of similar cases'. Obedience to the letter of the law was deemed to be of supreme importance, however ugly and unjust the consequences. The life of an innocent youngster was sacrificed for the greater good. It was shameful but not a mendacious act. The chaplain, however, was guilty of spreading a (benevolent) lie. He wrote to the parents that their son had been killed in action.

The element of indolence is a major factor — some assert that it is often a non-genuine excuse — for not disclosing the truth in sufficient detail. Experts find it time-wasting and irksome to provide copious information requested by non-experts. Hence C.E. Ayres's saying is cited so often: 'A little inaccuracy saves a world of explanation'. The member of a given discipline can convey a message to a colleague in a few sentences while the same exercise vis-à-vis a layman calls for a long lecture which, frequently, is not comprehended. For this reason, but also because of laziness, experts speaking to non-experts cut corners and do not reveal the whole truth. Medical practitioners wrestle with this predicament several times a day. While prescribing pharmaceutical remedies, they do not have the time (or inclination) to detail all the possible side-effects. Small talk with a patient, say about the weather, takes less time than spelling out the complexities of an illness.

Mention must certainly be made of a passive falsehood that is nurtured by a reluctance to be inconvenienced. Millions of our fellow citizens are guilty of uttering this kind of lie without even blushing. After witnessing an accident or some disturbance, they are approached by the parties involved or the police who inquire whether they would be prepared to give evidence as witnesses. They respond: 'So sorry! We would have liked to help but we did not really see what happened.'

Filling in questionnaires is a multitudinous burden and legal duty in our society; the respondents know that they are obliged or even statutorily bound to give full and honest answers. Politicians who use these returns, believing them to be meaningful, like to think that these forms are usually filled in with genuine answers even though furnishing accurate information costs money and time. Liars, however, prefer to supply 'guestimates', often a euphemism for not telling the whole truth. The valuable testimony of F. McFadzean, the CEO of the Royal Dutch Shell's UK operations, is on written record. Prime Minister Harold Wilson's (national) planners demanded that the UK's major companies should divulge in voluminous detail the contents of their five-year plans. Business firms were simultaneously 'advised' to revise their in-house projections in line with the official 3.8% GDP growth proclamation. (Only stupid executives were unaware that this figure was fanciful.) The majority of firms thought that it was in their interest to reply even when they had no five-year plans. Sheepishly, the forms were filled in with millions of numbers; the liars hoped that the authorities would be happy. Few threw the questionnaires into the dustbin. Why risk annoying politicians and powerful civil servants? McFadzean also realized that it was in the interest of Shell to be seen to participate in this hocus-pocus. He was, however, not prepared to utilize costly monetary and human resources in order to supply accurately the requested comprehensive answers: 'We did not in practice disturb our engineers with the counterproductive exercise of revising design and cost estimates; they were engaged in more essential work. We submitted the best guesses we could and carried on precisely with what we were doing before the [national] planners intervened.' McFadzedan did not announce this at the time. He waited until the British government had abandoned its sacred growth figure and after it had become near-certain that Shell would not be penalized for failing to respond honestly to the questionnaire. Only then did he proudly announce that his corporation had, disobediently, made no efforts to arrive at the whole truth.

We know from the memoirs of leading industrialists, who managed to climb to the very top, that it can be helpful to have a dishonest disposition. Some, in retirement, actually boast with relish of their deceptions. Business decision-makers must frequently make public observations on the future of the empire over which they rule. If they have no compunctions about bending the truth, they may find it sometimes propitious to outline with Machiavellian forethought projections that fall short of what they truly believe is likely to occur. Take the example of a CEO who had reason to believe that his company would earn in the coming year $100 m. However, there was a slight possibility that profits would reach only $90m. Were this to happen, his critics would attribute it to his incompetent stewardship. Far safer then to announce a mendacious forecast, i.e. to express the hope that in the coming year the company will earn $75m. If the results turn out to be much more favourable, as indeed he had had reason to expect, he will be praised for his entrepreneurial qualities. If he is a British citizen, the 'unexpected' rise in profitability might even result in his receiving a knighthood.

Spurious accuracy is a useful device employed by people who aim to give the false impression that they have meticulously researched a given project. These liars wish to be recognized as profound experts. In a tantalizing report on Turkey it was asserted that in the world league the country ranked sixth in the production of counterfeit goods; allegedly, the country accounted for 3.2% of such global output. How can this numerate conclusion have been seriously arrived at? Noteworthy is the decimal point in 3.2%. No doubt it was meant to feign learned accuracy to distinguish it from 3.1% and 3.3%. In an expensive business journal, readers were told that 'Spain has one of the biggest black economies of any rich country'. The writer probably thought that such a feeble generalization would lack credibility. To make it therefore look erudite, he cited an official source that 29.7% of the Spanish labour force was working in those parts of the economy where income 'is not declared to the taxman'. The precise percentage suggests that this too was an obviously bogus statistic. On the other side of the Atlantic, a consultancy firm provided its clients, US-based multis, with confidential forecasts. Printed on expensive paper, the data were said to be accurate to the nearest decimal point. For example, the clients were advised that the prospects of investing in India were bright: the country's GDP was calculated to rise over the subsequent *twenty* years by 107.8%. At the same time they furnished their clients with the vital prediction that Japan's GDP would, also after twenty years, be $361.1 b. At first sight one might think that the renowned clients would be repelled by these fatuous and deceitful predictions. Sad to report that many influential economic decision-makers are prone to be swayed, i.e. deluded, by forecasts spiced with decimal points. Henry Matisse would have it that 'exactitude is not truth'; it is more to the point to aver that exactitude in long-term forecasts is fraudulent.

Many individuals, eager to be proposed for desirable political posts or honorary public service appointments, lie about their wishes. They may surreptitiously scheme and intrigue to further their ambitions because they regard themselves to be highly competent to carry out the tasks which they are coveting. But the mores of our age demand that the candidates should in public give the false impression that they are not really interested in the vacant appointments. If these are finally offered to them, they are expected to say that, only under pressure, are they reluctantly taking upon themselves these burdensome civic duties. They lie when they say that the jobs were thrust upon them and that only their sense of public duty impelled them to serve.

Preparing a mendacious curriculum vitae, to obtain a job or membership of a club, is a practice of which many are guilty. In 1992 President Clinton received a large donation from Larry Lawrence for his election campaign. On the basis of the latter's assertion, that he had volunteered for the merchant marine and was wounded when his ship was sunk by enemy torpedoes, President Clinton secured a plot for him in the Arlington cemetery that is reserved for the martial heroes of the US. He was therefore buried there when he died in 1996. A year later his putative war record was exposed as a pack of lies. His body was disinterred in disgrace. According to the American press this was the first disinterment because of 'fabricated heroism'.

Anatole France would have it that 'without lies humanity would perish of despair and boredom'. This observation has been echoed by others who have spelt out why lying is such an important feature in making life tolerable: lies are deemed to be social lubricants.

Liars have justified imparting untruths on the ground that their audiences do not wish to hear the truth but relish being deceived.

Some liars defend their mendacity when, as they see it, the truth itself is bizarre or freakish. This also occurs when they regard the audiences as too stupid or biased to understand the truth. A raison d'etre for lying is therefore said to exist when the truth is unlikely to be understood and/or believed.

Institutional Mendacities

Throughout the ages many small and large corporations have flourished because their CEOs employed deceitful techniques to crush competitors.[3] This was only possible with the active and passive teamwork by senior employees who were ready to tell lies for the benefit of the institutions and corporations that employed them. These collaborators authorized the payment of bribes, sanctioned the cheating of customers, shareholders and banks, hoodwinked government inspectors and initiated a host of other mendacious tactics. A few did so primarily to safeguard their own positions and improve the prospect of collecting bigger bonuses and juicier stock options. Yet it is arrant nonsense to predicate that the majority of most Western employees lied solely and mainly for private material gain: they were often genuinely motivated to further the fortunes of their companies. The Church Committee in Washington and investigatory Euro-

---

[3] At the turn of the nineteenth century National Cash Register strove to build up a monopoly position by driving competitors into insolvency. William Rogers has set out in detail how the corporation sabotaged its competitors and spread disinformation about them; it was later prosecuted for violating the anti-trust laws.

pean bodies have publicized sordid cases where renowned executives of multis were involved in deceptions that held out no or only minute personal financial rewards for the high-powered liars.[4]

Internecine lying — accompanied by stabbing colleagues in the back with poisonous daggers — is pervasive in certain large organizations with unwieldy structures, such as the armed forces, universities, civil services, and (most pronouncedly) among the world's huge corporations. In *The Might of the Multinationals* I have shown how — under the umbrella of one corporation — executives attached to given departments, divisions and subsidiaries are prone to fight one another by resorting to lying, defamation, the preparation of false research reports and the contrived arousal of destructive national and ethnic animosities. Pepsico uncovered in 1982 a serious financial irregularity which obliged it to revise its already-published global revenues. Elaborate mendacious schemes had been devised by the executives in charge of its Mexican and Philippine operations. The managers of these subsidiaries had inflated the receivables, chosen not to recognize substantive bad debts, wilfully ignored some obsolete inventories and deferred the recording of legitimate expenditure. Layers of false documents had been furnished to cheat the controllers of Pepsico's parent company. The president denounced the guilty men for having perpetrated a 'fraud of such proportions' but he also had to concede that they could not be charged with committing a criminal offence. The liars had lied intramurally to deceive their colleagues. Why had they lied? The culprits, said the president, were motivated to 'improve the apparent performance of their operations. The misrepresentations were not designed to divert company funds to personal, improper or illegal use.'

---

[4] Why did a high-ranking legal executive launder abroad the money of his employer, a famous US oil company, and then personally carry the dirty funds across several national borders? He did so to enable his corporation (under duress) to make an illegal contribution to President Nixon's re-election campaign. The courier did not expect to receive a yacht. He endangered himself by furthering the fortunes of his corporation. The Spanish inquisitors tortured their victims to glorify God. In our age some corporate criminals lie and break the law to aggrandize the companies for which they work

The biblical command 'Thou shalt not bear false witness against thy neighbour' does not explain if 'neighbour' refers only to people in the immediate vicinity of one's tent or also to members of one's family, religious affiliation, ethnic group or nation.[5] We are told that we must not wrong our neighbour by telling lies about him. But when called upon to testify, are we told to lie in order to help our neighbour? There prevails a deeply-embedded propensity to lie in order to assist sinful, i.e. guilty, friends, neighbours, members of one's club or political party. Institutional and professional solidarity nurtures an esprit de corps that encourages refined mendacity. Among judges, doctors, surveyors, policemen there are those who feel duty-bound to act in accordance with this putative social obligation. Regimental honour often embodies the duty to lie in favour of a guilty fellow-soldier. During WWII, in a foreign land, the officer commanding the company in which I served saw to it that the civilian and military police were unable to lay a charge against one of our men who had committed a serious offence. Though we all held the soldier culpable, we protected him by not disclosing his identity and whereabouts. In 1894 Dreyfus was wrongly convicted of treason and sent to Devil's Island. It was the result of a malevolent conspiracy. Only in 1906 was he formally cleared though the evidence, on which he was convicted, had already been revealed as flawed shortly after his trial. The public campaign to exonerate him — associated with Zola's famous 'J'accuse' — may actually have prolonged his agony. The majority of officers, *including some who were convinced that he was innocent,* saw the agitation to free him as an affront to the honour of the French army. Hence, attempts to release Dreyfus were frustrated by a series of stratagems. This is a textbook example of how men, goaded by an institutional loyalty, can become guilty of evil mendacity.

Galileo was not tortured when he was pressured to disavow his opinion that the sun was the centre of the spheres and it is the earth which rotates. The request had come from the Holy Office but yet Galileo did not comply with it; he was accused of asserting matters which seemed to contradict

---

[5] According to Enoch Powell the literal translation of 'you shall love your neighbour' is flawed: he claimed that 'there is no distinctive force in "neighbour"'.

Scripture. Years later, after he had been subjected to intensive cross-examination at the commissariat of the inquisition, he changed his *public* stance. Again there is no proof that he was physically tortured before he gave in and on his knees recited the prescribed abjurations, declaring that henceforth he would detest his errors and heresies. Galileo had undertaken to lie. According to James Brodrick, a modern Jesuit who has not hesitated to call the then pope 'stupid', maintains that the pope had *in private* accepted the validity of Galileo's theses but yet wanted him to abjure his alleged heresies. Galileo died in 1642. In 1992 the full assembly of the Pontifical College in Rome was told that after 13 years of deliberations a papal commission finally concluded that Galileo had been right: the earth does revolve around the sun. It would be rash to surmise that only at the end of the twentieth century had the powerful and well-informed leaders of the Roman Catholic global empire suddenly discovered this, now acknowledged, fact. I offer two explanations why Rome nevertheless suppressed this truth for centuries. They are by no means unique as many other large institutions have chosen to lie for the same reasons though perhaps none did this so consistently and during such a lengthy period. In Brodrick's historical account Galileo's theories were deemed to be 'rash as things stood and unsettling to simple mind'. Like other institutions the heads of the papal empire may well have argued that 'for the good of the public' the truth should not be disseminated. Why reveal matters to the masses which they cannot really comprehend but may bring about unsettling mental consequences? The second reason has to do with the eminence of the institution: there is the justified fear that if one goes on record to announce the errors of its most prominent spokesman, this dark shadow may also weaken the credibility of other papal pronouncements.

The people at the helm of giant organizations depend on assistants to ration the information that reaches their desk. Dictators surround themselves with adjutants who, supposedly, convey loyally the pertinent truth however unpalatable. This is so in theory but in many cases personal, faithful confidants have faked messages by, for example, inserting notes of false optimism. There are authenticated instances where the entourages have suppressed important news that they knew would not be welcomed. This happened to Hitler and, most pronouncedly, to Stalin.[6] Why do high-ranking attendants behave in this disloyal manner? One motivation is a genuine concern for the boss who is thus being spared annoyance from reading messages with displeasing contents. But there are often also selfish reasons for such deceptions: these liars prefer to lie and live rather than take the risk of facing an unpleasant fate when transmitting truthful, but annoying, contents. It would be fatuous to propound that the conduct of megalomaniac, bloodthirsty dictators is analogous to the conduct of leading captains of industry in the Western world. Yet, even some of these influential men (and the generalization applies perhaps even more to women) are rarely prepared to reward assistants and advisers who consistently bring to their attention bad tidings. In the UK of the twenty-first century honest and dedicated assistants are not exiled to the Gulag for bringing distasteful facts to the notice of their masters. However, such awkward employees may be demoted or have their employment terminated. High-fliers in hierarchical institutions, conscious of who butters their bread and determines their future prospects, will not persist in telling their employers too frequently things which these eminent men and women hate to hear. Far better to massage the truth.

The following incident is another example where it was deemed holier to disseminate an untruth rather than tell an unpalatable truth. John Paul I, elected pope on 27 August 1978, died under strange circumstances on 29 September 1978. Autopsies are not performed on popes which added to the conspiracy rumours. The Vatican spread a false story about John Magee, secretary to Pope John Paul I (and later a bishop in Ireland), who allegedly had been the first to find the body. (Magee himself later denied this.) It was the custom that each morning a nun left a cup of coffee outside the

---

[6] An authoritative joint KGB and CIA study by Murphy, Kondrashev and Bailey documents how Cold War reports were filtered and revised until they were fashioned in a form which was sure to appease Stalin. 'Many intelligence reports on Berlin were never disseminated because it would have been politically risky to do so... KGB officials suppressed information that might have contradicted established policy or the party line.' One report on a British cabinet meeting, that reached the Soviet intelligence service, went only to Molotov and Zorin but not to Stalin as it would have been 'certain to irritate the irascible leader'.

Pope's bedroom. On the relevant day the nun found that the cup had not been drunk and consequently she opened the door and thus became the first person to see him dead in bed. According to Edward Stourton 'the idea that a woman had been the first person to see the body was considered so shocking that the John Magee story was put out instead. It is characteristic of Vatican thinking . . . that a female presence should have been thought less acceptable than a public lie.'

Some Writers Lie

Genuine fiction writers are not liars but those writers, who fabricate fictional accounts and present them as non-fiction, are. Since the invention of the printing press some writers have been marketing their wares under false colours. When the deceptions are exposed, the liars or their publishers have defended these bad deeds as 'harmless' as they were 'victimless'. Literary falsehoods are often soft-pedalled as being merely 'hoaxes'. Nigel West has devoted a whole tome to laying bare the truth about seventeen British, putatively autobiographical, books in which the writers publicly indulged their fantasies about intelligence exploits that they had allegedly carried out in WWII. They hawked their fiction, dressed up as facts, making use of doctored photographs, faked documents and manufactured records.

While the Stalinist and Nazi regimes imprisoned and murdered scores of writers who were deemed to be 'enemies of the state', thousands of obedient writers and journalists in the USSR and Germany produced mendacious accounts. (When the dictatorships were overthrown, some of them recanted and admitted that they had done so under duress.) But while one can find some words of sympathy for those who were prevented from writing truthfully by dictatorial regimes, this consideration does not apply to the many liars who lived in countries where they did not have to fear retaliation by the state. The English historian A.J.P. Taylor wrote elegantly about a famous academic without using the taboo word: 'In private conversation Laski had the amiable weakness of inventing facts to support his argument; and in his writings, too, he inclined to believe that the facts would conform to the ideas, if only these were brilliant enough.'

In the last quarter of the twentieth century numerous writers in the Western world behaved cravenly when publishers and the electronic media were unwilling to handle writings that were not in conformity with the current PC. These modern oppressors are powerful enough to bully writers who must then either forgo being published or having to lie obsequiously. In 1957 Peter Hall had been banned in London from directing the *Cat on a Hot Tin Roof* because the play had some homosexual undertones. He recalled this, almost 40 years later, when he prepared a drama series for the UK TV Channel 4 which was based on *Sacred Hunger*, written by Barry Unsworth about the African slave trade. When he sought a financial backer in the US, he was rebuffed by what he called 'liberal censorship'. One American TV company was actually happy to finance the project provided none of the slave traders were black. The book (and history) said otherwise: black barons did sell blacks to white traders. Those who imposed the PC condition did not suggest that the writer or producer had invented something which was false. 'The Americans were terrified that if we show a black slave trader, they'll lose money at the box office . . . they will be thought "incorrect" by a sizeable part of the dollar-paying public. They don't want to offend the black community.'[7]

With some exceptions,[8] publishing anonymously or under a pen-name constitutes lying. Writers who do so deceive their readers or, at best, suppress the truth about the identity of the author that may be highly relevant. Senior civil servants have used a nom de plume in order to portray their political masters in a bad light. Individuals with grievances against their employers, who are not courageous enough to come out openly as whistle-blowers, have published diatribes while simultaneously being paid by their victims. Those who thus pen diabolic attacks on institutions and individuals have a distinct advantage in that the injured parties cannot rebut ad hominem. The individuals who opt for these subterfuges, be they noble or nefarious, must therefore be categorized as liars. But there is another side to this coin. Writers may discover that they cannot find a trade publisher

---

[7] Simon Blow, 'Censorship then and now', *The Spectator* January 11, 1997.
[8] Some writers use a pen-name and *say so publicly*. Thus, a famous UK economist published his academic writings under his real name while his prolific output of detective stories was brought out under an assumed name. This openly declared compartmentalization was clearly not an act of deception.

who, for a variety of reasons, is willing (or able) to market their writings when their real name is cumbersome or the individual has an unpalatable past or association. During the McCarthy era, Hollywood studios did not dare to publicize the real name of writers who were suspected of being communists; they did however make use of their scripts when these were signed with a fictitious name. In the nineteenth century women writers were frequently persuaded that they could only became famous if they signed their manuscripts with an adopted male pseudonym.

One does not have to be a Moslem to write, located in Paris, serious articles about Saudi Arabia. However, from the commercial standpoint of a non-academic publishing house, it is more exciting to bring out a book by a writer who can say that he has lived for forty years in Riyhad and, now, relating his personal experiences, was penning startling revelations. Particularly, if his name is Muhammad and not Pierre, he will be preferred to the 'theoretician' in Paris. I illustrate this with a few of the many articles and books on record that illustrate this trend. Writers, who exploit the current PC atmosphere and are ready to lie in accordance with it, know how decisively this may enhance their chance to harvest book prizes which would otherwise elude them. Authors, who are allegedly from ethnic minorities and/or are disabled and/or have an unorthodox sexual orientation possess passports which can pave the way for the publication, and later raving reviews, of mediocre manuscripts. Several Australian publishers seem to have had the misfortune to have fallen prey to an infatuation with PC.

(a) Helen Darville, the daughter of English-born parents, who nursed literary ambitions, was fully aware how her mundane national origin was a definite handicap. As Helen Demidenko she won the top Australian literary prize. In her book, which she claimed was based upon stories of her relatives, she wrote of Ukrainian complicity in WWII. An uncle was said to have told her of his own crimes. Her father was said to have arrived in Australia crippled by polio while her mother had to work as a maid. In Australia there are grants for authors with a non-English background; she received these and earned also prizes. The publisher was happy when she appeared dressed in Ukrainian costumes at award ceremonies. It was of course all lies and lies — her middle class parents came from the North of England.

(b) The writer, who was originally known as Colin Johnson, gained fame as Mudrooroo, the revered voice of the Aborigines. His prolific writings about 'my people' were seemingly authentic as it was deemed in Australia that only a true insider, a genuine Aborigine, could have written meaningfully and accurately on the subject. The contrived public origin of Mudrooroo, a tear-jerker, was embedded in his (false) personal history. He was depicted as one of the blighted generation of 'stolen children' who were forcibly removed from their Aboriginal mothers. Those who believed this spoke of him as one who had overcome racism and other hardships — a model for his people! Mudrooroo, showered with prizes for his novels and poetry, was made head of Aboriginal studies at the university of Perth. When these personal tales were being debunked, the infamous liar's sister 'outed' him by revealing that they had a Negro grandfather from North Carolina but there was not a drop of Aboriginal blood in the family.

(c) The Rev. Toby Forward grew up in the Asian communities of Birmingham (England) and wrote short stories about girls in that environment. He was white, educated, middle class and wise. Hence he concluded that no UK publisher would be interested in a book by him — unless he changed his personal details. He chose the name of Rahila Kahn who, as an Asian woman, was deemed knowledgeable enough to write authoritatively on the subject. It was a success story until his agent divulged the truth.

(d) In 1939 Richard Llewellyn became rich as the author of a semi-biographical book on the hard life in a Welsh mining community. It became a best-seller in the English-speaking world. So famous was this book that the University of Texas bought his private papers in the 1960s. Some forty years after its first edition an American researcher discovered that his real name was Richard Lloyd; he had changed it for obvious reasons. He was of course not born in Wales but in Hendon, a borough of London. While his book would have it that he had worked in a Welsh mine, nothing could have been further from the truth.

(e) If Rigoberto Menchu had offered her mendacious story as a work of fiction, it might never have been published but as an autobiographical story it became a global best-seller and earned her the Nobel Peace Prize. She, who had been educated by Belgian nuns, portrayed herself as an illiterate poor girl in Guatemala. Her own brother was surprised to read that he had died while working for slave wages on a coffee plantation — one of numerous untruths.

(f) Even worse was the fate of the *Washington Post* which was duped by its reporter Janet Cooke. She wrote several articles about an eight-year old heroin addict who she claimed to have interviewed; he was a figment of her imagination. It was said that 'everyone wanted to believe her story . . . she was young, black and attractive'. Because her lies were believed, she was awarded the Pulitzer Prize.

(g) Kim Stacey was dismissed from a newspaper in Kentucky after she had written five articles about how she was dying of brain tumour. The pathetic series was sensational except that it was wholly untrue.

(h) *The New York Times* was forced to acknowledge in 2003 that one of its reporters, Jayson Blair, had fabricated stories; the publishers regarded it as so serious that it brought about the resignation of two of its editors.

(i) Even more scandalous was the experience of America's largest circulation daily *US TODAY* which discovered that its most prominent foreign correspondent, Jack Kelley, had to resign after it was found that during more than ten years he had invented stories. It happened more than once that his war reportages were accompanied by stories on how the reporter had risked his life under crossfire while he was in fact enjoying the safety of a hotel room, far behind the lines.[9]

(j) I have personal knowledge of how the editor of a newspaper unwittingly gave prominence to the fabled eyewitness account of a British journalist during the bloody fighting in country A. He discovered (but too late) that the dispatch had been composed in, and transmitted to him from, country B; the dishonest journalist had never been in A.

(k) Two affairs deserve to be quoted because they cost the naïve publishers — who ought to have been more sceptical — a great deal of money; the liars concerned did not lie only for vanity's sake but also to enrich themselves. Thus *Corriere*

---

[9] The *Daily Telegraph* and the *Sunday Times* have over the years published several (uncontested) exposures on these literary happenings in Australia and the US. I have drawn upon them in part for my cited illustrations.

della Sera published as a world scoop the faked letters of Benito Mussolini. *The Sunday Times*, *Paris Match* and *Stern* were jointly taken in when they published the (invented) diaries of Hitler that had been certified as true by renowned experts.

Plagiarism is clearly a mendacious endeavour. One of the worst examples has been revealed posthumously concerning the German playwright Bertolt Brecht. As a result of research in the USSR, the DDR and the US, John Fuegi has documented what several other critics had long suspected: a considerable percentage of his famous plays and 100% of his less famous plays are attributable to Elisabeth Hauptmann, his close collaborator whose contributions were not highlighted and sometimes not even mentioned by the celebrated Brecht. Particularly after the demise of the DDR, his dishonesty in claiming sole or major authorship was discussed in several German publications. Finally, mention must be made of a subject which has not had the attention which it ought to have had: the mendacious behaviour of some translators. In so far as they do their job badly, they are to be condemned as incompetent and not as liars. But, for a variety of reasons — and there are cases where they have acted in connivance with, or on orders of, publishers — translators have been known to sanitize the original language editions. 'Polishing' the text is sometimes deemed a holy task when an English-language translation is prepared of a book written in, say, French which contains derogatory remarks about the people in, say, America.

Certain scientific books and articles in learned journals have in time been revealed to be fallacious without the writers having been liars.[10] Those who perpetrate scientific fraud by the wholesale invention of data are of course liars but

---

[10] A number of scientists — the anthropologist Margaret Mead, who presented her seemingly revolutionary findings in *Coming of an Age in Samoa*, is an outstanding example — have made world-shaking 'discoveries' which proved to be wholly fictitious. Some were indeed premeditated liars but others have pleaded that they were duped and a few claimed to have been victims of a conspiracy. Gould has described the bitter fate which befell a German university professor who had boasted of his having detected the 'Luegensteine'. Johann Beringer announced that he had found fossils with features that were unlike any hitherto found on any conventional fossils. They showed frogs copulating as well as heavenly objects. Some were marked with Hebrew letters, spelling the name of God Yehovah. He wrote of all this in a sensational book where he rebutted the charges of critics that his

these are relatively rare. More frequently do scientific liars ignore or suppress drug trial results which do not suit their beliefs or hypotheses. In 2004 the *Journal of the American Medical Association* published an article by An-Wen Chan, an Oxford University researcher, who on the basis of one hundred scientific trials, presented findings which showed how 'inconvenient' results were often not published and of course not disclosed to the public. Alexander Kohn and Broad & Wade have assembled historical data on a host of scientists who, from Isaac Newton onwards, have been guilty of deceiving their readers. History has been kind to many mendacious scientists when their theories turned out to be correct though their writings about the actual testing in the laboratories had not been honest. Newton was found guilty but few remember him today for the lies in some of his writings because his motive had been 'to lie for the truth'. On the other end of the scale Cyril Burt was also induced to lie for the same motive. He had a theory that 75% of human intelligence is inherited. His mendacity consisted in fabricating data to support this theory. He is remembered for this because his theory was not validated. Those who falsify scientific data, thus argues Kohn, probably start and succeed with the lesser crime of 'improving' upon existing results.

'Minor and seemingly trivial instances of data manipulation — such as making results appear just a little crisper or more definitive than they really are, or selecting just the "best" data for publication and ignoring those that don't fit the case — are probably far from unusual in science.' Kohn has enriched our vocabulary of synonyms for lying by recalling the work of Charles Babbage, an English mathematician born in 1792. He is saluted as the trailblazer who first investigated systematically the mendacious activities of scientists. Babbage spoke of 'forging' when untruthful observations are published. The term is also applied to allegedly executed experiments which were never performed. 'Forging' is thus an outright lie. If genuine data are manipulated to suit the

---

fossils were not authentic and that his findings had only recently been carved. Alas, he was the victim of the dirty tactics by two colleagues who hated him and had gone to considerable trouble to plan this debacle. Beringer was indeed guilty of conceit and professional injudiciousness — but he was not a liar. When he finally concluded that he was bamboozled, he impoverished himself by buying back all copies of his book.

vested interests of the scientists, this is described as 'trimming'; when, for example, a number of animals are added to or subtracted from control or experimental groups. (Kohn reminds us that the current terms are 'fudging' and 'massaging data'.) 'Cooking' takes place when only those data are cited which back up the hypotheses of the researchers; data that do not fit are discarded. (Kohn reports that in today's jargon this is designated as 'finagling'; it tells only half the truth.) 'Cooking' is encountered also when scientific papers omit aberrant values, misreport actual conditions of experiments or alter ancillary data. A kindred type of lying is the omission of whole experiments which had yielded negative results, to wit were contrary to the hypotheses under test.

For Good and Bad Causes

Pro Patria

Plato wanted people to be punished when they lied for private ends; to him such behaviour was 'pernicious and subversive'. He postulated that the 'rulers of the state are the only ones who should have the privilege of lying for the benefits of the state; no others may have anything to do with it'. Ever since, politicians and obedient civil servants have boasted of the patriotic lies which they have disseminated on behalf of their country. This motivation is highly flexible. It is a relatively simple proposition when the sole intent is to help defeat an external enemy. But even then there is a case for moral restraint to keep patriotic lying in bounds. During WWII British intelligence officers, based in London, are rumoured to have lied to some of their agents who were parachuted into France: they were supplied with false dossiers relating to the invasion plans of the Allies. These lies were imparted to them because it was hoped that at least one agent would be captured and under torture reveal the planted (false) information to the enemy. Agents were ordinarily issued with poison pills so that they could commit suicide when caught. Allegedly, the agents concerned were given dud pills so that they would be unable to end their lives. Did the aim to dupe the enemy legitimatize this outrage against dedicated patriots?

The allies who fought Germany in WWII suspected that the rulers of the USSR had been responsible for the murder of some 10,000 Polish officers who were buried secretly in the Katyn woods. The Russians lied, asserting that these Poles had been butchered by the Nazis. In the midst of the war the Germans delivered convincing proof that the Russians were the guilty party. The Western powers, however, did not regard it as expedient to concede that their ally, the USSR, was the culprit. Hence the conspiratorial suppression of the truth. But why was this mendacious strategy continued after the defeat of the Germans? Some Western politicians did indeed break rank and stated publicly that the erstwhile enemy, Germany, had told the truth while the Russians had lied continuously. But most of the Western political decision-makers counselled that the truth ought still not be proclaimed officially lest it exacerbate the Cold War. For the (spurious) sake of détente, deemed to be in Britain's interest, the falsehood, which blamed the Germans for the Katyn massacre, was perpetuated.

Lying pro patria is sometimes a screen behind which politicians and generals attempt to promote their careers and/or disguise their failures. Napoleon set the tone for mendacious communiqués, issued by military commanders in the field. This precedent has been emulated by generals of different nationalities who have likewise released false news, ostensibly to deceive the enemy or to raise morale at home. Historians have unearthed numerous bogus alibis of this kind. They have also found that some generals even lied when they sent confidential assessments to their political masters. Several generals, who have boasted in their memoirs of the lies they told for allegedly patriotic reasons, did so in fact to cloak the military fiascos which they had caused.

Roosevelt, who considered in 1940 assisting substantively the UK in the war against the Germans, simultaneously entertained the ambition to be re-elected president. He knew full well that there was no chance of his being re-elected if he so much as dropped a hint about his intention to help Britain topple Hitler. Being a pragmatic fox, Roosevelt desisted from telling the truth about what he was striving to do if he won the electoral contest. Mendaciously, he appealed to the isolationist sentiments of many voters by declaring: 'your boys are not going to be sent into any foreign wars' which is exactly what he did soon thereafter. In 1964 President Johnson campaigned for re-election, fully cognizant that most of the electorate was hostile to US involvements in foreign theatres of war. He therefore portrayed his Republican opponent, Barry Goldwater, as a warmonger while presenting himself as a candidate who yearned for peace. Immediately after winning the election, he put into operation the covertly prepared plans to intensify the war in Vietnam.

In peacetime the morality of lying for one's country raises hard and puzzling issues. Is it moral to deceive not only foreigners but also the public of one's own country? May one lie to apprehend those who would corrupt our youngsters by importing heroin? What about lying to raise domestic living standards? Should we praise those who pursue a pro patria policy by falsifying statistics so that additional foreign aid can be squeezed out of foreign donors? Some beneficiaries of the Marshal Plan were the first to perform such a patriotic duty but since then the LDC countries have learnt how rewarding it is to cheat international agencies — some of which actually want to be cheated — by submitting false data in order to enhance the flow of unrequited foreign assistance. B. Gross had first-hand Washington knowledge of the applications for aid which were spiced with tailor-made data. He related that, when the Marshall Plan was being introduced, one of the chief European figures had told him: 'We shall produce any statistic that we think will help us to get as much money out of the United States as we can. Statistics which we do not have but which we need to justify our demands, we will simply fabricate.' In 1992 Turkey's Ministry of Finance reneged on a commitment to the IMF. Over a period of fifteen months it had employed a stratagem that camouflaged the real growth of the money supply; reportedly, the IMF turned a blind eye. Only in the year 2000 did an auditor's report reveal that, three years previously, the Ukraine's central bank had engaged in a series of clandestine transactions to overstate the country's foreign exchange reserves to obtain a greater IMF loan than it would have been entitled to if the IMF has known about them.

Politicians, contriving to hoodwink foreigners 'in the national interest' would often prefer it if in the process they did not also have to deceive their own people. But compartmentalization, involving the release of contradictory official accounts for domestic and foreign consumption respectively, is rarely feasible. In 1992 the Japanese government, in response to pressures from foreign countries to transform its economic policy, did play such a trick. To placate its foreign critics, the Ministry of Finance issued unrealistic forecasts, the absurdity of which was of course obvious to domestic cognoscenti. The Japanese public read in their newspapers that the announcement about the predicted magic growth was meant for 'foreign consumption'. A leader of the ruling party, Hiroshi Mitsuzuka, even spelt it out. He told the electorate that 'the forecasts were made for another country, not for our own'. There have always been incentives for politicians of certain countries to fashion the size and composition of the reported GDPs in a manner that, they hoped, would prove materially helpful to their economies. The smaller the announced national product, the lower the requisite financial contributions (for membership fees and other purposes) that need to be delivered to supranational organizations. The lower the per capita GDP, the more financial assistance is given to the 'poor' country by international bodies and the better-off countries. Hence LDC politicians find it opportune to exaggerate the estimated size of their population and to understate the volume of the GDP.

Suppressing the truth about infectious diseases and contaminated water supplies is a perverse form of mendacity by altruistic politicians who seek to protect their countries' tourist industry. In the days of Mussolini, when Italian newspapers were censored, the government was actually able to conceal a polio epidemic in Venice. Today such a patriotic 'game' can only be played in very few countries. In 2004 the Chinese government bullied its press not to report the full details of the SARS epidemic. Rebellious journalists were dismissed but, thanks to e-mail, the Chinese government failed to suppress the truth as effectively as Mussolini was once able to do. In the spring of 1991 Peru was ravaged by a severe outbreak of cholera. At first the news was hushed up but ultimately the official tourist agency confirmed it, adding the untruth that no tourist had become involved. A member of the government caught the disease and was sent to a military hospital; it was announced that he was suffering from laryngitis. In 1985 cholera spread from the countryside to the Ethiopian capital city. The rulers of the country refused to acknowledge the widespread incidence of the disease; official instructions were given to denote it as 'acute dysentery'. This patriotic lying was practised so as not to frighten off tourists. It was also meant to counteract the reluctance of foreign countries to import Ethiopian coffee. All countries must inform the WHO when highly communicable diseases are rampant. Sudan and Ethiopia did not comply with their duty to inform the WHO that they had a cholera epidemic. Instead, they referred to 'severe gastroenteritis' and 'acute diarrhoea'. The WHO knew this to be a lie but its charter prevented it from alerting the world.

Patriotic lying of an elegant nature is practised widely in rich and LDC economies where the governmental perpetrators have no compunction about lying if it helps to champion the export prospects of their domestic companies. Governments have been known to provide forged certificates-of-origin and false end-user documents for meritorious export firms. Export subsidies are furnished surreptitiously by governments which have signed treaties not to do so. 'Unofficially', mendacious trickeries with the object of stealing technological secrets from other countries are known to have occurred. In many countries the official trade statistics are not always truthful. Some of the numerate inputs have been falsified by traders and manufacturers in collusion with officials in the importing and exporting economies. Countries, which have instituted general or specific import restrictions, are nevertheless penetrated by supplies of the forbidden goods. This is described euphemistically as 'exporting by unconventional means'. It can entail smuggling, the corruption of customs officers or the presentation of false manifests. The last-mentioned technique brings it about that the official statistics report the import of industrial machinery when the goods actually brought in are luxury video-recorders; deadly weapons may be exported and imported by describing them as machine tools. To smooth the path for the export of goods which are subject to heavy import duties, manufacturers may denote $5,000 consignments as having a value of only $3,000. Under-invoicing and over-invoicing are important elements in the distortion of the records of international trade. Most politicians adopt a nonchalant attitude. If the national interest is not thereby affected adversely, falsified statistics on cross-border trade are seen to be, at worst, an unfortunate fact of life.

Until sterling was floated in 1992 all British post-war governments published misleading data on the UK's foreign currency reserves. None excelled at this practice more than Harold Wilson and (his partner) the Earl of Cromer, Governor of the BoE. Whistling in the dark, Wilson boasted in 1966 that his chancellor had given an 'absolutely frank, straight, honest statement' to the HoC; with a sense of humour he added — though nobody laughed — that the country had got 'pretty well used to accepting that we do tell the facts'. Even after Cromer had openly admitted his role in a long and persistent campaign of deception, there was a general tendency — at least in Britain — to fight shy of denouncing this strategy as lying par excellence. Some actually congratulated him for his patriotism. Even critics preferred flowery euphemisms to extenuate his monthly mendacious reports. Harold Wilson went on record to call the falsified numerate returns 'token figures'. When *The Economist* commented acerbically on the Earl's misdeeds, it did so in the implied belief that its readers would not stomach any overt reference to lies. Nothing was therefore written in coarse language. The journal was satisfied to castigate the BoE for its latest 'trickery' and the 'obfuscation of . . . reserve figures'; it said unkindly that the selections of these false data was akin to 'picking a figure out of a hat'.

Most civil service statisticians in the non-communist world, who obediently concoct misleading figures, had good personal reasons to comfort themselves that they are exemplary patriots. Declining to participate in these games may have led to some losing their job or at least the effacement of their good promotion prospects but none has been shot for refusing to do what they are told. Things were different in the USSR. Stalin lost no sleep when he arranged to send the globally known statistician Nikolai Kondratiev to prison where he was to die. Stalin aimed at hoodwinking the outside world and his people by disseminating falsehoods relating to the growth of the national output. He was also very eager to inflate the Russian demographic figures. Stalin announced that, thanks to the merits of socialism, the annual population increase was about 3 million — a completely unwarranted boast that was only buried ceremoniously in the days of Gorbachev. Kondratiev and his senior colleagues had not been sufficiently servile. They refused to produce the data, needed to back up this Stalinist lie, because the requested statistics were blatantly at odds with the (unpublished) censuses and surveys. After they were dismissed, it was officially stated that a 'serpent's nest of traitors in the apparatus of Soviet statistics had exerted themselves to diminish the population of the USSR'. Thereafter, Kondratiev's successors actively invented data that pleased Stalin. There was no consensus in the West on how enormous were these lies. The false statistics published by communist Russia did confuse the capitalist world but, incidentally, they also misled the USSR's decision-makers.

The Devaluation Cowards

In 1931 Britain's financial editors were called to the Treasury where one naughty man actually asked about the likelihood of a sterling devaluation through an abandonment of the gold standard. Douglas Jay remembers that the spokesman's face 'flushed with passion; he was like a housemaster who had caught boys exchanging obscenities'. He shouted at the questioner: 'Unthinkable ... an affront to national honour ... I hope no one will repeat such sentiments outside this room.' A week later the journalists were summoned to hear about the devaluation which the Treasury spokesman described as 'excellent news'. In July 1949 the chancellor of the exchequer told the HoC: 'His Majesty's government have not the slightest intention of devaluing the pound.' It actually happened in September. After Harold Wilson had become prime minister in 1964, he repeatedly condemned any talk of devaluation: to him 'it was almost a religious issue'. The last time that Wilson and Chancellor Callaghan denied any such intention was in October 1967 — it came to pass in November. At the instigation of Chancellor of the Exchequer John Major, who soon thereafter became prime minister, the UK joined in 1990 the Brussels-based exchange rate mechanism (ERM) which arbitrarily determined the official value of the shackled sterling. He appointed Norman Lamont as his chancellor who characterized the notion, that the UK ought to leave the ERM in order to devalue, as a recipe for catastrophe. In 1992 Major and Lamont were forced by events to abandon ERM membership and sterling was floated. Within weeks Lamont, who had previously declared himself opposed to any devaluation, now exulted over his new freedom to operate with a sterling currency, the price of which would be fixed by the vagaries of the market.

The motives of politicians who go out of their way to retain unrealistic parities are often said to be their concern for the 'the national interest'. Often this is a threadbare excuse. Wilson's disastrous and prolonged stance is explained in part by personal vanity. In addition, he and Callaghan believed that a devaluation would mar the electoral prospects of their party. John Major favoured fixed exchange rates because he believed that a stable sterling rate was a political virility symbol. Politicians are prone to delay overdue devaluations because they fear that if the price of the national currency is lowered against that of other currencies, they would be stamped as 'losers'. Wilson could have been helpful to the UK economy, without the Labour Party being severely damaged, if he had voluntarily devalued the British currency immediately on assuming office. Instead, he waited for more than three years. Margaret Thatcher too paid a heavy price for curtailing the free movement of sterling. Her Chancellor of the Exchequer Lawson had tied the pound to the German currency and she allowed his successor Chancellor Major to bully her into dragging the UK into the ERM. All these events were accompanied by lies and lies. The governmental defence of unsound, artificial, Sterling parities helped some sophisticated individuals and large corporation to amass fortunes by lawful and unlawful means. The losers were the ingenuous and law-abiding citizens who trusted the mendacious proclamations of the politicians.

I have always opined that it was not in the best interest of the UK to have fixed exchange rates. Those, however, who did not share this view were automatically obliged to condone the lies of politicians that were meant to prop an overvalued currency. There was, however, no reason why journalists, academics and independent public figures should not have spoken out to warn the country. If after 1964 these had done so *in public* and forecast that sooner or later a devaluation was bound to come, they would have done their duty and performed a public service because the agony of operating with Wilson's phoney sterling *would* have ended much sooner. However, in the then prevailing atmosphere it was not comfortable to decry the obstinate, but democratically elected, prime minister. The few who raised their voices were denounced by members of the government for even mentioning the possibility of devaluation; they could only whisper in private. Wilson prohibited the distribution of pro-devaluation position papers within the top echelon of his administration. He dreaded that any mention of the accursed word 'devaluation' might demoralize his warriors. The prime minister was amazingly successful — it could not happen nowadays — in muzzling individuals outside the civil service including almost all who occupied influential positions in the media. Few editors dared ignore the implicit ban on the publishing of discussion features which set out the benefits that would accrue from a devaluation. The editor of a banking review rejected an article by an Oxford academic on the forbidden theme. The editor praised him for his well-argued and well-written submission. But, he remarked, that 'at the moment' the magazine could not harbour authors who favoured his prescription. The *Observer* was disobedient in that it permitted a professor of the LSE to criticize the authorities for keeping the obsolete sterling parity that was set in 1949 and had not been adjusted since. Harold Wilson in person reprimanded the editor-proprietor for his lack of patriotism. For two years the paper desisted from this heresy until it actually advocated devaluation. The original admonition had been made in private but on this occasion the prime minister launched his attack in public. The *Observer*'s deplorable proposal was berated as a 'defeatist cry . . . a wet editorial . . . by moaning minnies . . . who will seek any opportunity to sell Britain short at home and abroad'. Despite such outbursts, historians will wish to defend Wilson for never threatening to garrotte the perceived enemies-of-the-state. If we are to believe the post-1967 confessions, the vast majority of academic economists, practically every serious economic journalist and numerous top civil servants had all been of the opinion that failure to devalue was detrimental to the British economy. Nevertheless, they chose to be passive liars and did not come out of the closet; not a single resignation on this issue appears to have occurred. After the devaluation event they related how they had always favoured it; this was to prove their cerebral aptitude. Very few felt honour-bound to say 'peccavi' and acknowledge their personal guilt in suppressing the truth.

The two most guilty parties were the luminaries of the *FT* and *The Economist*. If they had published the truth, to wit the strong belief of their editors that resistance to the inescapable devaluation was a calamity, their influential standing would very quickly have forced Wilson to abandon his dogmatic stance. But they feared the wrath of the government. The *FT*'s star writer Sam Brittan, then the UK's most distinguished economic commentator, had an international repute. He naturally disapproved of Wilson's policy — but stayed silent. (Of course the owners of the *FT* could have stopped him writing what he thought. But in that case, he could have resigned without thereby becoming a pauper.) After 1967 Brittan built up an alibi that did him no credit. He claimed that the press had been 'censored or self-censored' and 'for three years the public had been taught to believe that the devaluation was a disaster, a disgrace and a dishonour'. To fend off criticism he wrote (in the post-devaluation year) about one of his heroic deeds: he mentioned to his admiring public that, subversively, he had pierced the censorship. While the *FT* had never been an *overt* advocate of devaluation, he had nevertheless managed to pull the wool over Wilson's eyes. Brittan boasted that his paper had actually referred to the desirability of 'fundamental policy changes'. Who was to blame that this putative pro-devaluation message was not understood by 10 Downing Street or by anybody else? 'Our readers were not as quick to decode as we had hoped.' No doubt the readers of *The Times* must have been equally stupid. They also did not seem to have appreciated that Peter Jay, its economic editor, had secretly 'waged a coded campaign for devaluation' — so he declared after the 1967 event. What pitiful, unconvincing excuses!

The Economist repented shortly after Wilson had thrown in the towel. Its writers then felt liberated and belatedly elucidated why a devaluation had always been inevitable: 'It has been clear for some years that sterling has been overvalued.' Its readers were now enlightened that the devaluation had arrived because of the 'inexorable pressure of facts'. Unlike the *FT*, *The Economist* confessed to its sins unreservedly, lamenting that 'this has therefore been a beastly three years' for its editors. In a hushed style it conceded that 'in the past this newspaper has often visibly pulled its punches when discussing Britain's obviously crumbling exchange rate'. The laconic 'obviously' raises a discomfiting question. If it was so manifestly apparent, why did not the magazine let its readers discern the truth at a point of time when it really mattered? The editors craved for our sympathy because of their suffering during the beastly period. I think that commiseration should be reserved for the subscribers to a financial journal who were deceived by an intensive suppression of the truth.

There is no gainsaying that intellectual honesty was brushed aside by the UK economists who had not spoken up. Yet, despite Wilson's pompous blusters, no one had to fear being harmed physically if he did not join in the sponsored conspiracy to lie about the merits of a sterling devaluation though swimming against the stream would not have been pleasant. A few words must be said about young Nigel Lawson who had good reason not to annoy his political elders for he was then busily seeking a constituency which would adopt him as a parliamentary candidate. Nevertheless, despite all the poisonous barbs, he was a lonely heretic who disseminated the truth at his peril. He is an old man now but his period as editor of the *Spectator*, a weekly with a small circulation, was surely the proudest span of his life. For his 'disgraceful' advocacy of devaluation, both in the journal's editorials and in the features that he commissioned, Lawson was castigated widely. Some political 'friends' commended in private his unpatriotic conduct but rebuked him in their public pronouncements. The pro-devaluation articles in his journal were plain and explicit; they were not in a coded style. This separated him from his journalistic confreres who agreed with him but withheld the truth from their readers who were entitled to be told the truth. Alas, there is a codicil. When Lawson, after a significant period as an innovative chancellor of the exchequer in Margaret Thatcher's government, retired from politics, he penned a bulky volume of autobiography. In his memoirs he wrote, without any inhibition, about a particular deception, practised by the Treasury and the BoE. He mocked the naïve people who imagined that the foreign currency reserve figures, 'so conscientiously quoted and commented upon in the financial press', denote the true reserves. Lawson told of two Treasury books. The data in the SPOT BOOK were published while those in the FORWARD BOOK were not. He confessed that he, like his predecessors, had released to the public — but not to 10 Downing Street — misleading statistics:

> During 1987 I understated the size of the inflow of money into London by tucking some of it away in the FORWARD BOOK. The idea of making use of the FORWARD BOOK to conceal the true position was not an innovation of mine. I believe that during the acute run on sterling in 1976 under Labour the true reserves were completely exhausted and actually became negative; and that this was concealed from view. Whatever was concealed from the press or the financial commentators, it goes without saying that the Treasury's own market report, which was sent to Margaret every evening without fail, always gave the full and true figures.

Gollancz Lied For Stalin

Active revolutionaries scorn moralists who debate whether and when lying is allowed. It follows that one had no right to expect editors of communist journals to present the news fairly. The raison d'etre of the *Daily Worker* was to proselytize and dish up apologias for the Fatherland of the Workers — not to furnish information objectively. This kind of avowed mendacious propaganda proved, however, largely ineffective because only gullible persons could thus he duped. Hence the frantic efforts to enlist fellow-travellers in useful positions who could spout with greater credibility falsehoods about life in the USSR, China and the other communist paradises. They were exempt from the formal discipline imposed on members of the communist parties, did not have to swear allegiance to dialectical materialism and were even allowed, nay encouraged, to proclaim adherence to a religious creed. David Caute, Paul Hollander and Paul Johnson have published research studies on the thousands of prominent (mainly Anglo-Saxon) writers, scientists, politicians, religious dignitaries and academics who — not being members of the communist parties — managed to lie adroitly about the communist world. The manipulators in Moscow saw in Hewlett Johnson the globally most effective fellow-traveller. In the name of Christianity, he brushed under the carpet the atheism of the communist leaders and the persecution of the faithful in order to preach that communist societies were ethically on a higher plane than the capitalist countries. He obeyed his masters and, inter alia, spread the myth that the West was waging bacteria warfare 'to destroy the Chinese masses':

> From this capitalist world, where morals are outraged, we turn at last to the Soviet world. There is something singularly Christian and civilized in [its] attitude and intention. Russia is the most moral land that I know. Stalin is no oriental despot. His readiness to relinquish power shows it. [Communist] China is performing an essentially religious act, entirely parallel with the Christian abhorrence of covetousness, freeing man from the bondage of the acquisitive instinct. No persecution of missionaries or Christians has been countenanced by the government.

Stalin thanked the Red Dean (as he was called) in person by receiving him in audience. He was awarded the USSR's coveted Peace Prize. David Caute has noted that the Soviet authorities appreciated his services so highly that he was accorded more lines in the *State Encyclopaedia* than Jesus Christ. Why were the lies of Johnson of greater value than the mendacious testimonies by official and unofficial Marxist propagandists? His biggest lie was to allow his masters to connote him — as was indeed the truth — the 'Dean of Canterbury'. Many in the UK and almost all people outside the UK, who he ensnared with his malicious assertions, were deceived into thinking that he was the Archbishop of Canterbury. There was tremendous pressure on him to resign his clerical post but of course he did not respond for this designation was his main attraction. He ignored the joint appeal by all the five canons of the Canterbury Cathedral who had complained that his pro-Stalin propaganda was 'gravely impairing the spiritual influence of the Cathedral'.

When it was all over, the tribe of fellow-travellers produced a variety of excuses for their mendacity. Many have since claimed that at the time they were ignorant of the reality — something which was genuinely true of only a minority. Others now argue that the guides, who accompanied them on their journeys in the communist countries, were the ones who brainwashed them and should therefore be seen as the real culprits. The relatively few fellow-travellers who have recanted in public maintained that they had been fully aware of the evil which they were praising: they lied because they did not wish to assist the enemies of the USSR as they hated Western capitalism more than they loved the communist countries, the heinous depravities of which they chose not to denounce. Other motives have since also been cited. Thus a large number of fellow-travellers were actuated by the knowledge that if they said or wrote things that pleased the rulers of the USSR, their names would be publicized globally by the Stalinist propaganda machine. This pleased in particular political has-beens but was also at the back of the mind of the many unpaid liars who enjoyed having their vanity tickled. Jean-Paul Sartre, a grovelling apologist for Stalin's crimes, returned in 1934 from Russia; he told his audiences that there was 'total freedom of criticism in the USSR'. When asked in Paris why the Soviet Union does not permit its people to travel abroad, he replied that the Russian citizens have no wish to journey in foreign lands. Of course he knew that these were puerile untruths. But only in 1974, when he prepared himself to meet his Maker, did he feel the need to clear the desk: 'I lied. I wrote an article where I said a number of friendly things about the USSR which I did not believe.' It was not really an abject apology, but still an advance on the conduct of so many of his confreres who did not admit, even after the collapse of the Soviet Union, that they had been propagandist accomplices of the Stalinist regime.

The German writer Lion Feuchtwanger never said 'sorry' for his fatuous declaration which the Communist International reproduced in many languages: 'The air which one breathes in the West is stale and foul. One breathes again when one comes from the oppressive atmosphere of a counterfeit democracy into the invigorating atmosphere of the Soviet Union.' The American author Konigsberger persuaded some of his countrymen that China was 'a country almost as painstakingly careful about human lives as New Zealand'. According to Sweden's Jan Myrdal, Enver Hoxha — in reality one of the world's most blood-stained Stalinist dictators — was 'both respected and beloved [by the people of Albania]. He does not stand above or outside the people'. Warren Miller experienced the 'thrill of standing in the center of history' when he visited Castro's Cuba 'where every man was a brother'. A combination of vanity, exhibitionism and senility played a determinant role when Beatrice and Sidney Webb were found to be frantically intent upon recovering fame in their old age — the Stalinists happily provided this. The couple had once been the archangels of moderate British socialism — Sidney was a member of the first Labour government — who had naturally deplored the 1917 October revolution, compared the USSR with fascist Italy and denounced the diabolical communist labour camps. By the mid-thirties they no longer received the reverential attention which they been accustomed to. It seemed likely that they would be spending the rest of their lives in uneventful retirement but a good opportunity offered itself in 1936. After visiting the Fatherland of the Workers, they published two volumes on *Soviet Communism: A New Civilization*? which proved to be a cover-up of Stalinism by the world-famous erstwhile enemies of the USSR. As their love for the communist tyranny deepened, the question mark was dropped in later editions. The communists were delighted that the Webbs had introduced in their magnum opus some marginal, innocuous criticism of the Soviet Union — for which members of the communist parties would not have been forgiven — because this made their numerous lies appear so much more plausible. The Webbs showered praise upon the 'constructive work of the OGPU (the forerunner of the KGB) in the labour camps' but also lauded it for 'achieving a triumph in human regeneration' because of its prison reform and child rescue work. The journalist Louis Fisher eulogized Stalinism in his dispatches from Moscow. When he broke with the communists because of the 1939 Hitler-Stalin pact, he did cry mea culpa, but like others of his tribe it was not wholehearted: 'Why, instead of holding my tongue, did I not come out as a critic of the Soviet regime? It is not so easy to throw away the vision to which one has been attached for fifteen years. Moreover the Soviet government was effectively anti-fascist. I hesitated to throw stones in public.'

Alexander Werth, like Fisher, was a long-standing fellow-traveller whose Moscow dispatches were printed in several countries. He, like many other liars, denied the existence of *punitive* labour camps. By 1947 the mask had slipped and he had to retract; he now said that there were indeed such camps but they never housed more than two million prisoners. Werth could not plead ignorance for he spoke Russian fluently and had been a long-term resident in the Soviet Union. He knew that the actual numbers were between seven and twelve millions and that these figures were accepted in the West. How certain can one be that Werth was acquainted with the true estimates? In 1967, when he was finally exposed in toto, he conceded that he had lied when he at first said that there were no prisoners in the camp and then, in 1947, whitewashed the true numbers. He asked his duped readers to forgive him because he lied for a noble cause: 'My estimate was lower than most, I admit. But there was a good reason. There were no end of people in Britain and in the US who were advocating a war against Russia. Yes, I had every reason to pull my punches and I don't regret it.' The criminologist Mary Calcott came from the US to investigate a labour camp, the unfortunate prisoners of which were building the Moscow-Volga canal. (It has since been established that thousands died there because of the working conditions and the brutal guards.) She sent home a message to sceptics: 'I could never see what kept men in this camp unless they wanted to stay there. No convicts I have known would have any difficulty if they wanted to break away.'

The draconian collectivization of agriculture brought in its wake hunger to most of the USSR and death from starvation to millions, particularly in the Ukraine. The majority of Stalin's Western friends said nothing in public about the victims in the communist paradise. The British scientist Julian Huxley, imbued with love for Stalin, employed ridiculous hyperboles to tell his Western audiences about a visit to Russia where he received the 'impression of a population not at all undernourished, and at a level of physique and general health rather above that to be seen in England'. G.B. Shaw was advised about the lack of food in the USSR which is why his friends prevailed upon him to take essential food with him on his visit. When he arrived at the Polish-Russian border, he demonstratively threw away all his British food provisions. Soon thereafter, Shaw sent a message to his admirers in which he asserted that it was nonsensical to speak of food shortages. Shaw was not an unqualified success (from the standpoint of Moscow) because world opinion was divided on whether to write off his conduct as mendacious or extravagantly fanciful.

A host of fellow-travellers have spoken, to the detriment of their own country, of the superior justice which prevailed in the USSR. The English barrister D.N. Pritt gave as his professional view that in Stalin's Russia 'imprisonment must be reformatory and is not in the smallest degree punitive'. Maurice Hindus told his audiences: 'Punishment, torture, vindictiveness, severity, humiliation have no place in this system . . . indeed the prison exists not for punishment but for ministration.' The Webbs praised the prison administrators who, so they averred, 'were well spoken of'. In their investigations they discovered that communist prisons were 'now apparently as free from physical cruelty as any prison in any country is ever likely to be.' An American of considerable repute, Anna Louise Strong, would have it that the communist prisons were idyllic institutions: 'So well known and effective is the Soviet method of remaking human beings that criminals occasionally now apply to be admitted.' It is offensive to imply that Britain's esteemed professor of political science, Harold Laski, had such limited erudition as to buy at face value the medley of absurd stories that his Russian handlers had been selling him. He fits our definition of a liar, one who knowingly imparted untruths. Laski revealed that Russia had a much more progressive judicial system than Britain. He said that, unlike in his own country, the (communist) judges wanted the prisoners to lead a 'full and self-respecting life'. The English professor was struck 'by the excellent relations between the prisoners and the warders, and the sense of men who were living a useful life'.

The famous show trials of l936–8 elaborated how, through the good offices of Trotsky, the GESTAPO had infiltrated the leadership of the Russian communist party and the supreme command of the USSR's armed forces. Among the accused were top architects of the 1917 October revolution, prominent founders of the Communist International and contemporary generals of the Red Army. They were charged with murder, espionage, treason and sabotage, committed on orders from the Nazis. All who appeared at the public trials pleaded guilty and told the courts that they had conspired to restore capitalism. These ridiculous allegations were of course untrue and, by prior arrangement, the judges handed down mostly death sentences that were duly carried out. Had Stalin merely sought to eliminate old comrades and those who aspired to occupy his throne, he could have had them shot without the comedy of a trial. But he staged these morbid judicial performances both to terrify the citizens of his country and to send signals to foreign governments. For the latter purpose he asked fellow-travellers, lawyers and others, to attend the court hearings. These foreign guests were expected to send home emollient reports and indeed there was no show trial, however absurd, about which they did not make sympathetic noises. Without dissent, they extolled the purity of communist justice and stressed the guilt of the alleged traitors and saboteurs.

Bertolt Brecht compared the accused to 'scum and vermin' and affirmed that the trials had 'clearly demonstrated the active conspiracies against the regime'. The testimony of Jerome Davis — he was the head of the Legislative Commission on Jails in Connecticut — was circulated by the pro-Stalin lobby in North America. Davis established his credentials by relating how he had personally seen hundreds of American criminals who, when confronted with the proof of their guilt, had confessed. Based on these personal experiences, he concluded that the defendants in Moscow must also have been guilty. Davis rejected the obvious explanation that they were made to rehearse their parts: 'The accused were tried in open court; there was not then and is not now a scintilla of evidence that any of them had been tortured.' (Even when, after the war, conclusive evidence was available to indicate how the accused were made to confess in public, Davis stuck to his story). The pathetic Feuchtwanger was enlisted to coax 'progressive' public opinion. His fairy tale was as follows:

> The accused drank tea, newspapers stuck out of their pockets and they glanced frequently at the public. It was more like a discussion than a criminal trial, the kind of discussion educated people, who attempt to establish the truth, conduct in a friendly tone. The judges, the prosecutor, the accused, and this was no illusion, were linked together by the bonds of a common goal.

The most authoritative lies were furnished by solicitor Dudley Collard and barrister Denis Pritt. On returning from Moscow they refuted the 'totally unfounded' allegations that the proceedings had not been summary and lawful: 'We hereby categorically declare that the accused were sentenced lawfully. It was fully proven that there had been links between them and the GESTAPO. They quite rightly deserved the death penalty.'

Many of the accused had spent years in Czarist prisons; after 1917 they had stood at the helm of the Russian dictatorship. Why did they say in open court that they deserved to be shot? Some did so because they feared further torture and other hoped that they or their families would escape the death penalty as a reward for their sycophantic confessions. Arthur Koestler, in a semi-fictional book, suggests that a few were impelled by a peculiarly perverse motive. He created a character Rubashov, an amalgam of several leading commissars arraigned in Moscow, whose inquisitor successfully persuaded him to confess:

> We need waste no time on the accusations. You comrade Rubashov and I know that they are lies. But the world revolution to which we are both dedicated is in danger. China and Germany are planning to invade the Fatherland of Socialism.To defend achievements of the Fatherland we need the support not only of party comrades but also the backing of the simple-minded toilers who constitute the majority of our people. To impress them we need a story that appears credible to the illiterate masses. Your name means something to them. Because you are an old and respected leader of the Party, you are in a position to carry out a vital service to our cause. You have made so many sacrifices in your life — we are asking for a last sacrifice. Calumnies will be heaped upon you, the hero of the October revolution, after you have convincingly told how you were recruited by foreign capitalist hyenas who are waiting to destroy us. You must then go on to recant your crimes. Of course the judges and your old comrades will know that you are not guilty. Inform the court that you are not asking for mercy but are eager to be given a punishment which is commensurate with your treachery. But I promise you. After we have overcome our enemies, the truth about your final act of heroism for the glory of communism will be recorded in the history books.

Rubashov, as was asked of him, lied for the cause he had held dear all his life. He had no illusions that his life would be spared. It was not.

After 1933, till the Hitler-Stalin pact at the outbreak of WWII, the USSR appeared to many to be the only country which could be relied upon to resist Hitler. This was cited also by the Cambridge spies (Philby, Maclean, Burgess) as the underlying motive for their treachery. Anthony Blunt, the art historian who too became a Russian spy, said explicitly that he 'could best serve the cause of anti-fascism by working for the Russians'. Many individuals, who were drawn into the Stalinist web and voluntarily lied to condone Stalin's crimes, did so because the threat of Hitler took precedence over their negative attitude to the communist philosophy. Victor Gollancz, a relatively wealthy businessman, was one of them. He was guilty of evil misdeeds but yet these may not have barred him from entering heaven because of his compensating virtuous act, soon after the Hitler-Stalin pact was signed. When he left the Stalinist camp, he gave public testimony about his own past crimes. He chose not to defend himself by alleging that he had been duped or bribed with Russian gold or blackmailed by the KGB or held prisoner in Siberia or suffered from senility. Gollancz also chose not to affirm that he had innocently covered up the travesties of the Moscow trial because he was ignorant of the Russian language. Loud and clear he asked forgiveness for deceiving so many and having misused his influence and commercial strength to manipulate the truth. He had lied — and he said so. He added that he had been a knowledgeable liar. His daughters asked Ruth Edwards to write, twenty years after his death, a (partly critical) biography. This confirms Gollancz's motives in the light of documents that had hitherto been in the family vault. Much of the contents of this, now documented, material had already been available in his lifetime but not in published form because he did not hesitate to threaten his traducers with the libel laws. Harry Pollitt, the doyen of the Communist Party of Great Britain regarded Gollancz as the most influential UK fellow-traveller. Pollitt, though a busy person in charge of multifarious activities, acted as the regular carer of Gollancz. Despite many provocations, the latter acted obsequiously when beguiled by the country's top communist leader who spent endless hours flattering him — and this paid off.

In the inter-war years Gollancz's eponymous firm prospered from publishing mainly innocuous books, especially detective stories. (He even profited by marketing one of Trotsky's books, something which Pollitt would not have tolerated). In the spring of 1936, as yet a free man, he founded the Left Book Club [LBC]. He then had no idea that this institution, of which he was the financier and CEO, would bring him glorious political authority. Without the LBC he would have remained an insignificant figure and, in turn, without him the LBC would not have provided the Communist Party of Great Britain with an unrivalled propaganda vehicle. In the course of time Gollancz became an obedient tool but this, and the lies that accompanied it, were motivated by altruism. Gollancz did not gain materially from the LBC; he would probably have become richer had he not spent his energies and financial resources on the creation of the LBC which brought him in time both fame and infamy. Initially, he confined himself to publishing every month an inexpensively-priced leftist book.

Apart from himself, two admirers of the Soviet Union made up the triumvirate of book-selectors. Harold Laski was one of them. He was the author of a pompous book in which he praised the independence said to be enjoyed by Stalin's judges and defence lawyers; he eulogized Vishynski, the infamous conductor of the show trials: 'He was doing what an ideal minister of justice would do if we had such a person in Great Britain.' Laski's lies were unbounded: 'No one who has ever seen over a Russian prison, and compared that experience with a visit to one in England, can doubt that the advantage is all on the Russian side.' It is Gollancz who chose personally this celebrated academic who had reported that 'an eventual disappearance of crime is expected by Soviet authorities; the labour camps which supplanted prisons are themselves diminishing, partly because they have cured their inmates and still more because the normal free life of Soviet society is becoming strong'. Laski's other LBC colleague, John Strachey, was an even greater friend of Stalin. (It was widely believed that Pollitt thought it expedient not to have Strachey as a card-carrying member of the communist party; better to let him operate as a fellow-traveller.) Unlike Laski, Strachey openly acknowledged that Marxism was his creed. He told the British public about the 'exhilaration of living [in Russia] that finds no parallel in the world. To travel from the capitalist world into Soviet territory is to pass from death to birth.' The subscribers to the LBC became fellows of a national, political club which held mass meetings, set up discussion groups all over Britain, organized political lobbying and brought into being several journals with a wide circulation. There were tens of thousands of LBC subscribers, more than Britain's Communist Party had members. Gollancz found it expedient to deny that he had created a Marxist association; he maintained that the LBC was only an umbrella association for followers of various leftist groups. This was formally correct but in substance a lie. Most of the LBC branches were in effect controlled by communist activists. Gollancz's carer 'suggested' who should be appointed to the (paid) posts of the LBC. The astute Pollitt wanted to camouflage the Stalinist domination of the LBC. Hence, he proposed to the triumvirate that occasionally books by harmless non-Marxist writers should be commissioned. Pollitt thought it desirable that the perceived image of the LBC ought to be that of a broad, tolerant church but he excluded from it writers on the extreme left who were critical of Stalinism. Gollancz had been George Orwell's publisher; on returning from Spain the latter naturally turned to him first to publish his anti-Franco book. Alas, in it were some unkind references to the Spanish communists. Gollancz was pressured to reject the manuscript.

August Thalheimer, who had been a leader of the German communists, fled into exile when Hitler came to power. By that time he was no longer in the mould prescribed by Moscow though he remained a devout Marxist. Gollancz, who at first knew little about the internecine doctrinal conflicts on the extreme left, had contracted to issue a book of his on dialectical materialism. Pollitt insisted that the agreement to publish should be rescinded though advance publicity for the Thalheimer book had already been circulated. Pollitt did not challenge the contents of the manuscript but was merely concerned that no dissident of the Communist International should be published. Gollancz had to be bullied and, as he later himself confirmed, obeyed the order with a heavy heart. When Gollancz was once again free, he set out the facts. He related that many of his friends had criticized him sharply for suppressing a book just because the author was no longer an official communist spokesman. They accused him of delivering proof that the LBC was simply 'a part of the Communist Party. And then, when I got letter after letter to that effect, I had to sit down and deny that I had withdrawn the book because I had been asked to do so — I had to concoct a cock and bull story to explain the substitution. I hated and loathed doing this: I am made in such a way that this kind of falsehood destroys something inside me'. If moral condemnation is called for, I berate Gollancz and not Pollitt. At fault is the person who had a delicate soul and, without being tortured, agreed to be manipulated.

Russia's ambassador in London was under orders to accord him the requisite honours which fed his vanity. In 1937 Gollancz made the pilgrimage to the Stalinist Mecca. His hosts were not disappointed because he went on record that 'for the first time I have been completely happy ... there is a feeling that here is a piece of good on such a vast scale that, while here, one can forget the evil in the rest of the world'. Edwards mentions the 'moral agony' which he endured when the communist editors of the official LBC journal spread the Stalinist lies concerning the show trials. What makes Gollancz's conduct so deplorable is that he did not believe in the guilt of the accused though of course did not say so aloud. His humbug was even more unattractive when one recalls that, on principle, he was opposed to capital punishment for even the most atrocious crimes. He was the leader of the National Committee for the Abolition of the Death Penalty and used his private wealth to finance this movement. Yet, says his biographer, Gollancz — in public at least — never so much as hinted at qualms about the execution of the innocent victims of the Moscow trials. When he finally abandoned Pollitt, the Communist Party of Great Britain fell upon him with a vicious vindictiveness reserved for traitorous apostates. He replied in 1941, denouncing the Stalinists and composing his peccavi:

> Looking back, I think I erred more as a publisher than as a writer or speaker, and more by omission than by commission. I accepted manuscripts on Russia, good or bad, because they were 'orthodox'. I rejected others, by bona fide socialists and honest men, because they were not. It was in the matter of the Moscow trials that the inner conflict was greatest ... I published only books that justified the trials ... I am sure as a man can be — I was sure at the time in my heart — that all this was wrong: wrong in the harm it did to oneself and wrong above all in the harm it did to the sum total of truth and honest thinking.

Benevolent Forecasting Liars

The weather is not affected by accurate or inaccurate forecasts but the consequences of suppressing their publication could be helpful to interested parties. My story deals with an attempt to bully the government to do precisely that. The evil blueprint was not followed through but those who wanted the truth about the weather to be subverted deserve to be remembered with hilarity. When the electronic media announce in the morning that it will rain heavily during the day, people are apt to change their plans. They may thus abandon planned day-outings to the seaside. MPs have been known to attack the government because the state-owned Meteorological Office sometimes produces flawed forecasts. The MP Gresham Cooke once castigated the authorities for predicting sunshine on a Whit Monday when in fact a rain front was blown across the UK by a high-speed airstream. His complaint was only frivolous; it did not have the ominous implication of a resolution passed at a conference of the National Chamber of Trade. The motion spoke of 'concern at the damaging effect which adverse weather forecasts can have on the business of traders in seaside towns'. The indignant delegates who voted for this motion were factually right when they pointed out that radio announcements, foreshadowing imminent bad weather, deterred many people from visiting the seaside. Their displeasure, however, did not centre on the accuracy of the announcements. One trader noted that the 'weather forecasters took a sadistic delight in predicting bad weather'. The resolution demanded that the meteorological experts be 'urged to take a brighter outlook'. This could have been interpreted to mean that mendacious forecasts were to be concocted. The seaside businessmen knew full well that they did not have the influence to back such an unacceptable request and they settled for a lesser demand: the leaders of the Chamber of Trade were instructed to ask the authorities not to allow predictions of bad weather to be announced publicly during the holiday season.

The truth about past or current events is concerned with actualities; when knowledgeable people violate it or suppress its dissemination they are deservedly called liars. What are predictions? (Hopes, ambitions, homiletic spurs and targets they are not.) Most predictions are conjectures, surmises and guesses by forecasters who speculate on what is most likely to occur. These can be evaluated in accordance with their meaningfulness and numerate correctness; the performers can be judged by their past achievements and the organizations that have sponsored them. Lying does often play a role. We shall examine later when and how mendaciousness can creep in. To be treated seriously, conjectures should be definite and relatively unambiguous statements, such as 'the Irish GDP is set to grow in 2005 by 4%' or 'three inches of rain will come down in May of next year in Portugal'. Broad generalities may prove to be highly accurate but are not helpful to decision-makers. Likewise, conditional predictions — such as 'the Albanian national come will rise by 3.5% provided that the factors A, B and C function in a prescribed fashion' — are useless. Caveats, especially those in small print, only add spurious academic flavour to predictions and also provide incompetent forecasters with alibis. In some predictive exercises the past successes of individual forecasters do matter greatly; this is so when specialists forecast, for instance, the price of copper, the likely output of oil in Venezuela and the anticipated frequency of earth tremors in Peru. In all other predictions the customers are most interested to know who the forecasters are associated with. This obsession with 'authoritative predictions' is not an allusion to the competence, erudition or past attainments of the predictors. Customers make use of forecasts, which they regard as authoritative, in order to change their own perceptions and plans for the future. They will, however, only do so if in their eyes the promoting organization has such a repute that any predictions made under its umbrella convey instinctively an unwritten guarantee which makes lesser mortals think it is safe to rely on these forecasts. Who is authoritative? First and foremost the state and its agencies. What about macroeconomic predictions originating in the private sector? Those emanating under the imprint of *Fortune*-listed global corporations (and a few scholarly research agencies) are also considered to deserve serious attention. Shell, Sony and Hoechst are companies which are thought to have the resources to prepare meaningful predictions and are believed to have contacts with knowledgeable politicians. I have never quite understood why, apart from amour propre, corporate giants would want to share their 'knowledge' of the world's future with others. But, as they are frequently intent upon doing so, their prognostications are listened to with much deference and deemed to be dependable. If an individual, employed to formulate such predictions, leaves the corporation, the noteworthiness of any of *his subsequent* pronouncements counts for little. The senior economist of Pepsi-Cola, whose views on the growth rate of the Albanian GDP used to be quoted in the world press, will find that his vicarious fame has melted once he no longer operates under the umbrella of his erstwhile employer.

How are forecasts treated if the contents turn out to be abysmally wrong? They are often applauded when the accuracy criterion does not have an overriding virtue. The cabinet minister, Peter Shore, evoked hilariousness in the HoC when he repulsed attacks on his department for publishing extremely flawed forecasts. He enunciated that the dissemination of incorrect forecasts is not shameful: 'the important thing is which side of the forecast we are likely to be wrong'. He followed in the footsteps of Chancellor of the Exchequer Roy Jenkins who once disarmed a political adversary by boasting of the Treasury's very erroneous predictions: 'I am very glad to have been proved wrong... the export forecasts have been exceeded by a substantial margin.' In the City of London they also do not always put the emphasis on correctness. On a memorable occasion ICI was praised because it had 'got its forecast joyfully wrong'. The chairman of Costain was praised undeservedly for having circulated an unsound prediction: 'Nothing pleases shareholders so much as to learn that their chairman's uninspiring forecast turns out to be wholly pessimistic.'

There are two kinds of mendacity in the forecasting game. The first is a coarse type akin to fraud. If, based on inside knowledge, an individual *knows* what is about to happen or if he is in a position to determine how certain things will be in the future — as is, for example, the chancellor of the exchequer in some microeconomic fields — then his views on forthcoming developments are not predictions but statements. When he chooses to make public his knowledge, he can either tell the truth or resort to a falsehood; in the latter instance he is clearly an active liar. I am setting out only one (hypothetical) illustration because this type of mendacity is very rare. The chairman of a chemical multi planned to raise new capital through a rights issue on terms which were very favourable to his company. The documents that were issued detailed the corporation's excellent performance in the last three years; the CEO postulated confidently that in the current year the profits would rise by 11%. These truly attractive true assertions made it very likely that the corporation would succeed in recruiting the requested capital at a relatively low cost. The chairman did not, however, disclose that their main and most profitable product was about to lose the major part of its global market share. He had learnt something of which the City was as yet ignorant: a Japanese company was about to start the manufacture of a competing product which would sell at one half of the price which his firm is able to charge charge at present. If this news were released, it would not impact upon the profits of the current year but the share price would nevertheless slump drastically for it is determined by an appraisal of future profits. If the chairman did not reveal this, as yet secret, relevant factor, he deserved to be described an unmitigated liar.

The second kind of forecasting is practised very widely in the public sector, mostly appertaining to macroeconomic data. The state cannot determine how the balance of payments, inflation and the national products will turn out to be in coming years but it can *influence* their progression. How Western governments actuate this will be discussed below but first some words about credibility, the sine qua non of plausibility. In the Greek legends the princess Cassandra possessed an extraordinary faculty. The god Apollo had endowed her with the gift of prophecy in return for her promise to let him make love to her. She reneged on the bargain and Apollo punished her. He did not take away her superb attribute but ordained that she would not be believed. Cassandra was to predict correctly the downfall of Troy and she had the foresight to warn Agamemnon of the plot to kill him. Repeatedly, she warned of the dangers of the Trojan horse. All to no avail. While Cassandra had clearly not been robbed of her competence, she was no longer blessed with credibility and credibility is the linchpin of honest and dishonest forecasters. Can, without the gods interfering, credibility in forecasters melt away altogether? Murray

Kemp[11] is among those who subscribe to such a prognosis: 'To achieve economic objectives it may be necessary to hoodwink the public; but the possibility of hoodwinking derives from credibility, and even the most gullible will not be deceived indefinitely by the same confidence trick.' The attitude of the public in the defunct USSR to the pronouncements of its lying leaders constitutes an extreme and perverse example. Many of its citizens discounted entirely the veracity of any official statement. Some went so far as to infer that if a foreigner is praised by government ministers, ipso facto he must be a depraved person and vice versa. The South African Apartheid politicians enjoyed in the communist fatherland considerable adulations as honourable and wise men. This approbation was a political reaction which came about because the Russian government constantly churned out anti-Apartheid proclamations and reviled the white rulers of South Africa. The man-in-the-street believed that if the mendacious communist propagandists make out that these men are wicked, then the opposite must be true. Kemp's thesis may be validated too in other parts of the world but, in my view, it is not corroborated in most Western democracies.

Based on confessions by retired personalities, who had once been active in the public sector, one is left in no doubt that forecasts by state agencies are sometimes flawed because politicians have deliberately issued misleading figures — of course, they say, in the public interest. Alec Cairncross, head of the UK government's Economic Service, disclosed to the members of the Royal Economic Society what his masters had been up to: 'There is a real risk that the government will insist on cooking the forecasts rather than reveal how awful the situation is.'[12] Chancellor Maudling had no compunctions in boasting that he had put into effect a 'confidence trick': 'I thought of a number for the growth of the economy over a period ahead rather greater than had been achieved in the past. Then everybody would work on the assumption that it was going to happen and lo and behold it would happen.' He described his lies as 'ambitious'

---

[11] M.C. Kemp, 'Economic Forecasting when the Subject of the Forecast is influenced by the Forecast', *American Economic Review*, Evanston, June 1962.
[12] A. Cairncross, 'Forecasting', *Economic Journal*, London, December 1969.

for the country. Maybe this was so, but did it alter the fact that he abjured the truth? John Galbraith used strong language to warn that 'under all circumstances official American economic forecasts should be mistrusted . . . No government forecaster can say unemployment will worsen, inflation become more severe, etc. Yet these things, alas, do occur. It follows that our official forecasts are right only when things go right.' Sam Brittan, who had once volunteered to serve the Wilson government in the preparation of a National Plan, soon became disillusioned with the responsible minister, George Brown. When he was once again a journalist with the freedom to expose his former masters, he accused Brown of preparing a 'Virtuous Confidence Trick'. Brittan, the repentant sinner, reproached the minister for dishonestly inducing a 'favourable view of the future'; he maintained that the official, widely published, mendacious forecasting exercises had duped many people. Brittan argued that if the National Plan had consisted merely of some false macroeconomic projections, most industrialists would have cast it aside. But, to adorn the Brown confidence trick with spurious credibility, thousands of numerate statements were interspersed among copious and tedious prose: 'a big document full of figures is more likely (even if unread) to carry conviction than a short statement of objectives'. After the National Plan failed and was discarded, Brown was openly criticized for having circulated forecasts with an upward basis in order to generate faster growth. He said that he was proud of what he had done and his defenders averred that the National Plan had been a good idea, precisely because its numerate falsehood had served to inspire 'growth psychology'. Dishonesty along those lines is quite fashionable. *The Economist* once proposed that the British Treasury should publicly adopt a very high [though clearly unrealistic] growth rate in order that it could be 'burned into the nation's consciousness'. Academics and others who know of the pitfalls of (particularly economic) forecasts show contempt for the putatively intelligent CEOs of mighty corporations who swallow fictitious forecasts though they ought to know better. The wily dishonest predictors on both sides of the Atlantic know their trade only too well: many economic decision-makers can indeed be deluded by seemingly authoritative forecasts and particularly by those which are spiced with decimal points.

It is an established fact that, despite the wily invention of figures and the deliberate spread of falsehoods by some forecasters, the public's credence in the English-speaking countries has rarely plunged to zero. This is especially the case with governmental forecasts because — so spoke the experienced politician, Chancellor Nigel Lawson — 'they enjoy the imprimatur of the Treasury which are invested with a spurious authority'. S. Oh & M. Waldman have shown persuasively that in the United States there are enough trusting people to validate false predictions by the state. 'Our major finding is that if agents in the economy receive information which states that aggregate production is likely to be high in future periods, the information — even when based on false data — would have a positive effect on future movements of output.'[13] In the experience of Chancellor Reginald Maudling, 'if a government decries the prospects of the British economy, how can anyone else be expected to think otherwise? For it is a sad irony that governments are always believed to be speaking the truth when they are saying unhappy things.' In his doleful reminiscences he highlighted, as have others, that bad tidings are more readily believed than predictions of good tidings. But Maudling did not deny that official announcements, projecting rising prosperity, are also capable of creating reactions which help to materialize false governmental predictions. Chancellor Denis Healey was questioned on whether his personal credibility and that of the government had been damaged irreparably because of inaccurate forecasts. He replied that having to take responsibility for issuing a wrong forecast is a bruising affair. But, he went on to say, at the end of the day the government's trustworthiness is only blemished but not destroyed. Alpha Chiang has told of his research on false forecasts which bears out Healey's judgement. While contrived forecasts do impair the public's faith in governmental announcements, the credibility of official spokesmen is not forfeited altogether. Chiang admitted that the acceptance of state predictions is deteriorating: 'Most tools can be expected

---

[13] S. Oh & M. Waldman, 'The Macroeconomic Effects of False Announcements', *The Quarterly Journal of Economics*, Cambridge, November 1990.

to be blunted through use but official forecasts have still enough potency to exert influence.'

The overwhelming majority of the population in Britain's democracy would be shocked to learn — though they will not have the opportunity to find out — how academic economists relate to the accuracy criterion when, writing in esoteric language, they publish their prescriptions in learned journals. Were the Great Unwashed in a position to understand what is being plotted, the object of the exercises would be frustrated. It has been said in defence of Treasury's forecasts, which are released for public consumption, that they are indeed primarily window-dressing and are not meant to be true predictions of the macroeconomic future. To subject them to an 'accuracy-analysis' is largely an irrelevant exercise; the best that can be said of official forecasts is that they are indicators which display the direction in which the state would like to propel the economy. The mandarin Cairncross, who served Labour and Conservative politicians in office, has laid down that to prepare a forecast for political masters entails the preparation of advice that enables it to be 'judged in terms of the policy to which it leads, not in terms of the accuracy of the forecast itself'. Murray Kemp has accused the authorities in Washington that they are in the habit of preparing 'forecasts which are merely means to an end and [therefore] the most efficacious forecasts may be wildly and deliberately inaccurate'. G. Bombach[14] has outlined how politicians can benefit from flawed forecasts. He is disdainful of bashful academics who employ euphemisms when they advocate mendacious forecasting; he thinks they should be proud of what they are scheming. Bombach derides the honest economists who predict what they believe is likely to happen; having stated that the GDP is set to fall by, say, 3%, they exult at their intellectual attainment when this prediction has come true. He would have it that they deserve to be denounced mercilessly. What matters in an economic prognosis is not 'Richtigkeit' [accuracy] but the ability to help shape the future through effectively influencing the decision-makers. Before the two British economists R.J. Ball & T. Burns became prominent figures in the public sector,

---

[14] G. Bombach, 'Ueber die Moeglichkeit Wirtschaftlicher Vorraussagen', *Kyklos*, Basle, 1962.

they could afford to speak their mind freely and did so with muted intellectual haughtiness: 'The purpose of a forecast is to produce a policy. Forecasts cannot be properly judged in terms of some narrowly defined numerical criterion of accuracy. The critical question is whether they provide generalised signals for "appropriate" changes in policy.'[15] Two econometricians J. Ash & D. Smyth spelt it out explicitly: 'Perfect forecasting is not necessarily always beneficial.' They published a book on the subject in which they made the outrageous suggestion that governments may more easily obtain the desired level of demand 'through judiciously misleading the private sector'.

Malcolm Galatin, my last witness, took it upon himself to enlighten politicians on what consenting economists were in a position to do for them:

> If feedback effects are significant, then the question of the accuracy of forecasts is not the only important one. It is possible that forecasts may become important tools of economic policy when the forecaster wishes to influence the value of the outcome by his choice of forecasts.[16]

This conveys a truly sinister intent. Galatin is not alone in describing mendacious predictions, formulated to have a decisive impact upon economic behaviour, as 'instruments of control'. The first time that this theory was put to the test was in the US between the summer of 1944 and the spring of 1946. Leftist supporters of the New Deal publicized doomsday predictions on the post-war American economy. Some government economists predicted that soon unemployment would exceed 8m; a renowned research body foresaw that one third of the labour force was about to be without gainful employment; several trade unions forecast that there would be 20m unemployed. As to the GNP this was projected to stagnate or even to decline. In fact the (constant-price) GNP and disposable national income exceeded the predicted levels by 8–13% and unemployment hovered in the 2–3m range. When the dismal performance of these forecasters was probed, it was found that those who had rung the alarm bells

---

[15] R.J. Ball & T. Burns, 'The Need for Reflation', *Sunday Times,* April 2, 1967.
[16] M. Galatin, 'Optimal Forecasting in Models with Uncertainty when the Outcome is Influenced by the Forecast', *The Economic Journal,* London, June 1976.

had not actually believed in their own predictions. They had issued deceptive estimates because they favoured Keynesian policies and sought to lay the foundations for a US welfare state. Knowing that their fellow-citizens rejected these political prescriptions, they hoped to achieve their aims through the backdoor by frightening the public with mendacious messages of gloom: 'to get the cure, they promised the disease'. Their strategy, to create a backlash which would engender pressures that in turn would bring about the state interventions favoured by the schemers, was aborted. But the politically motivated US forecasters set a precedent that has since been emulated successfully in other countries.

How does the technique work? Unlike meteorologists, economic prognosticators can often influence the outcome of their predictions thanks to the reaction function that is also known as backlash or the law of feedback or the announcement effect. The strength of the targeted consumers' credulity or scepticism of governmental forecasts is a major factor appertaining to the scope of the 'reaction function'; it is indeterminate because the public's perception as to what is a lie and what is true cannot be presumed with accuracy. All that can be ascertained is that scepticism has not reached zero and that the credibility element varies as between customers. When the American statistician George Cline Smith formulated the nature of the law of feedback, he arrived at the conclusion that government forecasts do have an impact but he conjectured that these affect the outcome in a totally unpredictable manner. Thus a prediction of a 3% growth rate could alter events by bringing about either a 1% or 5% rate. If the Smith findings were to have general validity, no purpose would be served by dishonest predictions. The purveyors of mendacious forecasts can take comfort from the fact that there is a great deal of evidence that the theoretical Smith findings are not germane to developed Anglo-Saxon countries. There is a redeeming factor: the decision-makers do pay attention to government predictions and react thereto in the *direction* intended by the forecasters. J. Ash & D. Smyth were cynics about the accuracy of forecasts issued by state agencies. They told the uninitiated, who pondered over official growth predictions, not to regard the stated growth rates as correct. Nevertheless, Ash-Smyth exhorted them to study the (false) growth figures in order to discover 'the course', i.e. the line along which the government wants the economy to develop. Authoritative forecasts do make people adjust their mode of thinking; the reactions will be primarily a response to the perceived direction.

The dishonest government forecasters have long accepted that they are looked upon as potential liars. This has led them to pursue a stealthy, circuitous strategy. Take a situation in which the Treasury is apprised of a widespread belief in the private sector that next year's GDP will go up by 2% and that production, investments and labour recruitment is being planned accordingly. The Treasury has reason to surmise that there is enough slack in the economy to justify a 3% growth target. If the government were to forecast a likely 3%, it would not thereby induce the private sector to adjust its plans upwards because the acceptance weight of the government's credibility was such that it would not be believed commensurately; people would speak of mendacious politicians who are hawking a 3% figure though they expect a much lower rate. The solution consists in publishing forecasts which the forecasters regard as neither realistic nor desirable. Forecasts are therefore released that are based on the premise of a 4% GDP growth. Digesting these figures, many entrepreneurs will recall how badly they had their fingers burnt when they last trusted fully the official growth projections. They will, however, not ignore altogether the 4% projection for they take into account that Western politicians cannot afford to tell extraordinarily large lies which are so exasperatingly wrong as to rebound later upon them. The private sector will scorn the 4% figure and treat it as a deliberate lie and then ask itself how big the lie is. If they conclude that it may be wrong by as much as 1%, it would be interpreted to mean that the government is surely seeing 3% as a realistic target. Hence the private sector adjusts its plans not from 2% to 4% but to 3%. Without altruistic, self-effacing government employees, such a deception could never have been carried out. As soon as the ex post growth rate is verified to have been 'only' 3%, the media will rebuke the taciturn civil servants for their incompetence in predicting 4%. The discredited forecasters must then swallow their pride. They cannot tell the media what really happened. Only in private can the manipulators smile and congratulate one another on their contrived success; some will reveal the truth in their memoirs in which they can boast about how they lied in the public interest. It is the composers of their obituaries who will have to decide whether to depict them as dishonest forecasters or incompetent economists or benevolent patriotic liars.

Chapter III

The Convoluted Motives

> The truth is rarely pure and never simple
>
> *Oscar Wilde*

The Knots of Altruism

Those who reject the philosophy of the perfectionists and look favourably upon the circulation of particular benevolent lies, will have to justify themselves on the Day of Judgement. Will liars then be appraised in accordance with their intentions or the repercussions of their lies? (If the answer is 'by both', will the two elements have an equal weight?) Most — but by no means — all well-intentioned liars are motivated solely by pure altruism. Yet, a qualifying caveat must be taken into account for there are varying degrees of altruism, and benevolence is a vague, contentious concept. Because there are no objective criteria which are assured ubiquitous acceptance, benevolent and malevolent mendacity — apart from some salient exceptions — can only be assessed by subjective value standards. In this chapter the working assumption prevails that benevolent lies mainly generate good results though in real life this is certainly not always so. (In a section below we are dealing with well-meant lies and meritorious objectives which go wrong and disastrous consequences follow.) But already now we must take up a position with regard to those honest, and often fanatical, individuals who lie uninhibitedly to champion actively a religious faith, political party or a variety of causes such as feminism, Keynesianism, an end to anglers murdering fish, Marxism, the founding of a Kurdish republic. They like to be called 'conviction liars'.

Those observers, who passively favour the objectives, have no problem about connoting the lying of these activists as salutary while others, who consider the aims to be pernicious, will not wish to condone their mendacity. Must we, who reject the totalitarian creed of the perfectionists and accept that benevolent lying has an honourable place in society, treat with equanimity all those who lie altruistically for causes that we consider to be ignoble? I am not persuaded that all altruistic lies which are spread in support of 'good' causes should automatically be treated as benevolent lies. Much of altruism is a slippery concept that must be handled with deft fingers. The standard definition treats it as an antonym of egoism *and* concern for others. I do not share the view that both features must be present; the second one alone suffices. Of course it will usually co-exist with selflessness but this need not be so. If one required of altruistic practitioners, that they ought in no way to think *also* of their own welfare but concern themselves exclusively with the welfare of deserving individuals or causes, then the scope of benevolent lying would be very much restricted. I also discard the notion, which was first mooted in the 1930s, that altruism is not always the result of untrammelled personal decision-making. It was then suggested that certain human beings possess genes that determinately incline them to act altruistically. If indeed genetics determines altruism, there would be little scope to explore its moral and political parameters. With equal vehemence I denounce those who preach that, in the material sphere, *all* human beings are wholly 'pocket-book' selfish and self- centred.[1] One such definition of altruism describes it as an activity which 'promotes the fitness of the recipient at the expense of that of the provider'. It is certainly correct that selfless acts are frequently performed by individuals who suffer losses in order to do good. But I believe that one can be actively concerned with the welfare of others without this involving one in making personal sacrifices.[2] The benevolent lies employed by doctors, lawyers and priests belong to this category and I hope to demonstrate that

---

[1] There are individuals who pay the top marginal income tax but yet plead for even more draconian income tax rates. Though this would clearly hurt them materially, they favour punitive taxation for the rich because, in their altruism, they want the less well-off to benefit.

[2] In the German concentration camps the inmates were given only meagre food rations. From the accounts of survivors we learn that some prisoners chose to give part of their rations to others who they deemed to be especially deserving — these benefactors were clearly pure altruists. But what of those

it can also include the mendacious declarations of well-intentioned politicians.

I go further than that. While there are few instances of pure altruism, there are many grades of altruism which incorporate some elements of personal selfishness. I have no difficulty with this though it is correct that the altruism of such persons, who *also* stand to benefit, if often treated with suspicion. Donors of charitable gifts, which are *largely* financed by commensurate tax reliefs, are definitely beyond the pale. So are donations which are given in the expectation of thereby earning a knighthood or the political approbation of the public. What matters in each case are the relative weights of selfishness and concern-for-others. As I write this, the UK is blessed or plagued with professionals who lie and prepare forged documents so that illegal immigrants may settle here. Passionate pleas are entered on behalf of the former in which it is stated that while they obviously gain by charging large fees, they are also motivated by humanitarian considerations and the national interest of the UK which, allegedly, is suffering from a labour shortage. How are these liars to be treated? There is no hard and fast rule and only a personal value judgement determines whether the liars pass the test and are praiseworthy despite their material benefits.

The same conundrum, that needs to be resolved, exists when the wind blows in the opposite direction. Does it follow that an individual, who himself does not derive any material benefit but steals and lies to achieve a charitable objective, should automatically be extolled a hero? The public, police and judiciary are prone to regard it a mitigating factor when proof is delivered that his criminal lies were not uttered in order to enrich oneself. (The victims, however, are rarely prepared to think highly of a crook who deceives them but says in his defence that he acted illegally not to enrich himself but to serve some holy end.) A priest sells bogus shares in order to fund the building of a drug clinic with the proceeds of his fraud. Some of his parishioners buy the worthless shares. Was his altruistic deception a noble one?

---

who deprived the terminally ill of their rations? It may indeed have been logical to take away from dying men nourishment in order to sustain the lives of others who still had a chance to survive. If this was done by inmates who used the plundered food to feed themselves as well as others, such behaviour personifies an amalgam that embraces both selfishness and altruism.

The CEO of a textile company prepares phoney accounts to defraud the shareholders and the revenue. His soi-disant motive is unselfish. He wants to continue operating the corporation to safeguard many jobs. The culprit is a wealthy man and, materially, it is of little importance to him whether the business collapses or not. The CEO is certainly a criminal even though he did not falsify the accounts to store away in Lichtenstein the fruits of his mendacity. Should he go to jail or receive a medal for his well-intentioned striving to rescue the jobs of 1,500 employees? Was his mendacity benevolent? In 1993 a Dieppe bank employee was given a suspended prison sentence of 18 months and fined a tiny sum. He had stolen money from the accounts of depositors who, in his view, could afford it. The thief did not profit as the stolen funds were all given over to 'deserving' persons. The residents of Dieppe and the local judiciary were eager not to discomfort someone who in their eyes was an altruistic saint. To ensure his anonymity the court ordered that he be known as Monsieur X. The only journalist at the trial, who lived in Dieppe, consented not to identify him by name in the dispatches he sent to the Paris newspapers. He did, however, report that the accused, who had cheated the bank for 12 years, was treated as a hero. The bank did not dare to dismiss him and allowed the lying thief to resign in dignity. A collection was made to help Monsieur X return the stolen money to his former employer. Everyone, including the prosecutor, portrayed him as a well-meaning person — 'scrupulously honest' — who merited praise and not condemnation.

The benevolent lies, which are set out in this paragraph, run counter to the prevalent view that altruism is a sine qua non for the sanctification of lying. To cite but a few definitions of altruism: 'devotion to the welfare of others'; 'opposed to egoism or selfishness'; 'uncalculated consideration of, or devotion to, others' interests'; 'a concept that holds that the interests of others, rather than of self, motivate an individual'. I am about to relate examples of real people who lied — sometimes in a perverse fashion — with one objective in mind: in their selfishness they wanted to save *themselves* from death. They did not have others in mind but only their own welfare. Though most of my readers are likely to approve their mendacity, saying that the liars have nothing to be ashamed of and I agree with them, it is a hazardous conclusion. These lies cannot be called benevolent but as they are not repulsive it may be asserted that they were uttered for a just reason. They involved breaking the law of the land for personal salvation; the decision to do so was made by the potential beneficiaries. The perpetrators may be applauded though they did set a conjectural precedent.

Very shortly after the end of WWII, I was in an army unit in Klagenfurt where I came across a Jewish youngster who had escaped the Holocaust by enlisting in the Hitlerjugend, something which entailed telling many lies. He did not do so as an altruist; he did not sacrifice himself for others. He took a big risk for the sole purpose of remaining alive. I do not fault him for doing what he did and in my view he does not deserve to be castigated in the spirit of St Augustine. Only in the year 2002 was published a remarkable research study, which included interviewing actual survivors, by an American academic B.M. Rigg. He found that many hundreds of half-Jews and even some 100% Jews — in the language of the racialist Nazi laws — saved themselves by serving under false pretences in the German army. A few Gentile German officers covered up for a minority and these may well be commended for their passive benevolent lies. The majority, however, depended entirely upon complicated lies, intended to disguise their Jewish provenance; some even made use of a legal subterfuge in which they and/or their mothers gave mendacious declarations on oath. This saga began in 1933 when the Gentile mother, married to a Jew, of the State Secretary of Aviation Field Marshal Oskar Milch went to court to testify to a lie: she 'confessed' that she had betrayed her husband and it was a Gentile lover who fathered her six children. Oskar's documents, which had hitherto shown him to be a 50% Jew, were consequently modified to make him a 100% Christian. Until 1944 many others — 42 in the town of Hamburg alone — turned themselves mendaciously into full non-Jews by virtue of the mothers being blamed for a putatively illicit relationship. One young man cheated the gas chambers by telling the Gestapo that his mother had been a slut; he said that she had been an active prostitute. In that year Himmler's office disseminated a warning that judges should not be misled because 'every mother is willing to commit perjury when it is a question of the German [to wit, Aryan] ancestry of her child'. It is not easy to describe these lies as benevolent but I treat them as useful lies.

I reject the wild sophistry according to which altruistic deeds can *never* be an unselfish act since the charitable donors and the purveyors of benevolent lies are always rewarded with personal happiness and smug satisfaction. The English Utilitarians opined that doing good to others was itself a source of pleasure. There are Biblical allusions which suggest that more happiness is created by giving than by taking. Such rewards are of course enticing but I treat them as an incidental element. On the whole, they are not the main factor which determines the altruistic motives of well-meaning persons — though there are weighty (mainly religious) exceptions. In any case these non-material rewards are vague in nature and at best can be described as part-payments for good deeds. Much more significant, when exploring genuine altruism by charitably-minded individuals, is the decisive role played by deferred non-material benefits which accrue after death. Rubashov, the falsely accused Bolshevik hero in Koestler's semi-fictional account of the Moscow Trials, agreed to give up his life and cooperate with his tormentors after he was promised that his good name would be restored at some point in the future. Cynics will say that Rubashov took a big risk. How could he, the purported atheist, have been sure that they will keep their promise?

For devout individuals it is not a matter of an uncertain speculation when the apostles of Christianity, Hinduism, Islam and Judaism promise that posthumous payments await the doers of good on earth. (While faithful believers obviously rely on this, it is not necessarily the only — or even main — motivation for their altruism.) Sidgwick has written about the deferred pleasures of the monks who thought to ingratiate themselves with their deity by exercises which consisted of tormenting themselves. If asked what motive there was for doing all this, they replied: 'You are not to imagine that we are punishing ourselves for nothing; we know very well what we are about. You are to know that for every grain of pain it costs us now, we are to have a hundred grains of pleasure by and by.' In Matthew 19.21 Jesus is cited: 'If you wish to go the whole way, go, sell your possessions, and give to the poor, and then you will have riches in heaven.' This sentiment is replicated by John Mason Neale:

> Wherefore Christian men be sure,
> Wealth of rank possessing.
> Ye, who now do bless the poor,
> Shall yourselves find blessing.

The message, that altruistic sacrifices on earth spells the deferment but not the abandonment of riches, is spelt out in several prayers and hymns; yet the remuneration is not detailed:

> I know not, oh, I know not,
> What joys await us there,
> What radiancy of glory,
> What bliss beyond compare.

A Welsh hymn, sung in Sunday schools, is a little more explicit:

> I am a little soldier
> Who learns to draw the sword,
> To battle for my Saviour
> Till death brings my reward.

In the Talmud there are references to 'credits' that are earned for good deeds and which are accumulated for the afterlife. Zangwill has explained that the Jewish poor 'felt no shame in begging. They knew it was the rich man's duty to give . . . They regarded themselves as the Jacob's ladder by which the rich man mounted to paradise'.

Muslim scholars have elucidated that there are afterlife rewards when 'one enters the Garden' where one is recompensed for good deeds on earth. Bouhdiba has promised those whose terrestrial actions warranted entry into paradise that it was 'a place of sexual pleasure'. Max Weber has formulated a universal generalization which centres upon 'the hope for and expectation of just compensation, envisaged in various ways but always involving reward for one's own good deed and punishment for the unrighteousness of others. This expectation of just compensation, a fairly calculating attitude, is the most widely diffused form of mass religion all over the world.' He has dwelt particularly on Hinduism, where the virtuous 'expect an improvement in their chances of rebirth, i.e. the ascent of the soul into a higher caste'. This, he maintained, applied in particular to the lower Hindu castes: 'the more depressed the position in which the members of the pariah people found themselves, the more powerful became the salvation hopes'. All religions seem to fine-tune the value of good deeds on earth by propounding that anonymity enhances the intrinsic altruism of charity and multiplies the rewards that are given for charitable deeds after death. Thus, a Talmudic maxim sets forth that 'The rich should not know to whom they give and the poor should not know from whom they receive.' Thus the poor are spared the indignity of having to appear grateful to altruistic donors.

Believers who sacrifice themselves to help others are piling up brownie points which will stand them in good stead when they meet their Maker. On the day of reckoning God is expected to be generous to those who have treated well their fellows on earth and especially those who have brought non-believers into the fold. Missionaries, in anticipation of being seated in heaven in the front rows, have on occasion had recourse to mendacious and sometimes even illegal tactics in order to maximize the conversion of heathens. What about their records which were bolstered by the deployment of deplorable devices? What about the hypothetical priest, mentioned above, who deceived his parishioners to build the drug clinic? Even worse, what about the criminals who amass wealth, spend part of it on themselves and hand over some of it to a good cause? Some religious organizations are known to refuse unclean donations; the founder of the Rockefeller dynasty was hurt when his financial gifts were not accepted by the congregants of his church. Most charitable organizations have no such compunctions. The scholarly Yusuf Al-Qaradawi has described the Islamic position. If an individual has accumulated riches through something forbidden, e.g. forgery, usury, gambling, and uses the money to build a mosque or do any other good deed, the guilt upon him of having done something unlawful or forbidden will not thereby be lifted from him: 'In Islam good aims and intentions have no effect in lessening the sinfulness of what is forbidden.' While it is not affirmed explicitly, one can infer that, while Moslem charities may accept gifts from unrighteous donors, 'the burden of sin remains' upon the sinners.

Some bien pensant altruists forcibly 'enhance', as they would have it, the welfare of others by means that do not please the beneficiaries. There follow two illustrations. The first refers to altruistically-minded persons who see it as their mission to curtail smoking. Those who bring about prohibitions to ensure that smokers do not discomfort non-smokers are on the whole praiseworthy. The same cannot be said of do-gooders who introduce laws that are not primarily intended to safeguard non-smokers but are targeted to make life more onerous for smokers and thereby punish them. The altruists claim of course that it is done for the good of those who smoke. By imposing oppressive taxes on smokers, most of the potential 'beneficiaries' are not deterred from smoking but are made relatively poorer which leads to their having to cut down on their consumption of food; the poorest smokers may have to give up their annual holidays. This is a typical instance in which unselfish persons with a benevolent inclination force their values and prescriptions upon adults who abhor what is being done, allegedly for their own good.

My second illustration refers to a society of American altruists who, unselfishly, collect money for a poverty-stricken area in Africa. They were advised that in the long run more good would be brought about if their funds were not spent to augment current consumption but, instead, used to finance capital projects, such as flood barriers and steel plants. A commissioned cost-benefit analysis showed that, computed over a fourteen-year period, the capital option would optimize the benefits accruing from their aid funds. The nannies acted accordingly, thereby depriving the present-day indigenous poor of the type of aid (food, medicines, hand tools) which these relished to receive. The idealists who imposed their will had a clear conscience. Personally, they had nothing to gain by choosing to help the poor country in a manner they thought propitious even though it clearly did not meet with the wishes of the recipients. These well-meaning nannies still merit being described as altruists. However, the resentment by the objects of their benevolence, does somewhat blemish this altruism.

Reciprocal altruism can be described as mutual egoism or disguised selfishness. Though reciprocal altruists often appear to act entirely unselfishly, their true motivation is frequently more prosaic and, spiritually, not always uplifting. One is dealing with persons whose seemingly charitable demeanour is enveloped in a selfish apprehension: the putative altruists are staking a claim to a moral entitlement in order to obtain benefits when they fall on bad times. They do not enter into a contractual bargain but their expectations hinge on unspecific, mutual, moral-cum-social obligations. Thus David Reisman, among others, has denied that a 'counter-gift' can be categorized as a benevolent deed. The biographer of the leftist Richard Titmuss, a professor at LSE, said of him that 'altruism was the moral key word of his political activities'. Titmuss wrote a book on the way blood was obtained for medical purposes. He denounced the system of 'mercenary donations' which prevailed in capitalist North America and contrasted it with what he thought was 'sheer altruism' in the UK. Titmuss reported that in the United States only 10–15% of the blood supplies originated with individuals whose only reward was a cup of coffee; the overwhelming majority came from mercenary donors and family credit donors. (In the US a patient receiving blood is ordinarily obliged to pay for it or required to donate an equivalent amount of blood which is frequently given by a suitable relative.) In the UK donors are not paid and all the blood flows into a national pool. It is probably true that this is a superior system but, as Titmuss unexpectedly learnt, his original belief that in Britain 'sheer altruism' motivated all the donors proved not to be not true. Titmuss was forced to admit that many UK donors were not really pure altruists for they were impelled by one of two non-altruistic motives. Those who had been in a hospital where they were given blood transfusions felt that they were repaying a sacred debt. Others mentioned as their main motive the speculative contemplation that in the future they might find themselves at the receiving end. A large proportion was honest enough to testify that the reason for their donation had been a 'calculated' one which related to their own lives; they were not driven to do good for others. The British trade unions have adopted Dumas's motto: *tous pour un; un pour tous*. Let us assume that to demand redress for the unjust dismissal of one of their members, one thousand Welsh postmen went on unofficial strike and consequently lost ten days of pay. Sanctimonious TV commentators on the TV point to this as a noble, unselfish act. This is a highly misleading obvservation. The outstanding motive of most of the strikers was a tactical consideration. They were buying an insurance policy. If a similar fate befell them, they hoped that fellow-members of their union would actively campaign for their reinstatement.

Altruism, the caring for others, frequently entails rendering positive assistance. In some very rare cases selfless individuals lie, in the hope of preventing bad things happening, and cause damage to the very people they wish to help. Several honest, caring policemen strove for weeks to bring to trial a nasty child molester. As experienced detectives, they surmised that their failure to persuade a key eye- witness to give evidence, would almost certainly lead to the culprit's acquittal. They were of course not permitted to tell the jury that the accused had already twice been sentenced for similar offences. The officers resolved to lie on oath and declare falsely that the accused had made a detailed confession which he later withdrew. Their reason for lying was clear. The aim was to ensure that the accused was not set free. Unless he was incarcerated, he would probably again assault sexually young children. We shall return to their altruistic conduct in the next section.

The Consequential Effects

Both Matter

The nature of lying has so far been discussed primarily in relation to the intent of the liar. If his motive was holy, then the accolade of a benevolent liar might be bestowed upon him. The purer the altruism of the liar, the greater the magnificence of his lies. But if the focus is solely on the intent of the liar, one can find oneself in very deep waters. Should a saint be blessed when he spreads holy lies without taking into account both the good and the bad ensuing effects? Jean Jacques Rousseau replied in the affirmative. He evaluated lies exclusively by the goodness or malevolence in the mind of the liar, a notion that most thinking people will find difficult to take on board. To atone for one's failure to buy a suitable wedding present, it is banal to plead that 'the thought counts' because a considerate donor considers not only the giving of a present but also its suitability. Equally, one need not respect craftsmen who, failing to perform as expected, defend themselves by whining: 'I meant to do good and did not envisage the bad results which I have brought about'. Perhaps such apologists do not deserve to be sent to prison for reckless conduct but they should definitely not be rewarded for their negligence just because they had meant well. Persons who set out to deceive in the 'hope' that only good will come from it, are not automatically entitled to be garlanded as benevolent liars. Unless *reasonably certain* that pleasing results will be brought forth, they should not have lied. The cockles of one's heart are warmed by giving alms to a beggar. But has something commendable been achieved if he spends the money on drink? The incompetence of benevolent liars, and the fact that they can cause unintentional damage, make it imperative not to depend entirely on the intentions of liars.

But telling the truth can also be hazardous. The absolutists fail to stress that the truth can unwittingly engender rotten results. ('The worst libel can be the truth.') Modern pedagogy stresses the need to encourage children by playing down bad examination results; those that fail badly are comforted: 'you have tried and that is what matters'. This is not a good preparation for life because employers appraise their employees by their accomplishments. What matters is not the intention but what they deliver; the emphasis is almost wholly on consequences. To return to our subject of mendacity, some lies are so vile that they are not to be countenanced despite any good effects. Some lies spawn so conspicuously good consequences that, even despite the bad character of the liar, most people (except rabid absolutists) gladly commend them. Most lies fall between these two stools. They are neither outstandingly good nor spectacularly bad; the merits and demerits of their consequences are rarely clear-cut. My conclusion is that in almost all instances lies need to be examined by intention *and* the ensuing result. Unfortunately, this generalization — though probably sound in principle — is flawed in practice by two imponderables. How certain must a knowledgeable benevolent liar be that the consequences of his mendacity will be laudable? The consequences may not appear for a considerable time after the lie has been disseminated. How far ahead in time must a benevolent liar consider the likely results which flow from his lying?

In this paragraph, that compares four kinds of liars, I am assuming for the sake of the argument, that 'good' and 'bad' are meaningful adjectival descriptions in accordance with

the prevailing consensus view in a given society at a given point of time.
(1) An acknowledged altruist lies to produce results that are adjudged to be good and he is successful in his aim.
(2) An acknowledged altruist lies to produce results that are adjudged to be good but he fails and creates bad results.
(3) An acknowledged selfish, unpleasant individual lies to produce results adjudged to be bad and he succeeds in his aim.
(4) An acknowledged selfish, unpleasant individual lies to produce results adjudged to be bad but he fails; inadvertently he creates good consequences.

The only liar who will surely go to heaven is (1). The only one who should be stoned and sent for eternity to hell is (3). There is room for a difference of opinion about how many doses of moderate praise should be allotted to (2) and (4). My gut reaction is to admit these two types of liars to heaven but only after they have served a short spell in purgatory.

In the real world things are more complex, for with good or bad intentions there are sometimes simultaneously *several* consequences. A doctor may think that he ought to tell the truth to a mentally stable patient, to wit that he will very soon succumb to his illness; this disclosure is made to enable the dying person to arrange his affairs in anticipation of an early demise. The patient is grateful to the doctor and we may therefore call it a good consequence. But the man informs his mother who becomes so upset that she suffers grievously even before her son has actually died.

Fuchs was a communist agent who was unwittingly sent during the war by the British to the United States to assist in the preparation of the atomic bomb. When he returned to the UK after the end of WWII and his spying activities were exposed, he was put on trial and given a long prison sentence. It was long believed that the scientific information which Fuchs passed on to the Soviet Union had been of great significance and this applied in particular to the H-bomb secrets which he betrayed to his communist masters. In the 1990s a US physicist, W. Poundstone, wrote a book in which he decried the role of Fuchs. The H-bomb designs, which the spy managed to convey to Russia, had turned out to be unworkable. The Americans found this out only just in time.

The USSR scientists believed that the designs were workable because Fuchs had in the past been a reliable informant. The ultimate workable American device for the H-bomb was conceived only in 1951 when Fuchs was already behind bars. This demands a revision of the value of Fuchs's service to Russia. Of course his mendacious intentions had throughout been ignoble but the consequence of his flawed H-bomb information proved beneficial to the Western allies as it misled the USSR — at least for some time.

Historians are now agreed that the Chancellor of the Exchequer Harold Macmillan deceived his cabinet colleagues during the Suez crisis by producing frightening economic data which were untrue but appeared so convincing as to contribute to the British government reversing its military operation. To the chagrin of the French and some leading British Conservatives, the UK announced its intention to withdraw from the jointly planned military project. Why did Macmillan lie? He had selfish reasons to discredit Prime Minister Anthony Eden and his devious lies helped him to become prime minister. Decades after the event, a very plausible commentary was published on the consequences which flowed from the Macmillan intervention. While conceding that Macmillan had of course lied, the author maintained that by swamping his colleagues with misleading information he brought about a change in British foreign policy which, as the years since have attested, was indeed in the national interest of the UK. His malevolent lie had a pleasing end result.[3]

The Tablets of Bentham

The postulate that the merits or demerits of each falsehood can be ascertained by the repercussions is superficially attractive. Its advocates cite Pareto, their mentor, who propounded that if, when lies are told, one makes no one worse off but improves the lot of some, the dissemination of such meritorious lies should be encouraged or at least tolerated. Such thinking is but one step away from the seductive doctrine of Jeremy Bentham. Many philosophers, politicians and economists have indeed welcomed his Utilitarianism because it espoused consequentialism. Bentham appeared to

---

[3]   Diane Kurz,'Did Macmillan Lie over Suez', *The Spectator*, November 3,1990.

have provided a useful measure with which to fathom the overall value of state actions (and perhaps also the deeds of individuals and private bodies). State interventions were to be appraised by the way in which they impact upon the totality of all adult citizens within a given jurisdiction. What matters is the balance of advantages and disadvantages, the score of pluses and minuses. Bentham's first article of faith was the power of reason in human affairs. The second article was his belief that there is no good without evil; hence he naturally wanted politicians to prefer the greatest happiness of the greatest number.[4] Bentham did not dwell on the vexed question of who is to undertake the calculations. He also failed to take into account that setting off unhappiness against happiness is a barren exercise if one ignores their relative intensities. The underlying — in my opinion false — assumption that certain bad consequences are *automatically* whitewashed by more substantial good repercussions is quoted until this day to justify lying. Trotsky was asked to justify a certain statement of his which the questioners suspected was a lie. He replied:

> It was not the genuine truth. It was imposed on me. I am a political man. In our society everybody from time to time is obliged not to say the truth... I believe the question can only be decided by a comparison of the lies... and the truth. I believe that in the balance my truths are more heavy than the lies.

If the benevolent liars of the twenty-first century seek certainty from Bentham and his followers, they will be disappointed. Bentham was born into an age with no universal suffrage and where the majority of the population was still largely obsequious 'to their betters'. We have already noted that statisticians cannot help to appraise mendacity and that one must rely therefore on subjective, hopefully informed, value judgements. In modern democracies the votes of the majority of the population determine who should be an MP though justice is still meted out by individuals who are deemed to be wise and erudite; their judgements are expected to ignore the opinions of the masses though some

---

[4] Bentham covered himself with a caveat, according to which his famous axiom was only valid when 'the happiness of each party is equal'. This is an unlikely occurrence. His axiom is thus merely an abstract notion of little use in the real world.

judges do not always live up to this ideal. If we were to rely on populist sentiments, wild and unreasonable evaluations of the consequences of lying would frequently come to the fore. There is a close parallel with theft. Many of our fellow-citizens believe that stealing per se is not always a deplorable act — they often consider that it depends on who the thief steals from. The-man-in-the-street feels no compassion for 'deserving' thieves when they are caught burgling his home. Depraved thieves who rob blind old people are also widely condemned. But robbing General Motors, the state and millionaires is deemed to be less immoral; sometimes such stealing even meets with approval. Gallup polls in the UK found that the public treats thefts from big chain stores as less heinous than stealing from small shopkeepers. Most of the questioned respondents thought it more acceptable to remain silent when undercharged in a big department stores than in a family-owned shop. This warped morality knows no national boundaries. It highlights how dangerous it is to play in a minefield where the crimes of lying and stealing are judged by the calculus of consequentialism as determined by the majority of the population.

At best, Bentham's approach is theoretically helpful in providing pragmatic guidelines. But even these were never meant by him to be perfect. Bentham did not designate governmental edicts (and by inference lies) as being either wholly harmful or wholly beneficial. He conceded that actions which are good for one group of citizens may at the same time be bad for other groups. However, his conclusion, that the benefits accruing to ten million people outweigh the suffering of five million, can often be flawed. The happiness which has been accorded to a formidable majority of the population may weigh less than the pain that the minority[5] has been made to endure. Objective criteria can indeed be employed to determine who, in a material sense, is better or worse off. What is not quantifiable is the (factually accurate or inaccurate) perception of a beneficiary that the material benefits he has received make him feel that he has become better off than he had been in the past. Bentham's measuring

---

[5] Manning sums it up succinctly: 'Once Jeremy Bentham had come to the conclusion that the will of the majority is the nearest pursuable approximation to the will of all, he proceeded to treating minorities as a nuisance.'

tool is a crude gadget. It does not, for example, take cognizance of the fact that, despite the improvement in his material situation, the beneficiary has actually become unhappy. He is suffering because he compares his new benefits with the bigger benefits received by his neighbours. The episodes, sketched below, bear upon the vaunted ideal of weighing merits and demerits and are meant to be scrutinized with Bentham in mind.

Seven Exemplifications

(1) An importer was arrested for bringing unlawfully into the UK garments from low-cost Bangladesh in contravention of the prevailing quota system. The intent of the culprit was undisputed. His sole motive was to enrich himself. He admitted that he broke the law for which, he recognized, he must be punished. His lawyer asked for certain matters to be placed on the scales in mitigation. While the accused conceded that, as a result of his mendacity, no benefits accrued to the UK, he maintained that it was also pertinent to note that no harmful effects had been caused. Ergo, the importer sought to be rewarded for his putative virtues by receiving a relatively lower penalty for his offence. The judge was invited to note that, apart from breaking the import laws and preparing false documents, the importer could have done other bad things but had chosen not to do so. The lawyer explained that his client had not defrauded the Treasury of any taxes and had also not attempted 'to bring in drugs or pornography'.

(2) 800, mostly poor and old, people were defrauded when they acquired the worthless shares which were sold to them by a well-intentioned priest. In the two years of its existence the clinic, set up with the funds obtained from selling bogus shares, treated — mostly with success — some 200 drug addicts. The intent of the mendacious priest had been noble; he personally did not benefit. Later he justified himself by suggesting that the virtuous outcome of the fraud, without which the clinic would not have been established, outweighed the pain of the deceived investors.

(3) I knew the ambassador to an LDC, the ruler of which imagined himself to be a competent chess player. The ambassador was in fact a very much better player — in his youth he had been a junior champion — but the ruler strove to prove

that he could beat him. The foreign diplomat was invited to the palace for this purpose and it is there that the ruler was deceived by the ambassador. The latter told me that he abhorred lying but in this case his high-minded intent was patriotic: he let the ruler win and it was done in a convincing manner. The diplomat made it appear as if he had to struggle hard to ward off his opponent and that only after strenuous efforts was he forced to concede defeat. Thereafter he became a weekly guest of the ruler. I record with regret that my acquaintance, the ambassador, had become a perennial liar. Deviously, he made his mendacious tactic credible by occasionally arranging to win. He was an unselfish but clever liar. Indeed, as a direct result from his close proximity to the ruler, his country gained commercially from his crafty chess games. It opened many doors, led to several contracts and furnished many import licences. News of the trickery reached the ruler by a fluke. The sophisticated liar was overheard boasting of his scheming. The ambassador was asked to leave at once. His country was penalized economically for several years thereafter. The wrathful ruler saw to it that the valuable benefits, gathered during the two chess-playing years, were soon more than offset.

(4) The historic trial of 1931, involving the Royal Mail Packet Company, is recalled because of the perceptive reasoning in the judgement given by Mr Justice Wright. The company's chairman Lord Kylsant, Knight Grand Cross of the Order of St Michael and St George, was found guilty and sent to prison for one year. All were agreed that he had no personal pecuniary motive for the ruses he had initiated. He deceived the company's shareholders and the subscribers to a debenture stock by publishing accounts that made the company's fortunes look somewhat healthier than they really were. He was also responsible for the dividends being financed in part by transfers from secret reserves. All this occurred during a depression when the chairman hoped to keep the company afloat till the tide would turn. Kylsant was portrayed as a 'paternalistic dictator'; he sinned as a benevolent liar. Nevertheless, the court found that he had committed a crime by deceiving with fraudulent intent; he had infringed the law by presenting the accounts in a fashion that concealed the precarious position of the company. Kylsant pleaded that it was only a temporary expedient and, in any

case, his decisions benefitted the company. His lawyers maintained that by not telling the truth about the accounts, as the law demanded, he did only good and definitely did not harm the shareholders. The judge referred scathingly to the view that shareholders do not have a just reason to complain if the annual accounts fail to report the real profits that had been earned. He also repelled the notion that shareholders were not entitled to grumble 'if the position of the finances of the company were better than the accounts disclosed'. What mattered was the truth. In the judgement it was conceded that the deceptions had been well-intentioned and 'may work very well in many cases'; furthermore, it was agreed that directors who issue false accounts may in fact be generating commendable consequences. But, the judge warned, that 'on the other hand, it may be the subject of almost intolerable abuse'. Sending Kylsant to prison was regarded at the time as shocking, especially as the judge had stated that his motives were noble. The Court of Appeal confirmed the sentence. Their reasoning was even more harsh. The judges ignored entirely the consequences of Kylsant's deeds and based their judgement entirely on the fact that lying in this context was a criminal offence. In their stated view lying was not to be condoned, not even when it was benevolent lying. They condemned the publication of these inaccurate accounts as it opened the door for future malevolent liars.

(5) I previously referred to a group of policemen who, by mendacious means, had brought about the conviction of a child molester; without their mendacious testimony, he would have gone free with dire consequences for the community. I connoted them as altruists who had lied on oath for a good cause. This, however, is only half the story because I have so far failed to speak of the totality of consequences that ensued from their falsehoods. That they managed to have the molester put behind bars is per se a virtuous consequence but they also, indirectly, brought about consequences that were certainly not commendable. Their doings did not remain a secret for long. Colleagues of the mendacious policemen were apprised of what had happened. One can only surmise that this may have spurred them to emulate their confreres in other situations where lying on oath could not be justified. Worse than that, the officers who actually

achieved their aim relating to the child molester, had thereby learnt an unsavoury lesson. It would only be human if they did not say to themselves: 'We had no choice but to lie in order to bring the molester to court — and it paid off. What about future cases of a different kind where we also lack judicially acceptable proof? May we then not act likewise?' The one good consequence must therefore be appraised against the background of the many bad consequences which, one fears, were generated in the wake of the lies told in a benevolent conspiracy.

(6) The Wilson government devalued sterling in November 1967 but delayed the public announcement for a few days. In the interim period, Chancellor Callaghan faced a veiled parliamentary question on the subject. The MP, who raised the matter, was told: 'I have nothing to add to, or subtract from, anything I have said on previous occasions on the subject of devaluation.' Several government ministers were not happy with this reply for they wanted him to lie outright; they scorned his moderate mendaciousness. Crossman recounts in his *Diaries* that, after the principled cabinet decision had been taken, Callaghan was asked how he intended to answer those who would publicly demand an explicit statement. Crossman personally challenged him: 'If necessary, will you be able to deny that devaluation is taking place?' He cites the chancellor as replying; 'I certainly should have to.' Crossman complained to the prime minister that the government had been let down: Callaghan's answer had been equivocal 'and made confusion more confounded . . . what the hell was Jim up to? If soldiers can be asked to die in battle, politicians should be prepared to die politically in battle . . . this kind of softness is pretty expensive [and] probably lost us £200m that day.' Crossman was angry with his colleague for not lying with greater vehemence. He had been urged to deceive the HoC but had not done so in the prescribed manner. If he had, implied Crossman, the impact of the lie would have been greater and therefore more beneficial. Fewer people and companies would then have taken preventive actions to hedge the losses they faced from a devaluation. Crossman did not mind their being disadvantaged for his 'us' did not refer to the British people. If foreigners and British residents had reason to suspect that a devaluation was pending, they would have been able

(despite exchange controls) to reduce the losses which they were bound to incur from a devaluation. Who did benefit from the non-disclosure of the truth? Crossman and Callaghan sought to suppress the truth in order to buy time to prevent the coffers of the Treasury being affected adversely and they also aimed to defend the reserves of the BoE. Despite the vagueness of the chancellor's reply in the HoC, there were nevertheless cognoscenti who comprehended that his fudged statement signalled an imminent devaluation. Those who realized what the chancellor was betokening were mostly wealthy, intelligent and privileged individuals. The losers were the poor, the naïve and those who found it hard to accept Callaghan's disingenuousness. The bottom line reads as follows: the deception was practised for the collective good of the UK by giving the pertinent agencies of the state an advantage at the expense of the British population and those foreigners who had invested in sterling. It may well be argued that the Labour politicians were benevolent liars. But there were of course also bad consequences. Honest individuals and law-abiding companies were made to suffer. Which of these consequences were paramount? There must surely be many who will say that in substance the benevolent effects of the Chancellor's lies were outbalanced.

(7) The memory of Robin Hood sustains the prevalent belief that liars are to be admired — or tolerated — when they are agents of justice, i.e. when their mendacity redistributes wealth from the undeserving to the deserving. On the Berlin underground I witnessed an incident in which an educated native hippy, caught by the transport police, explained why he thought it morally legitimate to cheat by travelling without buying a ticket. They argued with him and stressed that if some passengers do not pay for their journeys, others have to pay commensurately higher fares. The hippy accepted that, arithmetically, this was so. However, he insisted that his doings were fair because the 'others' were relatively well-off while he was not. He actually quoted Robin Hood, saying that he had enriched some while impoverishing others. The nature of Robin Hood's robberies are somewhat clouded but the concomitant morality is more engaging than that of the Berlin hippy. There are putative moralists who condone lying when the state is cheated

through tax evasion — especially, when the gain is remitted wholly to a charity and the culprits, unlike the hippy, are themselves not beneficiaries. Populist sentiments apart, it is not right to assume that the consequence of giving to a given charity is necessarily more laudable than the good which the state might have engendered if all taxpayers acted honestly. Furthermore, the benevolent liars (to wit, the tax evaders) can be challenged on the ground that they are not proper persons to enforce arbitrarily social priorities. Why ought money, obtained mendaciously, go to charity A, which is not aided by the state, rather than to charity B which exists largely thanks to subventions from the Treasury? There are no scales to weigh satisfactorily the *comparative* consequences of benevolent lies.

Passive Lying

Passive lying is a more tortuous topic than active lying because it is circumscribed by numerous caveats. Two overlapping themes account largely for the withholding of the truth: (a) the omission to release available information, collected statistics, etc., and (b) attempts to prevent others from spreading messages which they had intended to do. The most vital proviso, which qualifies whether the suppression of the truth constitutes lying, has to do with the conundrum of who has the right-to-know, an entitlement that varies with time and the mores of each society. Rousseau has pioneered the concept — which to a large extent I consider to be valid — that 'to conceal a truth which one is not obliged to divulge is not lying'. Some have expanded Rousseau's dictum and aver that one may actually disseminate an untruth to individuals who are not entitled-to-know.[6] A widely discussed aspect of this proposition concerns doctors. When a practitioner is asked a specific question by a patient about his medical well-being, must he tell the truth and, if the answer is in the affirmative, in what detail? An ethically even more complex issue is whether the doctor is obliged to take the initiative and inform an ignorant patient that he is afflicted by a given disease and the consequences thereof. The recipient of the news

---

[6] It is akin to giving a counterfeit coin to somebody, for example a beggar, to whom you owe nothing. The donor may be castigated as an unpleasant deceiver but is he guilty of a crime?

may not have wanted to know about it and the doctor's gratuitous information therefore makes him unhappy and perhaps depressed. Ought a doctor to ignore this consideration and always go out of his way to tell a patient the relevant truth of which he is cognizant? The psychiatrist Marcel Eck, who specialized in the phenomenon of lying and penned an excellent book on the subject, has set out certain guidelines appertaining to when doctors can and should divulge, and when to suppress, the truth. He opined that one should not generalize for it often depends on the type of patient, his intellectual and nervous characteristics. But Eck maintained that in certain situations a doctor is obliged to make full disclosure to his patients. He asserted that while in the past no one would have a reproached a doctor for not taking the initiative to warn his pregnant patients of the extreme danger of German measles, today a doctor should be condemned as an unethical passive liar if he did not do so in all such cases.

When a colleague applies for a loan and submits personal data to his bank that I know to be false, I am neither legally nor morally obliged to tell the bank about his lies. A freelance contributor to the *Leeds Journal of Geology,* who is ill with AIDS need not apprise the editor of his affliction. But he ought to divulge this to his dentist if he does not wish to be a passive liar. The editor of the *Glasgow Pop Journal,* who has definite information that Sterling is about to be devalued but does not share this knowledge with his readers, is not a passive liar. Another yardstick must, however, be applied to the behaviour of the editors of prominent financial journals who advertise their specialist expertise, thereby attracting readers who expect to be supplied with news, opinions and forecasts on exchange rates and allied matters. Such editors — having appraised at editorial meetings the pros and cons of a devaluation and/or obtained information about impending changes in the parity of sterling — who designedly choose not to print what they know are blatant passive liars.

In many countries laws have been enacted, and many non-state bodies have laid down rules, which explicitly govern the suppression of the truth. In 2005 the Inland Revenue is not allowed to publish the income tax returns of any individual while in some countries such data are released. (Will this convention still exist in the UK in 2015?) Where an entitlement-to-know prevails, it implicitly imposes an obligation on the disseminators to express themselves in a manner which most of their audiences or readers are able to understand. If the truth deserves to be communicated to outsiders, the disclosure must take place with no inordinate delay. It is no use praising the British government for informing the public of a nuclear accident at Windscale thirty years after the event. In 1942 the Royal Navy submarine Sahib torpedoed an Italian troopship, not knowing that it carried hundreds of captured Allied soldiers who were being transported from Africa to Sicily. The accident was investigated and evidence was taken from the crew of the submarine and a few survivors. The next-of-kin of the 800 victims were told that their relatives had died in Italian captivity. Considering that this happened in the midst of the war, one would classify it as a benevolent lie. Though consistently pressed after 1946 to divulge the truth, the Ministry of Defence persisted with its ignoble 'pack of lies' until 1996. The pre-war prominent French politician Pierre Cot was always suspected of being a Stalinist fellow-traveller and in 1960 the authorities in Paris obtained irrefutable evidence that he was an agent of the USSR — but only in 1996 was this embarrassing fact officially acknowledged. The details of the Chernobyl nuclear disaster would probably have been suppressed for even longer if foreign countries had not become aware of it and demanded an immediate account from Moscow. The communist rulers had been brought up to be contemptuous of the right of the public to know. Hence they did not disclose heavy losses of life in train and air disasters with in the USSR. Their immediate reaction to the Chernobyl disaster was therefore traditional. The initial passive lying brought it about that the distressed population in the vicinity of the nuclear reactor suffered grievously because of the failure of their rulers to tell the truth at an early stage. Thousands, victims of passive lying by politicians who did not spell out promptly the ramifications of the incident, died and/or experienced serious ill-health because they had not been told the truth. For three days after the disaster the authorities issued no statement at all. When they had to abandon their policy of saying nothing, a few sentences — reporting a 'fire' at Chernobyl — were broadcast on the radio but the seriousness of the happening was even then not explained. In the subsequent weeks further information was released grudgingly but even the full truth, known to the authorities, was not released. Lives could have been saved if people had been encouraged to flee instantly from the affected area. When the government finally did commence evacuating the population, some refused to move because they were not fully aware of the implications of the horrible truth which had not been spelt out.

Diverse Suppressions of the Truth

In 1753 the HoC refused to permit a census of the British population because it was argued that overt knowledge of the number of people living in the country would reveal to potential enemies how small an army the government could muster. Hence Britain's population remained uncounted until 1801. The modern state — in democracies and dictatorships alike — excels at passive lying and is clearly well equipped to do so. The politicians in office always insist that what they are doing — or failing to do — is due to their conviction that they act in the national interest. No doubt many of the government decisions to withhold the (full) truth are inspired by altruistic motivations. But in numerous other cases their lies are less well-intentioned. The trouble is that government ministers are also the decision-makers who define what is in the national interest. In 1994 a former minister, who then no longer had to seek the approbation of the electorate, openly divulged a practice which politicians on active service would not dare to have mentioned. Lord Trefgarne said that political announcements 'should be made in circumstances and terms which suit the government of the day . . . it is 90% pragmatic. I am certain that pragmatism must be the right approach. Of course you must not tell parliament an untruth or mislead but you don't tell them everything — certainly not.' The UK is of course not alone in this. In 1983 when Germany boasted, and with great justification, of its democratic credentials, the American press ridiculed the attempt by the Bundesbank (the state-controlled central bank) to hide the country's balance-of-payments data; at that time no industrialized Western power formally withheld the publication of such figures. Germany was then running a very large deficit for a simple reason. US interest rates were higher than those in Germany and this generated a massive outflow of funds. The Bundesbank chose to disguise the situation by halting the publication of data which indicated the size of the overall deficit. The Western financial press was amused by the antics of Otto Poehl, the president of the mighty Bundesbank. He was not the kind of public servant who advocated the announcement of fabricated statistics but, as the *Wall Street Journal* noted derisorily, he took a 'more pragmatic, and at times, restrictive approach to the release of information'.

How far should politicians be accorded privacy relating to their private lives? Do they have the moral right to suppress wilfully the truth about *certain* personal deeds or attributes which jar with their political views? There is of course no universal answer. Some years ago an important member of the British government entered hospital for a minor operation. In our age he was certainly under an obligation to release this news but in the context of the UK it was still proper for him to give instructions that the nature of the surgery should not be disclosed.[7] In the US a minister would have been expected to 'reveal all' because the American electorate regards itself as entitled-to-know such matters. Political observers outside the US note with awe that hospitalized presidents allow or order that disclosure is made to the public of the quantitative flows from their bladder and bowel. The failure of British politicians to follow suit does not constitute passive lying, but their unwillingness to disclose other relevant private details does constitute a sinful suppression of the truth. British political decision-makers are fond of claiming that they and their families are entitled to privacy just as all other citizens. This is dangerous sophistry.

---

[7] On February 29 2004 the BBC screened a documentary on the 'Downing Street Patient' which dealt with the disclosures (and non-disclosures) made by all post-WWII prime ministers (except the current one) and leaders of the opposition relating to their own medical circumstances. Almost all of them did not tell the truth. They used to describe themselves as robust, hyperactive, healthy characters, even when they knew that they were ill and sometimes even dangerously ill. At best they underplayed their maladies. Once their masters had retired, the politicians' aides, press officers and doctors, who had of course been in the know, admitted shamelessly why they had been party to these lies. They were not at all contrite about misleading the public and justified their suppression of the truth by claiming that they had acted in the national interest. Though in the US the illnesses of politicians receive more informed publicity than in the UK, presidents and their nearest advisers still manage to disguise debilitating illnesses. Kennedy was highly successful in preventing the public from knowing about his enfeebling afflictions.

The elected representatives have voluntarily taken upon themselves a vocation which bestows upon them the right to determine how other people are allowed to shape their lives. This in turn entitles voters to receive information which they can use to denounce politicians as charlatans if their personal, disguised conduct is incompatible with their professed political and moral outlook.

In the ethos of three Labour governments between 1964 and 1979 the NHS was a holy edifice. The ministers of the Wilson and Callaghan governments regularly preached about the ethical beauty of the NHS and fulminated against anti-social creatures, to wit those evil person who paid for private medical service. Such enemies-of-the-people, accused of jumping the queue, deserved to be brought to book. Hence, in accordance with Labour election manifestos, draconian legislation was being prepared to bring about a total ban on private medicine within the NHS — except for dollar-payers from abroad. Existing private hospitals were to be curbed; the expansion of private hospital beds was to become subject to licences granted by the (distinctly hostile) minister of health. Those MPs, who did not favour such policies and publicly urged that the NHS should co-exist with private medicine, had no cause to disclose if and when they used private medical facilities. They were thus not on par with the members of the government who promoted the mentioned measures: these can rightly be connoted passive liars when they omitted to reveal that they were surreptitiously partaking of the joys provided by the private sector. The most rabid fighter against private medicine was the Minister of Health Barbara Castle who was personally preparing these far-reaching laws. Investigative journalists found out that she herself had in the past consulted doctors outside the orbit of the NHS. After first denying this, Castle conceded that this had been so. By far more outrageous was the conduct of her cabinet colleague, Denis Healey, who arranged for his wife to undergo a private hip operation. He had never opposed in public the measures being planned by Castle which were of course important planks in Labour's published programme. Nevertheless, he had no compunctions about helping his wife to jump the queue. More importantly, being a clever man, Healey — fully conscious that his behaviour was improper according to the tenets of his party —

schemed to keep secret the operation and succeeded in doing so for a considerable length of time. After the truth finally surfaced, Healey was indignant when people criticized his inconsistent behaviour. In his autobiography he relates how he had once walked out of a television studio in which 'he was questioned about the private hip operation Edna had had two years earlier. I was so angry . . . my loyal research assistant . . . was able to prevent me hitting the journalist responsible only by interposing his body.'

Perjury, to save the skin of an errant relative, is very common. It is even practised by members of a family who are estranged from the wrongdoer. *The People,* in 1908, printed an article about Lloyd George, who was about to be named in a divorce suit as a co-respondent in a divorce suit, in which it was alleged that he had bought out the petitioner for £20,000. The Liberal leader had no choice but to sue for libel. As the newspaper could not produce as their main witness, the bribed petitioner, Lloyd George was bound to win — as indeed he did — though he had good reason to believe that his character would nevertheless be stained. He approached his estranged wife, Maggie, imploring her to help him because there were strong rumours that she was about to leave the marital home. His deeply religious spouse 'was in torment' for she did not doubt that her husband had indeed been guilty of adultery and now planned to perjure himself by denying the allegation. Their son was to reveal later that his mother had confided in him. She did not care to advance his (threatened) political career but was moved 'simply to help him because he was hurt and frightened and in grave trouble'. To this end the couple drove together to the court and throughout the proceedings she sat at his side without uttering a word. There are historians who think that her passive lying was decisive for her husband's political future. It is a superb historical illustration of Robert Melson's generalization: 'The silences — what is not said — may be even more important than what is said.'

Another instance of intra-family passive lying relates to Sigmund Freud who at the beginning of his professional life had been on friendly terms with a Dr Wilhelm Fliess in Berlin, who with hindsight, is today regarded a crackpot. (Fliess has maintained that some sexual disorders could be cured by operating on the nose.) All the letters which he sent to Freud were at some point of time destroyed by the recipient but Freud's many communications to Fliess have survived. Anna Freud, the loyal daughter who sought to suppress material that might affect adversely her father's intellectual standing, left out controversial letters Freud had sent to Fliess when she edited a selection of Sigmund's letter. In Jeffrey Masson's explosive book there are details of Anna's tendentious editing. He accused her also of deleting vital passages in letters that she did reproduce when these, in her view, reflected badly on her father's repute.

Employers, requested to provide a testimonial for a former employee, risk being sued if they write the whole sordid truth. To be honest, the ex-employer would have to say that the individual had been found guilty of repeatedly stealing from the firm and was therefore discharged with ignominy. If, however, the testimonial merely mentioned that the said employee had worked for the company x number of years, this constitutes an obvious falsehood though formally what it does say is not inaccurate.

It was factually true though hardly a very serious matter that Prime Minister Harold Wilson not only smoked cigars but also relished the pleasures that are obtained from drinking cognac and whisky. He did not need spin doctors to tell him that this awesome truth ought to be suppressed. If at all possible, the public was to remain ignorant of his vices. Wilson tried to ensure that in publicity photos he was shown to smoke a pipe and/or drink a glass of beer. Why? In the early 1960s the 'natural' supporters of the Labour Party drank beer and smoked cigarettes as well as pipe tobacco. Would some of them have become alienated if the leader's elitists tastes were publicized? There was the famous occasion when Wilson allowed the television cameras to come into his room in a Liverpool hotel where, surrounded by family and political friends, he awaited the results of the general election. Wilson was tired and anxious. He fortified himself by gulping down some of the proscribed alcohol. It was an unfortunate lapse by an experienced television performer. But Thomas Balogh saved the day. Viewers at home found suddenly that their vision of the Labour leader was momentarily blocked. Balogh, his personal friend and comrade, had contrived to place himself between Wilson and the cameras.

It is a moot moral question as to whether I ought to lie actively to help convict a person who, *in the case before the court was blameless* but in other respects was a depraved, unpleasant individual. Am I to give honest testimony in his favour and thus bring about the collapse of the prosecution? Or should I act as a passive liar by declining to appear as a witness? The following is about a man who, despite painful temptations to remain silent, opted not to be a passive liar. It was to cost him dearly. Israel Kastner had a remarkable record as a saviour of Jewish lives during the Holocaust. He had no weapons in his armoury with which to kill the enemy. Instead, Kastner bribed known murderers, deceived Eichmann and told lies to Hitler's henchmen who were organizing transports to the gas chambers. Kastner later pointed out that his operational mode had not been in a romantically heroic mould: he found it tactically expedient to drink and play cards with Nazi executioners. But his endeavours saved the lives of numerous Jews. Among the prominent Nazis sent to Hungary, to carry out the extermination of Jews and the organized robbery of their material resources, was the SS colonel Kurt Becher from Hamburg. Kastner cultivated him and this bore fruit. As the war was drawing to a close Becher thought less of Germany and more of the fate that awaited him. This accounts for Becher's providing help for Kastner's rescue ventures. Shortly before the German army capitulated, the SS colonel took Kastner (attired in an SS uniform) with him to various concentration camps, a perilous affair which, however, had positive results. The real nature of Becher's relationship with Kastner can only be inferred. There were no written contracts. The SS colonel was intelligent enough to apprehend what the victors would do to him. It is very plausible to assume that Kastner induced Becher to assist him in saving Jewish lives by promising to testify on his behalf if and when Becher was put on trial as a war criminal which, undoubtedly, he was. Kastner emigrated to Israel with the ambition to pursue a political career in the new country but he faced many hardships: he had no money to even buy a modest flat and was not fluent in the local vernacular. Those were the years when tens of thousands of the remnants of European Jewry sought revenge for the Holocaust. No one in Israel disputed that all means to save Jews from the gas chambers had been commendable, and this included making (false) promises to the exterminators. Perhaps not surprisingly, very few Israelis were after the war ready to stomach the notion that a Jew would want to keep his word by telling the truth which favoured an accused SS colonel. Most of Kastner's friends were shocked with dismay when he honoured the surmised implicit promise. He journeyed to Germany to give the Allied lawyers in Nuremberg an account of what Becher had done to help him rescue Jews. This destroyed Kastner's political prospects in Israel. His physical existence was terminated in March 1957 by bullets of assassins; he was Israel's first Jewish political murder-victim. Becher was indeed released from captivity and quickly became a prosperous businessman during the German economic miracle. Kastner, who refused to be a passive liar, was only officially rehabilitated by the Israeli government a quarter of a century after his murder.

Prime Minister Edward Heath strove to drag the UK into a supranational United States of Europe. He himself was fully aware that this is what the signatories of the Treaty of Rome had in mind, but he was also convinced that if the British public learnt what was being hatched, it would probably not have followed his lead. Heath saw to it that at the 1975 referendum the votes would be cast with reference to a relatively innocuous issue, that of joining a Common Market. Heath did not reveal what was being planned in Brussels. His disingenuous strategy was successful. In the 1990s he no longer had to cover his tracks and it was then that he told the real truth. Heath now revealed to questioners that at the time he took the UK into the Common Market, he had already envisaged the near-certainty of its evolution into a political union, the adoption of one currency, the creation of a European army and many other things about which he had remained silent when he asked the electors to vote 'yes' in 1975. He did not, however, clear up a related query which was frequently put to him. Did he, during the referendum campaign, share his vision-cum-knowledge with the voters? On more than one occasion he was challenged to produce *explicit* particulars from his speeches, articles and television interviews which would verify that in 1975 he had already unequivocally outlined what the future would — and did — bring. Apart from some oblique and ambiguous references, he was unable to authenticate that he had not been a passive liar par excellence. Ignorance had worked in Heath's favour. His strategic passive mendaciousness is an egregious example of how a politician can gain the approbation of voters when these are deliberately not told what they should have been told.

When the Berlin Wall crumbled, a group of sceptical government statisticians from West Germany raced to the Alexanderplatz in East Berlin where many of the statistical data of the defunct DDR used to be stored and processed. The West German civil servants expected them to be as phoney as those of the USSR. To their amazement the data corresponded in most respects with the actual facts.[8] Apart from a few sensitive exceptions, the DDR collected true statistics. Stalin in his days released statistical falsehoods and executed recalcitrant statisticians while the DDR only did some 'polishing' of numbers but did not invent data. The DDR rulers did, however, practise passive lying. A vast amount of genuine — but politically unhealthy — statistics, stored in secret vaults, were only made available to a select group of politicians and bureaucrats; their release to the public was banned. The state statistical office was only allowed to publish a yearbook with harmless contents. Nothing illustrates the suppression of the numerate truth so well as the administrative treatment of the (true) data on suicides per 100,000 of the population. Until 1961 the collected figures on this subject were printed in the yearbook. In the subsequent years the collection of the figures was continued but the communist masses were no longer to be trusted with the information. After the demise of the DDR, the German Society for the Prevention of Suicide convened a conference in Dresden where papers were read on the comparative post-war trends in East and West Germany. This was made possible because the hidden files for the thirty-year period, during which their contents were a state secret, were found intact. With Teutonic thoroughness these established that the East German suicide rate was at least one third higher than that of West Germany. The communist ideologues had seen this as an implicit compliment to capitalist West Germany which is why they had determined that the dissemination of the truth must be

---

[8] Statistisches Bundesamt, *Untersuchungen zur Validierung der Statistischen Ergebnisse der DDR*, Wiesbaden, April 1991.

halted. In 1996 the government of Sri Lanka — then, allegedly, the country with the world's highest pro rata incidence of suicides — also forbade the publication of such statistics. No official reason was given for the ban but it was thought that the government opined that by suppressing the truth, it might restrain many persons from voluntarily ending their lives.

Galvanized Bullying

In 1967 Claus Moser became director of the British central statistical services. It was assumed at the time of his appointment, made personally by Prime Minister Wilson, that he would always act as a loyal supporter of the Labour Party. Moser left this job in 1978. Only ten years latter, in 1988, did he go on public record to detail how he had been subjected to improper pressures by Labour ministers. He averred that he had not succumbed but had threatened to resign. Several entries in Crossman's *Diaries* pinpoint one of the vexed affairs. This centred on the release of true and pertinent immigration data, a hot political potato. Crossman, a senior member of the cabinet, had convinced himself that adversaries of Labour, orchestrated by the registrar-general — 'a mild, willowy creature but obstinate and no friend of mine' — were up to something wicked. He wrote of him that he had a 'real ideological' motive for wanting to publish detailed data, based on the census, which projected to 1981 the number of new Commonwealth immigrants who would settle in the UK. Nicholas Kaldor, a leftist professor from Cambridge who advised the Labour government, was largely responsible for Crossman concerning himself with the professional domain of UK statisticians. As the following quotation shows, the intervention by Crossman was not impelled primarily to arrive at the factual truth. His main complaint was with the *presentation* of the relevant statistics, the accuracy of which was not being questioned. How would the public react if these data were published? Would it harm the Labour Party? Clearly Crossman shared Kaldor's fears; he cites the latter's outburst: 'There are some fascists in that office. These figures would do incredible harm because they would confirm [Enoch] Powell's accusation that we [the Labour Party] are flooding the country with immigrants.'

In most of the post-war years Queen Elizabeth broadcast a Christmas message to listeners and viewers in the UK and the Commonwealth. In 1973 she prepared a text in which she mentioned in the mildest possible language the difficulties that the British people were facing because of the current strike by the mineworkers. Prime Minister Heath, who was shown a draft, was determined that her address should not even hint at industrial unrest and the economic crisis. He censored her speech. When she sent him a toned-down version, Heath was still not satisfied and insisted that any reference whatsoever to the current economic crisis had to be excised.

Baldwin was able in 1936 to order the British press not to publish a single word relating to the King's relations with a married woman who he intended to marry after her pending divorce. The papers (and this included the communist *Daily Worker*) obeyed the unwritten edict until the day when the prime minister prevailed upon the sovereign to give up the throne. This successful bullying took place while the rest of the world reported the affair in considerable detail.[9] The competence of British governments in the twenty-first century to bully individuals, the press and associations in the private sector still exists but it is very emasculated when compared with what even Prime Minister Wilson was still able to accomplish.

International organizations are in a delicate position when, at the behest of member-states it is demanded of them to suppress the truth. Of course the bullying by powerful countries is particularly effective but these supranational bodies are obliged, sometimes by statute but always by pragmatic convention, not to do anything which even the smallest country deems to be inimical to its national interests. So while the officials know the truth, they often dare not publish it. The OECD regularly publishes economic country reports and forecasts. Its prestige is such that the politicians

---

[9] In this period powerful individuals and firms were indeed able to bring about the suppression of news items which they considered to be undesirable. Newspaper proprietors took seriously blackmailing threats to withdraw advertising. The owner of the *Express* group, Lord Beaverbrook, was able to persuade all the other press barons not to print the news relating to the arrest of Tom Driberg (later to become an MP) who had been found guilty by a court of a homosexual offence.

of its member-states, who finance the institution, care enough to protest bitterly if the performance of their national economy is not painted in bright colours. Governments are rarely able to induce the OECD to publish positive falsehoods but they can and do induce it to soften certain criticisms or exert pressure to omit relevant truthful assertions. In 1970 London learnt that the OECD was about to release a report on the UK in which was mentioned a possible increase in inflation. The then occupants of 10 Downing Street opined that if these unpalatable, though true, projections were published, this would damage the PR fortunes of the ruling party. *The Times,* allegedly on the basis of an official leak, disclosed that

> Prime Minister Heath's first thought seems to have been in terms of cutting off British finance for the OECD. It is understood that he ordered an immediate investigation of the UK's financial contribution to the OECD and membership of it. Government officials understood that he was at one point thinking in terms of withdrawing Britain from membership.

In 2003 Germany, once the mightiest economic power in post-war Europe, behaved in an even more dastardly manner. This brought it about that the OECD actually doctored the current report on Germany. The OECD even allowed its spokesman to confirm that Germany had indeed requested changes in the official draft. The German government, perhaps out of a sense of humour, agreed that it had exerted pressure but said that the aim had only been 'to avoid mistakes'. The *Handelsblatt* cited an OECD official as saying that, in his experience, Germany bullied more vehemently than any other country had ever done.

The UN feels that it must automatically treat the statistics issued by its member-states as statistically accurate. In one case — I have been told that there are many other instances — an LDC, where the unofficial markets dominated the economy, demanded that the UN statisticians should only refer to the official output and the artificially low prices thereof. When confronted with this incongruity, the UN said that it was well acquainted with the true facts but 'you cannot expect us to incorporate black market activities against the wishes of a member-state', i.e. the known truth had to be suppressed. Until 1972 Taiwan was treated as a separate state for statistical purposes. The People's Republic of China felt that its national prestige was being impugned and demanded that Taiwan be treated as one of its provinces. The UN, faced with bullying by the largest country in the world, had to give in and has stopped publishing data about Taiwan — a pure politicization of statistics. The Red Cross and the WHO, both headquartered in Switzerland, are in a similar quandary. They cannot always proclaim the truth when the government of member-states (or countries in which they operate) dictate what may or may not be said. Countries are supposed to report epidemics of deadly diseases to the WHO. But unless they do so, the WHO cannot officially alert the rest of the world.

Biblical Prophecies

An Immemorial Precedent

The Bible does not enable one to state with any certainty whether benevolent lies are, or are not, evil. There is testimony to sustain either view. In Proverbs 12. 17 & 22 it is said: 'He that speaketh truth shewest forth righteousness: but a false witness deceit. Lying lips are abomination to the Lord: they that deal truly are his delight.' In evidence for an opposite point of view one can point to several descriptions of individuals, such as King David, who told wicked untruths. In one story in the Old Testament three persons — Jacob, his mother Rebecca and his uncle Laban — are depicted as conspirators who set out to deceive. Adam and Eve disobeyed the Divine order not to partake of the forbidden fruit though God had said explicitly that if they did, they would die. Adam blamed Eve for leading him astray and Eve justified herself by relying on the serpent which had maintained that God would not be so cruel. The serpent was right. Adam and Eve were punished but God did not carry out his threat.

This, the last section of Part A of this book, is a bridge that leads to Part B, in which the probity of politicians of contemporary Western democracies is analysed. May one employ imperfect means to achieve good ends? This is not a query which has only arisen in modern times when universal suffrage prevails. The Old Testament proves that from the beginning of mankind human beings have had to wrestle with this ethical enigma. The Bible also demonstrates that it does not suffice to make use of expedient means to attain commendable objectives — the pronounced tidings must arouse persuasive credibility. This mattered as much in the olden days when the prophets spoke to the masses as it does in the twenty-first century when politicians can only achieve good ends if their messages *appear* to be plausible and trustworthy.

The Biblical concept of 'false prophets' has a specific meaning. It does not refer to preachers whose foretelling the future is later shown to have been flawed and who, therefore, are assailed for having misled their audiences. When Matthew exclaimed 'Beware of false prophets', he did not seek to castigate that kind of forecaster. Matthew warned the faithful to beware of impostors, to wit those who foretold the future although they were not authorized Divine heralds. Jeremiah cited God's censure of non-genuine prophets:

> Behold, I am against the prophets, saith the Lord, that use their tongues, and say, He saith. Behold, I am against them that prophesy false dreams . . . yet I sent them not.

The Bible recognizes as genuine prophets only spokesmen who are directly instructed or inspired by God. Ezekiel spoke of his own experience:

> The word of the Lord came unto me, saying, son of man, I have made thee a watchman unto the house of Israel: therefore hear the word at my mouth and give them warning from me.

When Jeremiah was made an accredited prophet, God told him:

> Thou shalt go to all that I shall send thee, and whatsoever I command thee thou shalt speak . . . Behold, I have put my words in thy mouth.

After receiving their marching orders, prophets have been known to argue with God and some have expressed displeasure at the messages they were instructed to communicate. Yet, at the end of the day, they declaimed precisely what God wanted them to say. They were expected to be obedient.

Biblical prophecies, spread by those who were commanded by an omnipotent and omniscient God, can be classified under two headings: they are either conditional or unconditional predictions. The former tell of defined consequences that ensue if people continue to behave iniquitously. But the sinners are also told that if they modify their conduct, or exogenous circumstances have changed, then the repercussions will not be punitive. This is illustrated in the prophesies which God urged Jeremiah to proclaim when addressing the people of 'backsliding Israel' and 'treacherous Judah'. The Bible records long verses with itemized savagery which delineate the horrible future: 'I will bring evil from the north and a great destruction . . . thy cities shall be laid waste, without an inhabitant.' This, however, was a qualified prophesy for, concomitantly, Jeremiah told the apostates and idolaters that if 'thou put away thine abominations', life will become so joyful that other nations will have cause to envy Israel and Judah. However, the shortcoming of these conditional prophesies is that they do not generate the same kind of feedback and backlash that are the consequences of the unconditional prophesies. This is confirmed in the Bible when Moses reported on the message that God had sent to the Israelites:

> *I will raise them up a prophet from among they brethren and will put my words in his mouth; and he speak unto them all that I shall command him . . . And if thou say in thine heart, how shall we know the word which the Lord has not spoken? When a prophet speaketh in the name of the Lord, if the thing follow not, nor come to pass, that is the thing which the Lord has not spoken.*

Thus, according to Deuteronomy, the accuracy criterion helps to expose false prophets.

The Maligned Jonah

Jonah's assignment consisted of a definite assertion that offered only a single version of the immediate future: 'And the word of the Lord came unto Jonah. Arise, go into Nineveh, that great city, and preach unto it the preaching that I bid thee.' Jonah began to enter into the city and proclaimed: 'Yet 40 days and Nineveh shall be overthrown.' There is nothing in this unconditional prediction which suggests that God might yet change his mind. It even lacks a hint which permitted the citizens of Nineveh to infer that if they repented, the determinate forecast would not come to fruition. Jonah was not ordered to mention that animals and children would be spared during the certain slaughter. Nor was there any affirmation in Jonah's message that God would differentiate between repentant and unrepentant sinners. Jonah uttered no threats or warnings. He only disseminated what he had been told would occur. God demanded that the sinners of Nineveh be 'denounced in the words I give you' and indeed Jonah shouted from the rooftops when and how it would occur.

We are told that Jonah's utterances carried weight. This happened in part because his unconditional forecast had an appurtenance that, designedly, made its contents even more plausible. Jonah did not tell the sinners in a vague manner that they would be punished at an unspecified point in time. Had he prophesied that God planned to destroy the city 'in a few months' or 'sometime in the future', the impact would have been very much less striking than his specific avowal that it would happen on a given date. (The twenty-first century secular practitioners of contrived forecasting are well aware that it is expedient to disdain woolly declarations for it is much more rewarding to spell out a specific, detailed prediction.) It was a master stroke that the Jonah prophesy contained the unchallenged item of 'forty days'. Consequently, due to the unconditional nature of the prophesy, enlivened by the specific item of 40 days, Jonah's mission proved a thundering success. As he was seen to be God's acknowledged messenger, there was a far-reaching, immediate backlash. Again we quote verbatim from the Bible:

> So the people of Nineveh believed God, and proclaimed a fast, and put on sackcloth. For word came unto the king of Nineveh and he arose from his throne and he laid his robes from him, and covered him with sackcloth, and sat in ashes. And he caused it to be proclaimed let neither man nor beast, herd nor flock, taste anything; let them not feed, nor drink water. But let man and beast be covered in sackcloth, and cry mightily unto God: yea, let them turn every one from his evil way.

Based on this account Nineveh indeed repented and in doing so invalidated Jonah's forecast for the compassionate God then withdrew his threat to annihilate the town. The Biblical assertion that the people of Nineveh 'believed God' was, however, not wholly accurate. Had they really believed in what Jonah told them, the described acts of repentance would have proved to be irrelevant.[10] If the citizens had really believed in God's message, which reached them via Jonah, it might have been sensible to flee from Nineveh to locations where they were not about to be exterminated. Alternatively, the depraved sinners might just as well have continued to sin because it was implicit in the prophesy that being covered in sackcloth would not avert the ordained fate — nothing could. Knowing all this, was the king a sceptic? He was certainly convinced that God was angry with the town and had pondered how to punish Nineveh. The king's actual reaction shows that he did not take seriously the most significant feature of the prophesy. The king is said to have spelt out his doubts: 'Who can tell if God will turn and repent, and turn away from His fierce anger, that we perish not?'

A few theologians have gone so far as to characterize the Book of Jonah as the 'noblest book in the Hebrew Bible'. Others have praised it because it highlights the power of repentance. Heaton regards it as unique among the prophetic books in being a work of didactic fiction which indicates that God was no less interested in the Gentile nations than in His Chosen People. The majority of exegetes throughout the ages have, however, attributed ignoble motives to Jonah. They allege that he was not a genuine prophet of God and had acted on his own. To many he was a prophet who lacked the compassion of his Master. In fact Jonah did not rejoice at the prospect of Nineveh being destroyed. Initially, he resisted going to Nineveh to prophesy and ultimately did so only under duress. When his forecast was disowned, he realized that he had played an active role in an episode which unfairly blemished his character. His credibility as a professional prophet was impaired badly and his amour propre was dented. Jonah was depressed because he had been involved into doing something he had not wanted to do. If we ignore the feelings of the prophet, one can only admire that — however inadvertently — he had been instrumental in executing an efficacious strategy. Accuracy had been sacrificed on the altar of consequentialism. Had Jonah been dispatched to unveil a conditional forecast,

---

[10] In his play L. Housman makes the prophet Jonah, say: 'Let them repent; but their repentance comes too late, if the word that I spake was true.'

his sermons would not have produced the results that his unconditional prophesy had brought forth. The strategy had therefore been sound. In my view there is no reason to conjecture that the Lord of Mercy ever really intended to destroy Nineveh. But had He confided fully in Jonah, would this noble man with a gentle soul have agreed to carry out this strategy? God was probably right in doubting that he would have done so.

PART B

Chapter IV

The Blotted Democracies

> Only he has the calling for politics who is sure that he shall not crumble when the world, from his point of view, is too stupid or too base for what he wants to offer. Only he, who in the face of all this can, has the calling for politics. *Max Weber*

From Pericles To Blair

At the outset four provisos must be set out. (1) Though the present chapter appears to be unrelated to the central theme of this book, its subject matter will, in the follow-on chapters, be recognized to have been a harbinger that elucidates some of the reasons why democratic politicians are nowadays obliged to behave deviously. (2) Democracy is nowadays something sacred which all decent people are expected to praise (without having to define what is meant by it). To be traduced as an opponent of democracy is akin to being called abusively a fascist or racist and marks one out as a pariah. (3) Neither in the US nor in any other large populous country has Lincoln's pithy maxim been actualized: 'government of the people, by the people and for the people'. Only the first of the three attributes is in part true; the second is an absurdity for it implies that the Congress, the White House and the Washington civil service do not (jointly) constitute the effective government of the US; the third can only be meaningful in a country ruled by a dictator or a one-party government because genuine democratic regimes harbour several political parties, each one with a distinct programme on what is 'good for the people'. (4) twenty-first-century politicians are fond of praising democracy up to the hilt; they also extol the wisdom and decency of their electorate. Once they are retired, they often change their tune and, unsavourily, speak disparagingly about the system and the voters who they once flattered insincerely.

Inefficient and Unfair Governance

The beginning of democracy is traced to an aristocrat, the sculptor Pericles, who ruled the small state of Athens. He submitted himself annually for re-election. His admirers said of him that he governed by consent though he neither flattered the masses nor appealed to their prejudices. Pericles had no party machinery at his disposal and there were no intermediaries between himself and those entitled to vote at the Athenian assembly. He enunciated that as not all people are equal, there are certainly many who are not competent to govern. Nevertheless, he thought that everyone, irrespective of their social origin, should have a part in political decision-making. He opined that 'only a few may originate policy, [but] we are all able to judge it'. All residents — but not women, slaves and foreigners — ought to be given an opportunity to vote and thereby express a judgement. At the end of his life he had personal reasons to doubt the pioneering value of his political credo. He had urged the people to support him in the Peloponnesian War – which, initially, they did. Unfortunately, things did not go well for Athens; the plague broke out and killed up to a third of its citizens. The people held him responsible for this and other mishaps. He, who had been once been so adored, was now humiliated by the ungrateful masses. One year after he died (of the plague), Plato was born. Sneering at Pericles's naïve faith in democracy, he served as the pristine symbol of anti-democratic thought throughout the ages. In his pronounced anti-egalitarian philosophy — that stressed the paramount need to maintain social harmony — he warned that if one lets the masses have a decisive say, then horrible consequences will ensue: instead of democracy, they might even opt for a dictator.[1] From Plato to Hitler, from John Stuart Mill to Kadar, many influential thinkers and very powerful personalities have castigated democracy when the system entailed universal suffrage. To illustrate this, here is a small sample.

---

[1] Plato propagated the myth that when human beings were created, gold was included in those qualified to become the rulers (the guardians), silver in the auxiliaries (the executives and administrators of the Republic), iron and bronze in the workers (the common people).

- *Though Plato* called the common people his brothers, he emphasised that God had made them differently: 'a few are born to rule, the majority to be ruled'. In an ideal republic 'the subjects are to obey any law the rulers lay down even if the rulers frame laws that do not work well or badly or make mistakes'.
- *A.N. Wilson:* 'The idea had got abroad that democracy meant not the freedom to ask someone more engaged or better informed to make decisions on your behalf but the freedom to make those decisions for yourself.'
- *Nigel Lawson* before he was appointed Thatcher's chancellor: 'While freedom is a cause to die for, there is no reason to be starry-eyed about democracy . . . Democracy was never intended to bring better or wiser government — nor has it. The oppression of the majority has been replaced by the oppression of the minority. The two minorities which suffer most are the successful and the really poor.'
- *Adolf Hitler*: 'Democracy, whose meaning could only be the mastery of the herd over the intelligentsia, the mastery over true energy through the dead weight of massed numbers.'
- *John Stuart Mill*: 'The problem is democratic society. Because in principle there is equality, it poses a threat to excellence and encourages mediocrity. Individuality is constantly at risk, in danger of being swallowed by the mass.'
- After the bloody suppression of the 1956 Hungarian uprising, the new dictator *Janos Kadar*, who was enthroned over his recalcitrant countrymen with the help of Russian tanks, explained why he was not only opposed to bourgeois democracy but also rejected workers' democracy: 'The task of leaders is not to put into effect the wishes and will of the masses . . . the task of leaders is to accomplish the interests of the masses.'
- *Walter Bagehot's* 'gloomy forebodings' centred on 'the effects of enfranchising an ignorant and greedy electorate'.
- *Samuel Brittan*, who referred disparagingly to the 'manifestations of the herd impulse', conjectured that as 'liberal representative democracy suffers from internal contradictions which are likely to increase in time, the system is likely to pass away within the lifetime of people now adult'.

- *C. Northcote Parkinson:* 'The pursuit of democracy does not end in perfection but in that chaos from which dictatorship offers the only means of escape.'
- *F.A. Hayek:* 'There has often been much more cultural and spiritual freedom under an autocratic rule than under some democracies — and it is at least conceivable that, under the government of a very homogeneous and doctrinaire majority, democratic government might be as oppressive as the worst dictatorship.'[2]
- *Lord Hailsham:* 'It is only now that men and women are beginning to realise that representative institutions are not necessarily guardians of freedom, but can themselves become engines of tyranny. We need to be protected from our representatives no less than from our former masters.'
- *Niccolo Machiavelli*, not surprisingly, came out against democracy and in favour of some form of dictatorship. His reasoning revolved around the question whether the governing elite should aim to be loved or feared. He opined that obviously it would be best if the two could co-exist. But, 'because hardly can they subsist both together, it is much safer to be feared than to be loved. Men, we say this in general, are unthankful, inconstant, dissemble, avoid dangers and are covetous of gain. Fear restrains with a dread of punishment which never forsakes a man.'
- *Edmund Burke*: 'A perfect democracy is therefore the most shameless thing in the world.'

The step by step journey from Pericles's direct democracy to the current representative democracy took many centuries. The most important post-Pericles innovation was the introduction of intermediaries between the eligible voters and the rulers; this enabled parliaments to become more effective in holding the government accountable. The Athenian notion of annual elections was dropped and replaced by terms of three-four-five years; without this reform the democratic rulers would have had to operate constantly in a feverish electoral atmosphere. The enlargement of the electorate also proceeded piecemeal. The disqualifications, on account of religion, gender and other grounds, were abandoned in stages and rather reluctantly. Despite strong opposition

---

[2] Hayek has written of the 'misleading and unfounded belief that so long as the ultimate source of power is the will of the majority, that power cannot be arbitrary'.

from most of the leading intellectuals of the day, a relatively recent change granted the right-to-vote to all sane individuals, even though they were uneducated, owned no substantial properties and paid no income tax. John Stuart Mill, representing the views of the majority of his contemporaries, had advocated the award of the franchise to all adult males but only subject to a number of exceptions. The receipt of parish relief was to him a good reason for disqualifying a citizen. More significant still was his view that only those men should be entitled to vote who could write, read and perform the 'common operations of arithmetic'. He thought that the right-to-vote should depend on the ability to 'copy a sentence from an English book and perform a sum in the rule of three'. John Stuart Mill and many of his generation were of the opinion that as the HoC has the power to make citizens pay taxes, the MPs ought to be chosen only by those 'who pay something toward the taxes imposed'. Nowadays such notions would be dismissed offhand as anachronistic. The system of unconditional universal suffrage is today propped in different countries by postal voting, the state subsidization of political parties in accordance with the number of votes cast for them, various prohibitions relating to political donations, penalties for those who do not exercise their privilege to vote in national elections, extending the franchise also to residents with a foreign nationality.

Our Full Democracy embodies the danger of the 'tyranny of the majority' over small and large minorities. We live in an era where the majority is oppressed simultaneously by several vocal minorities which the rulers of democratic societies expediently opt to appease. In the 1970s Lord Hailsham described the insidious inroads into British democracy which were generating instability. (Since then the dimensions of this phenomenon have become even more threatening):

> Whole geographical units show signs of wishing to opt out. Organized minorities clamour to be heard, and what they cannot win by the ballot box, seek to extract by violence or by depriving the population of their rightful needs. In the world of universal franchise, loyalty is at a discount. Self- discipline is a dirty word. Law and order have become objects of ridicule. Every restraint must be removed and the anarchic total

described as liberation, permissiveness and even humanism.

Religious concessions are given statutorily to gain the favour of small groups. The Sikhs have scored a precedent-making success. Nobody had suggested that the wearing of their headdress should be banned but tolerance was not enough for this minority which embraced less than 1% of the British population: they asked for, and were given, positive discrimination. Based on a consensus in the HoC, a law was being prepared which made it incumbent upon *all* motorcyclists in the UK to wear a helmet for safety reasons. It was thought so salubrious a measure that the MPs agreed to interfere blatantly with personal freedom. But, fearing unpleasantnesses from the Sikhs, who asserted that wearing the helmets would interfere with their religious headgear, the proposed legislation was amended to make it legally binding on all motorcyclists — except the Sikhs.

The introduction of universal franchise was justified on the airy assumption that abolishing electoral inequalities would make for a more just society. This in turn was thought to make parliamentary legislation more acceptable to all segments of the population because adults were now entitled to choose the intermediaries, to wit the MPs, who would have the determinant task to decide which legislative proposals should, or should not, become the binding laws of the land. It has not worked out as expected. Governments — from the prime minister to the most junior minister — now have to spend a great deal of their time, not on governing but on paying attention to the (real or imagined) grievances of the electorate. The governing politicians must demonstrate publicly how much they care what the masses — and not, primarily, the legislators — think about this and that. A tremendous waste of time but even so it is not the biggest handicap of representative democracies. Universal franchise has brought it about that neither the government nor the parliamentary representatives can consider the merits of given proposals solely on their merits. It is no longer a question of what the rulers should do but rather what they can get away with without arousing the wrath of the masses. Nowhere is this more pronounced than in economic affairs. Keynes once naively boasted that it is political philosophers and economists who play a paramount role in the governance of Britain. To some extent this was true in the past but today this assertion is unadulterated balderdash. The masses believe nowadays that they are able to comprehend the purport of economic policies and therefore insist that their views should prevail. Some economists have the illusion that the rationale of their discipline can still be influential through the 'dethronement of politics'. Though Churchill analysed this correctly in 1930, he merely managed to pose the right question but he too had in time to accept the disagreeable reality. He asked whether parliamentary institutions, 'based on adult suffrage, could possibly arrive at the right decisions upon the intricate propositions of modern finance and business'. To him universal suffrage spelt wild populism. He dared to say that, hoping that the threatened consequences could be fended off. If this did not happen, Britain would be like some other countries which are ruled by 'military chiefs or dictatorships'.

National Parties

All modern societies are governed with the *implicit* consent of the governed — only the essence of the consent varies from country to country. This generalization applies also to dictatorships, commanded by Franco, Hitler, Mussolini and Stalin. These despots were happy if their subjects only displayed passive consent. What the man-in-the-street perceived in silence or only murmured to his wife in the privacy of his home, was not of great importance to these dictators. Of course they wanted to be loved and enjoy a genuine popular esteem and to attain this they established ministries of propaganda. But, unlike prime ministers in democratic societies, it is possible for autocrats to survive without active, positive consent by the masses. They can therefore afford to shrug off the displeasure of grumbling, sullen, bad-tempered citizens who, though unwilling to cheer the dictators, are not prepared to revolt because they fear the reprisals that await them. An arrogant communist ruler summed it up: 'those who are not against us are for us'. Dictators sleep comfortably unless they have convincing evidence that a large number of their subjects are actively conspiring to overthrow them. In Western democracies politicians must woo electors to obtain their positive assent: 'those who are not with us — by at least voting for us in free and secret elections — show that they are in effect against us'. The fear of rulers in democracies, that they might possibly be penalized by the voters for acts that have aroused popular hostility, are real. Therefore, if at all possible, why take the risk? Playing safe, or cloaking the meaning of new laws in mendacious garbs, are obvious expedients. Even Margaret Thatcher, who historians will judge to have been a relatively highly principled prime minister, did on several occasions react to anticipated adverse popular opposition by altering, or abandoning altogether, legislative proposals in the pipeline.

Once democracy evolved as parliamentary democracy based on universal suffrage, the need for political parties was paramount. It became a sine qua non. No Brititish government could have ruled meaningfully for more than a few weeks if the 600 members of the HoC examined individually all proposed laws on their merits and then voted accordingly. No reasonable budget would have been approved by parliament if each representative voted for the various revenue and expenditure items in accordance with his personal likes and dislikes. Governmental stability demands that — apart from occasional exceptions — the leader of each party is in a position to enforce discipline, i.e. he can make his party's representatives cast their votes as instructed, even when they disagree with the policy of their party on given issues. (The leaders have today many impressive tools at their disposal to make almost all recalcitrant MPs toe the line.) The UK constituency system — where the victor is the first-past-the-post and the votes for the other candidates finish up in the dustbin — has hitherto brought it about that the representatives of two towering (alternate governing) parties constitute together the overwhelming majority of the elected parliament.[3] With two important stipulations the same happens when there are national party lists, provided there are no transferable votes and the votes for any party attaining less than a given percentage of the total votes cast

---

[3] A small party cannot expect to return an MP if its supporters are evenly distributed throughout the country. Under proportional representation the Vegetarian Party, speaking in the name of the British people, might get up to 31 MPs while at present they get none. Plaid Cymru, the Welsh National Party, is supported by only a minute percentage of the British electorate. Yet, as their potential voters are concentrated in a few constituencies within the Principality of Wales, it therefore manages to elect MPs to the HoC.

— say, 6–10% — are disregarded. Both systems therefore obviate the formation of peacetime coalition governments. The position is radically different when the system of national party lists allows for transferable votes and/or operates with only a very low barrier. This produces a plethora of parties and a government can then only be formed by a coalition of several parties. Poland before WWII provided an extreme example. Its pre-war parliament had representatives of religious, territorial and political parties and of occupational groups (farmers, workers, landlords). In situations, where the parliament has a medley of small parties, the inauguration of a coalition is preceded by horse-trading which often makes a grotesque caricature of democracy. To get the best bargain the party leaders must be proficient in logrolling: 'You roll my logs and I'll roll yours.' Thus, the parliamentary representatives of the religious groups may offer to join a coalition which promises the most luscious grants for their seminaries; the peasant organizations may be ready to support a government which will substantially increase the subsidies for fertilisers; the Senior Citizen party may demand of any coalition, which it is prepared to support, that it enact a law whereby older citizens can travel free on the state-owned railways. Sectional parties do not claim to be acting in the national interest; they do not formulate manifestos which are addressed to the majority of the population. Those who lead the sectional parties are not interested in whether their demands engender social injustices or harm the overall welfare of the nation. They merely have to prove to their supporters that they are optimising the benefits accruing to the people who they represent. In consequence, the leaders of the sectional parties are fortunate that there is less pressure upon them to articulate the kind of humbug that the leaders of the national parties in the two mentioned electoral systems must impart.

Countries with a voting system that produces two towering parties tend to produce benevolent lying. As their politicians do not cater for segments of the population, the national parties must formulate programmes which, hopefully, appeal to 95% of the electorate. This is only feasible if wholesale fudging prevails and their messages are verbalized in a language that is not offensive to any large group of voters. Thus, trying to please as many people as possible, the political tidings must frequently be ambiguous. When their leaders have to abandon the use of trivial generalizations and are compelled to be specific, they may have to be economical with the truth. The two-party system with its nationwide appeal operates with representatives who (mostly) obey the dictates of their leaders. Hence there is little need for the pork-barrelling which is so endemic in the US where cross-party voting flourishes because the respective leaders of the Republican and Democratic parties are often unable to discipline their representatives. In the UK the constituency MPs can indeed bring to the notice of the public and parliament local problems. But when it comes to the crunch, most MPs will have to act in accordance with the instructions emanating from the headquarters of their national party; reluctantly, they will have to ignore the wishes of their voters and swallow hard to disregard their own predilections. Why? To ensure being chosen (or confirmed) by the members of the constituency party, the aspiring and sitting MPs depend very largely upon gracious testimonials, issued by the leadership of the national party organizations. If they seek office, this becomes almost a necessity. As Prime Minister Edward Heath once articulated, the British government does not therefore have to take as much notice of interest groups and lobbies as does the government of the US. Another leading Conservative, Ian Gilmour, concurred: 'the government has to worry about its general popularity, not about its popularity on a particular issue'. How does it affect the potential voters? Let us assume that each of the two towering parties has a programme which outlines its stance on twenty topics. It is highly unlikely that there are a large number of voters who will agree wholeheartedly with all twenty. The majority of the population selects one of the two towering parties because it favours a large number of the points outlined in the manifesto: voters express their electoral preferences 'on balance'. In the polling booths electors exercise an overall judgement; they choose that party which has scored, in their eyes, more pluses than minuses — but they have to buy the whole packet.

It is only recently that a tragicomedy has been besetting the democracies that are not ruled by coalition governments. A political party has a raison d'etre if it propagates a set of policies which differ in substance from those of other parties.

If this is not the case, then its leaders are not conviction politicians but guilty of opportunism and personal self-seeking, attributes which, alas, are nowadays forced upon many of them. The one-time ruler of the Ford corporation, who had achieved fame for his success in manufacturing the Mustang, had little time for market researchers. According to his biographer, he did not think much of asking customers about their preferences. 'They don't know what they want,' he said some years after the Mustang had pretty much proved him right about such research: 'Ya gotta have an idea and ya gotta push it down their throats.' This is an unusual attitude that is dismissed with disdain by the CEOs of most large manufacturing companies. Their marketing executives are idolized and often enjoy greater prestige than those in charge of making the goods. The former are concerned primarily with what consumers are believed to want; the production department must adapt itself to the perceived wishes of the potential buyers. There is no moral ground on which to criticize businessmen for leaning so heavily upon the findings of market researchers. But should one be equally tolerant of politicians who are seeking salvation by 'listening to the people'? The reason why they are doing so is not in dispute. The vivid decline in obsequiousness has led to a diminishing trust in politicians and has also come to the fore when obedience is demanded in response to the leaders of non-political (ethnic, occupational, religious) groups. The Pope is said to have been disturbed when in an Italian divorce referendum professing Catholics demonstrated that they no longer went to the polls as automatons who blindly conform to the orders of their priests. Trade union bosses have learnt that even when they have the formal authority to conclude binding agreements with the employers, they can nowadays threaten strike action only at their peril unless the members have given their overwhelming consent.

Richard Klein was one of the first to elucidate this changing relationship between the masses and political decision-makers. He hypothesized that 'the deferential politician would seem to be well on the way to replacing the deferential voter'. Klein showed that, as a result, politicians are no longer so adamant in formulating policies which *they* believe to be in the national interest. Instead, they search the minds of the voters in order to gauge their sentiments, prejudices and feelings. Bundespraesident Richard von Weizsaecker has concluded that Germany is now a 'Demoskopie-Demokratie', a representative democracy that is strongly moulded by the messages of the opinion polling agencies. He has spoken disparagingly of the political parties which use these organizations to ascertain the wishes of the electorate and then utilize the information for the formulation of party programmes which regurgitate the popular wishes. I am a great believer in the idyllic supermarkets which are a very attractive face of capitalism in that they allow the consumer to choose what he wants. I do not, however, accept that the modus operandi of chocolate companies and the vendors of packaged holidays is a suitable vehicle for democratic politics. It must be stressed that when CEOs act on the advice of their marketing managers, they have merely been told about the preferences of the customers and not about what is really good for the customers. Provided they act within the law, corporations have no reason to interest themselves in the latter. If they have access to scientific research, which would have it that the expressed views of the customers are flawed because their thinking is irrational, that is not a consideration that a commercial firm must necessarily take into account. This, surely, is — or ought to be — the great difference between the makers of cornflakes and conviction politicians; the merits of political policies ought to be evaluated in relation to the public interest and not by the criterion of what ignoramuses think is good.

In anticipation of the 1966 general election, Harold Wilson — then the prime minister and leader of the Labour Party — asked his cabinet to prepare proposals 'that would be popular but not costly'. This was relatively innocuous. When Neil Kinnock became the leader, he surprised his erstwhile supporters by the manner in which he changed the face of the Labour Party. What he did has few parallels in British political history. Previously a definite leftist, he pledged that ideology would be erased from the party's dictionary. Henceforth, the focus would be centred on the attainment of power. He wanted all policies, including those he still believed in, replaced by other policies that were in accord with popular sentiments. In the past Kinnock had been a great believer in the benevolent power of the trade unions, was strongly opposed to the UK's membership of the EU and had demonstrated against Britain retaining its nuclear deterrent. He sent all these shibboleths to the slaughterhouse. Labour's transmogrified leader then fashioned a campaign which, unlike past ones, did not aim to convert voters to the socialist way of thinking. It was highly original of Kinnock when he proclaimed that he did not seek to preach and disseminate his political messages. He ordered the members of the shadow cabinet to attend 'targeted events', not in order to proselytize but to listen and be guided by what the people at large said. Meetings were organized under the umbrella of the 'Ask the People Campaign'. (A full-time 'Labour Listens Unit' was set up at the party's headquarters to collate the expected thousands of responses.) It was a woeful innovation which proved a dismal failure and had to be wound up quickly, and the Labour Party had once again to rely on privately commissioned opinion polls.

Despite this debacle, his successor, John Smith, remained converted to the idea that Labour ought henceforth be a consumer-led party and stressed the virtue of listening. The prime minister and leader of the Conservatives, John Major, did not hide his ambition to abandon the kind of conviction politics which his predecessor, Margaret Thatcher, had espoused. Following in the footsteps of Kinnock and Smith, he declared his faith in the virtue of listening to the public and shaping the governance of the country accordingly. The editor of the *The Spectator* described this stratagem as 'modern mass politics in all its superficiality . . . the triumph of packaging over product'.[4] In 2004 there was no let-up. Tony Blair had remained faithful to the concept that his party's policies should be determined at consultation meetings all over Britain. Once again ministers were sent out to such two-hour meetings at which they were not allowed to speak about the government's achievements and future plans; their duty was to hear what people said to them. Blair called these consultations 'Big Conversations'. It is not only morally offensive, but can also turn out to be a dangerous game, if politicians are really guided by the reports of opinion pollsters and by what they hear at these so-called consultations. The information may indeed reflect accurately the genuine opinions voiced held by the majority of the population at a

---

[4] *The Spectator*, London, July 7 1990.

given point of time. It does not, however, follow that these good people are necessarily cognizant of the implications which would ensue if their prescriptions were carried out. The politicians, who feel impelled to act in accordance with the expressed wishes of the masses, may well be knowledgeable enough to appreciate a priori the dangers on the horizon. What occurs when the chickens come home to roost as the politicians were convinced they would? The very voters who were once appeased will now vociferously reproach the party in office. It would be fatuous to advise the politicians, who are being blamed for the debacle which, intellectually, they had anticipated, that they could then rescue their reputations by telling the voters: 'we are not at fault — we only did what you inspired us to do'. Such apologias are suitable for academic controversies. In real life attacks on one's flawed record cannot be repelled by rebuking the electors for their past misconceptions.

The Crosses Borne by Democratic Politicians

In 1921 H.L. Mencken, one of America's renowned commentators, asserted that the 'average democratic politician is a scoundrel and a swine'. It is noteworthy that 85 years later his offensive declaration is still being cited. Such a populist sentiment, when voiced today by numerous academics, is of course ventilated in a more elegant fashion. Gordon Tullock and James Buchanan are the illustrious founders of the Center for the Study of Public Choice, located in Virginia. Tullock has explained that it is mere realism to depict the elected representatives as 'men who serve their self-interests'. The adherents of the Virginia school would have it that, by definition, politicians are corrupt — if not always in a pecuniary sense then certainly in a moral context. They lack principles and behave like 'vote-maximising entrepreneurs'. Politicians in office are said to focus on the market-place where, with public expenditure, they buy votes to remain in power. Friedrich von Hayek, in his disenchantment with representative democracy, was one of many economists who acclaimed Tullock's tenet: parliamentarians are participants 'in a bargaining process in which they bribe a sufficient number of voters'. To Anthony Downs, Western politicians are Machiavellian creatures who do not seek to gain office in order to promote a better or an ideal society; he debunks the primitive belief that the elected representatives would 'maximise welfare once they knew how to do so'. When Buchanan came to England, to hold forth on the diagnostic revelations pouring out of Virginia, he sneered at the naïve mentality of the native economists who had 'held on longer than most to the romantic notion that governments seek only to do good'. He mocked the British luminaries — 'notably Lord Keynes' — because they offered policy advice to UK governments on the implicit assumption that they were talking to 'benevolent despots'. The eminent missionary from America aimed to disabuse the British of the illusion that there are honest, dedicated politicians. He charged his hosts with being 'blind to what now appears so simple to us, that benevolent despots do not exist'.

These cited opinions of learned political scientists are replicated in more coarse language by a large segment, perhaps even a majority, of the unlearned electorate. It is widely believed that politicians are in the game because of the money and it follows that these corrupt individuals are neither altruistic nor idealistic. There are in my view only few grains of truth in these grotesque exaggerations. Nevertheless, it was necessary to quote the expletives because they are highly relevant to the kind of environment in which politicians in democratic societies have nowadays to subsist — and why they must often resort to lying. However, both the academic and populist myths are factually flawed in so far as they depict the motivations of the elected representatives. Political activities do not have job security and their emoluments are usually below those that many of them could earn in other walks of life. Instead of the abuse which is their portion, they could be enjoying favourable personal public publicity, influence and job satisfaction in non-political jobs. But they are genuinely enamoured with the notion that, through a political career, they can help to improve the lot of mankind. My seemingly idyllic assertion must be qualified in an important respect as I draw on the experience of another profession. Medical students are dedicated to the saving of human lives, an ideal which thrusts them to undergo a lengthy, onerous training. But after having been active as doctors for, say, twenty years, quite a number become blasé and some seriously consider changing their occupational pursuit. At that age, however, this is rarely practical and they are thus by default obliged to continue in their discipline without the idealistic motor that once propelled them. Politicians face today a parallel dilemma, one that did not plague their predecessors. In the olden days MPs were effectively part-timers and most of them could therefore continue to remain actively involved in a businesses or profession. Retaining links with their non-parliamentary pursuits gave them some economic independence and sweetened the pill when they wanted to resign or lost their seat at an election.[5] When today's politicians advance in age and, consequently, the likelihood of finding a good position outside the HoC is diminishing, they become more restrained and therefore less prone to defy the orders of their party leaders.

MPs in the twenty-first century, as compared with their confreres in the nineteenth century, are very busy. Among other things they are now expected to be glorified welfare officers, looking after their constituents.[6] Members of the HoC are saddled with time-absorbing chores which they must deal with because the electorate insists upon it. Voters do not recognize the right of politicians to have regular non-political weekends and reasonably long vacations. Yet, the victims dare not complain in public lest they offend those who 'hired' them. To have a ministerial assignment is even worse. After he retired, Lord Hailsham gave vent to his anger: 'When Gladstone was prime minister, he was able to spend about five months of the year at his country home in North Wales. Today, if a prime minister takes time off to spend a weekend on the water on his yacht, there is an immediate outcry that he is only working part-time.'

---

[5] In the days of Trollope, MPs could more easily refrain from having to agree to unprincipled compromises because, economically, they were in a position to withdraw from active politics and in any case had non-parliamentary occupational interests. Andrew Roberts has compared these MPs of a bygone age with their successors: 'Today's leaders in Britain and America are more and more drawn to politics as a profession and have less and less non-political outside interests. It undermines the public's respect for their leaders'. This may be true but, in my view, does not explain the current widespread disillusionment with politicians.

[6] Paxman has unearthed that in the 1940s and 1950s, MPs received two or three letters per day. After 1997 MPs were sent over six million letters a year, perhaps half of them from constituents, an average of 30 letters a day for each MP. Some MPs were claiming to have mailboxes bulging between 100 and 200 letters each day.

Before facing the actual electorate, the novice must first be adopted as a candidate by a constituency party. This can only be achieved when his name is on the national party list which indicates that he is an approved individual who is fit to serve in parliament. The people, placing his name on the list, are professionals in the central office of the national party. These selectors choose individuals not on their personally attractive merits but mainly in relation to two factors: (a) does the applicant have an unattractive and undisclosed past which, when discovered by the media, would vicariously discredit the party? (b) will he be loyal voting fodder and obey the orders of the party leaders during vital ballots in parliament? The officials in the national headquarters are careful not to be seen to be depriving the constituency parties of their autonomous privilege to determine who will be their candidate. When there is a vacancy, scores (and sometimes hundreds) of persons apply. The executive officers of the local party branches arbitrarily ferret out two to five applicants. Based on their own prejudices, the local party bosses estimate who would be most popular with the electorate at large. The names are then submitted to an 'adoption' meeting at which the party members cast their votes. Until the last decade of the twentieth century gay, non-white and female applicants had a hard time. Even now, the headquarters of the two towering national parties are not satisfied that a sufficiently large number of adoption meetings select candidates from these groups. The Labour Party found it necessary to issue binding numerical instructions whereby a stated proportion of the short-listed candidates must be female. The Conservative Party has not followed suit but its leaders bully constituency chairmen to favour applicants from the mentioned categories.[7]

---

[7] I have attended three adoption meetings; at each of them politics was not the dominant issue. The first meeting was still at a time when the selectors chose only one person and the branch could either confirm or reject him. The selectors' choice was a local Conservative activist whose past efforts were much appreciated. He did, however, have an important handicap. Having reached the age where one was expected to be the father of children, he was still unmarried. To allay the fears of the many sceptics in the audience, the leader of the party's women's section rose and explained maternally that she and her colleagues would put this matter right and find him a wife — as indeed they did. At another meeting one of the proposed candidates was a female solicitor. When asked why she should be chosen in preference to her

In the next chapter I shall detail the many benevolent mendacities disseminated by established MPs who cheat the voters in order to bring about benign accomplishments in the public interest. Here I am dwelling on relatively innocuous spicy lies, told by politicians in office as well as by novices who aspire to be MPs and have yet to jump gracefully over the first hurdle: *their expedient aim is to present an acceptable populist image.* George Walden, an MP who resigned disillusioned, wrote with ill humour: 'Anyone aspiring to a position of dominance in today's society would be inclined to wear the masses' clothes, affect their accents, hum their tunes and sympathize with their daily concerns.' Charles de Gaulle, who was offended when he was denoted a politician, exhibited cruel cynicism: 'In order to become the master, the politician poses as the servant.' The most astounding testimony was provided by John F. Kennedy, who himself was an outstanding liar in his personal life while he was an influential senator and later president. In a book on courage he chose examples from the US Congress where he cited the conduct of some individuals who suffered greatly for their honesty. He neither suggested that they were typical of American politicians nor did he assert that he himself was one of the heroes. Kennedy only admitted how much he admired these few. This is why he went out of his way to distance himself from the generalized 'harsh judgement' of Walter Lippmann who for decades had observed the behaviour of American parliamentarians and ultimately concluded that democratic representatives 'advance politically only as they placate, appease, bribe, seduce, bamboozle or otherwise manage to manipulate the demanding element in their constituencies; the decisive consideration is not whether the proposition is good but whether it is popular and the active-talking constituents like it immediately'. In his book Kennedy countered with an idealistic philosophical observation: 'democracy means much more than a system of political techniques to flatter or deceive powerful blocs of voters'. One of Kennedy's heroes, Senator Robert A. Taft, was depicted as an honest man. 'He once told a group in the heart of Republican farm territory that farm prices were too

---

two male competitors, she mentioned her sex; this, she averred, was especially important in our constituency where the local Labour Party was fielding a woman candidate.

high' and, on another occasion, denounced the farmers in his own state by saying that 'he was tired of seeing all these people riding in Cadillacs'.

We too have had such exemplary figures who are noteworthy because they were so relatively rare. Enoch Powell, who was chosen as a parliamentary candidate for a constituency in Northern Ireland, was one of them. He announced on the eve of a general election — to the chagrin of his political sponsor, the Unionist Party — that he was strongly opposed to Harland & Wolff, the province's largest industrial enterprise, receiving hefty subsidies from the British government. He declaimed this while aware that without this subvention the firm could not have operated and would have had to lay off many workers. As an apostle of free enterprise he felt he owed it to the public that he should state his, highly unpopular, opinion though he knew that it would not be helpful electorally.

Trollope tells of his fictional Liberal nineteenth-century prime minister George Plantagenet Palliser who

> was born heir to the highest rank as well as one of the greatest fortunes of the country. Though surrounded by all the temptations of luxury and pleasure, he yet devoted himself to work without any motive more selfish than that of being counted in the role of the public servants of England. He was not a brilliant man. He rather prided himself on being dull. He never allowed himself a joke in his speeches, nor attempted even the smallest flourish of rhetoric. He had taught himself to believe that oratory, as oratory, was a sin against honesty in politics by which he strove to guide himself.

One may assert with vigorous confidence that today Palliser would have no chance of sitting in the HoC. Universal franchise and the changes in the sentiments and demeanours of the electorate largely account for this. Palliser's old-fashioned honesty would also have worked against him. His wealth, elitist educational background, dullness and refusal to play to the gallery would have barred him ab initio from even being interviewed in the twenty-first century by the selection committee of any constituency party. Harold Macmillan, in the tenth decade of his life, drew attention to this change in Britain's political climate. He deplored that the new tribe of populist Conservatives had abandoned the 'paternalistic elements and traditions of the Tory party'.

With nostalgia Macmillan recalled the past when the British people had 'trusted those whom they regarded as their natural leaders'. Of course he could never have said this when he himself had to appeal to the Great Unwashed for their electoral support. But it did Burke no harm, when as a sitting MP, he publicized the famous dictum that he owed his constituents no duty except to listen to them. Two hundred years later there are still elected representatives who subscribe to his philosophy but they do not acknowledge this aloud lest the voters should listen in.

In *Survival of the Prettiest*, Nancy Etcoff cites Aristotle, who had pronounced that 'beauty is a greater recommendation than any letter of introduction'. Two thousand years later Michel de Montaigne asserted: 'I value beauty as a quality that gives power and advantage. It takes first place in human relations, seduces our judgements, exercises great authority and is marvellously impressive.' Beauty may indeed have all these adorable characteristics, but does it therefore constitute a criterion by which to judge who shall involve us in a war and who shall have the right to tax us to the hilt? Alas, there is a wide consensus in Western society that the answer must be in the affirmative. Banal personal external attributes are today determinant factors which politicians must reckon with. When an American academic addressed the British Psychological Society on 'faces', he asserted that in the US good-looking villains tend not to get picked out at identity parades. In part this was due to the populist perception according to which guilty men look bad: 'in the States defence lawyers always get their clients to shave off beards and moustaches and look neat and tidy'. This is precisely what happens in the world of politics in democratic countries. When appearing at selection procedures, it is naturally an asset to be properly dressed (and shaved) but many other non-political considerations count even more. Thus, applicants are obliged to present themselves together with their spouses. The woman is frequently a plus or minus factor in the selection of her husband. But what if the candidate has no wife or fiancée? On his own admission, a very suitable Conservative candidate, who was chosen and then elected an MP, had no wife or fiancée which would have condemned him outright but for his genial notion to ask a young lady acquaintance to come with him. At no stage did he explicitly deny his real sexual proclivity; he merely misled his audience by falsely giving the impression that he was heterosexual. Women applicants face even harder tests. They too are expected to be accompanied by their spouses and have to face questions, sometimes on very intimate matters, particularly from hostile members of their sex. In the past constituency parties wanted to know how much money the applicants, if chosen, would contribute each year to the party funds but this is now no longer the case. Instead, it is demanded of them that they acquire a dwelling in the locality. In the past it was only at Labour adoption meetings that the applicants had to prove their plebeian credentials but today the other parties also make similar inquiries. Did you go to a private or a state school? What kind of school do you send your children to? Do you make exclusive use of the NHS or do you sometimes pay for medical treatment?

In 1990 three members of parliament, Douglas Hurd, Michael Heseltine and John Major competed in the contest for the leadership of their party; the winner would automatically take the place of the deposed Margaret Thatcher. The electorate — only the sitting Conservative parliamentarians — was very restricted but was of course very sophisticated politically. Apart from those who had distinct personal reasons for supporting one of the three, the majority was motivated by a pragmatic consideration. They wanted that candidate to win who, *in the eyes of the public at large,* had the most attractive populist credentials and was thus the most suitable person to lead their party to victory at the next general election. Hurd and Major were both in the Thatcher cabinet. The style of their campaigning — though elegant and subdued — elucidated the profound metamorphosis that the Conservative Party had undergone. The two were said to be friends. Neither Major nor Hurd could fight one another on grounds of policy. There were no differences of substance, and if they existed, they certainly did not surface. As evident from their publicity and television appearances, the core of their rivalry was singularly non-political. John Major was one of several ministers in the Thatcher administration who had for some time gone on public record to tell the British people how much he personally valued the NHS; he let it be known that he and his family made regular use of its services. Such seemingly innocuous confessions can be interpreted to imply that Conservative leaders, who blaze abroad their personal association with the NHS, are more virtuous than their colleagues who have recourse to the private medical sector or benefit from NHS facilities without relating this to the voters. Major's campaign had commenced with an avowal in a 'genuinely classless society'. This dedication was enhanced whenever his supporters referred, as they frequently did, to his humble family origin. His campaign managers — according to Major, it was not done at his wish — spoke of his background in the relatively poor borough of Brixton. This was meant, by default, to denigrate Hurd's candidature and had the desired result. Major was portrayed as a future prime minister who, on the hustings, would be able to score well because he could appeal to the crowds as a man-of-the-people. Matters came to a boiling point when Hurd was interviewed on the BBC and tried to make light of his privileged upbringing. While he could not deny having been a pupil at Britain's most exclusive school, Eton, he attempted to attenuate this handicap by saying of his father that he had not really been so wealthy, claiming that he had been merely a tenant farmer. Despite this apologia, Hurd still felt himself needled by the BBC's further questioning about his parents' material circumstances. He burst out: 'This is inverted snobbery. I thought that I was running to become leader of the Conservatives and not some demented Marxist outfit.' Bruce Anderson, who has penned a first-hand account of the Hurd–Major rivalry, claims that Hurd's schooling at Eton undoubtedly damaged him. The fact that this issue had become a bone of contention among the Conservatives in the HoC outraged many 'in the traditionally-minded quarters'. Despite this, so Anderson maintains, 'Major's classless rhetoric did not deter a small but significant group of Etonian MPs and sons of peers from endorsing him'.

This mania of judging politicians by their looks begins at the adoption meetings and continues to haunt prominent politicians till retirement. The television era has made this a momentous feature. Trollope — if not he, then definitely Palliser — and Bagehot could not have imagined that there would come a time when decent, well-intentioned and competent English gentlemen would be ineligible to occupy high-ranking posts because of certain extraneous flaws.

They could not have apprehended that in the twenty-first century it was essential for a politically ambitious individual to be coached by experts before facing the voters on television. If he cannot shake off certain mannerisms that irritate the audiences, have his protruding teeth seen to and the ugly pimple on the nose removed, he is a liability to his party. In the spring of 2004 it became a vexed issue, aired in public, whether Prime Minister Tony Blair had been wearing too much make-up. Denis Healey, a former chancellor, would have liked to be Labour's leader but he lost out to Neil Kinnock. Healey spoke disparagingly of his rival, asserting that 'a lot of people, especially women, did not think he would make a good prime minister because of his physical appearance'. Martin Rosenbaum quotes a dictum coined by the famous spin doctor of Margaret Thatcher (who proved to be an obedient pupil): 'It is hard to get people to listen to words, it is the image that counts. So we put efforts into thinking how everything would look.' Thatcher's advisers also worked hard to reduce the pitch of her voice. Nevertheless, on the tenth anniversary of her entering 10 Downing Street, 24% of the people, asked by public opinion pollsters about her, replied that the 'most annoying thing about her was her voice. It was objected to more than any other feature of hers including any of her policies'. When Roy Jenkins, the rightist Labour minister, was attacked ferociously by the leftists in his party, they rarely missed out mentioning that he played tennis (to wit, a non-proletarian game) and loved imbibing claret of which he was a connoisseur.

Only in February 2004 did the secret come out that the French president had hidden so assiduously: he suffered from a hearing loss and a small hearing aid had been fitted into his left ear. This sparked a debate about whether as head of state he had been remiss by not announcing this disability. A constitutionalist, Guy Carcassonne, proposed that henceforth a team of doctors should examine Jacques Chirac regularly and report their findings to the electorate. Chancellors of the Exchequer, so tradition has it, are annually invited to speak at a festive dinner in the City of London's Guildhall to the financial establishment of the country. Evening dress and medals are of course obligatory. When Tony Blair appointed Gordon Brown his chancellor, the Scotsman was in a dilemma. Many of his policies were anathema to his erstwhile supporters on the left of the party. His image builders used the publicised and televised Guildhall affair to trumpet to those who sang the Red Flag that he was still one of them. Demonstratively, he was the only person in the ancient building who sat on the platform not properly dressed for the occasion. While he thus offended his hosts, he 'proved' to his comrades, who do not have evening dresses in their wardrobe, that he had not become a toff but had remained a simple man-of-the-people.

A politician with ministerial responsibilities must deport himself as a compassionate person. It is a difficult challenge to ministers who must be seen in this light when a disaster, say a burst dam or a fatal train collision, grips the public's attention. By immediately rushing to the scene, they are of course guaranteed wide media coverage though they do not help meaningfully with the rescue operations. The opposite is more often true for they invariably take up the time of the top officials who are actually dealing with the emergency. Ministers (and the leaders of opposition parties) have been mauled in the press because they were accused of having visited the scene with a self-seeking motive. Yet, what if the minister with pertinent departmental responsibility does not fly by helicopter to view in person the tragedy? He runs the risk of being denounced on TV for his failure to turn up, a clear proof that he is not a 'caring' politician. It is hard for those who reside in illuminated glasshouses to discern wisely what course is likely to earn them the approbation of the censorious public. PR specialists offer degrading but sound advice: far better to do something which per se is not exemplary but earns publicity than to labour hard and produce beneficial results in the national interest that are not reported in the press. Parliamentarians are well aware that pollsters regularly survey the electorate in Western democracies for the purpose of preparing tables of famous politicians. How is their fame evaluated? Certainly not by their political deeds. The top of the tables are reserved for those politicians whose names and faces — but not necessarily their portfolios — are recognized by the largest number of polled citizens. In other comparative surveys the pollsters ask which politician was the most outstanding in a given number of fields. Research findings, published in the *Chicago Tribune*, exemplified how populist images in the US are heavily influenced by the impact of youthfulness, good looks and bearing. The respondents had to rate the political performances of nine American presidents (from Roosevelt to Reagan) and also choose the 'most appealing personality'. Kennedy did not excel in the various political domains but 60% of the questioned people made him the outstanding victor in the non-political sphere. The runner-up was Roosevelt with 11% and Johnson came last with 1%.

It seems to be an established fact that the photogenic looks and demeanours of public figures on the TV screens often matter more than what they are saying or have achieved. There is also another adjunct that is electorally significant, namely the apparent physical stamina of the politician, as portrayed in the media. Because of bad weather, an aeroplane, returning Prime Minister Harold Wilson from Washington, was once diverted from London to Manchester. The cameras were on the spot to interview live the prime minister. Viewers heard the BBC journalist apologizing politely for troubling him at a time when he was surely tired and probably jet-lagged. Wilson, the experienced political fox, replied with indignation. He reprimanded the interviewer for even hinting at the possibility that he might be tired. Historians will never know if he had been or not. However, they will note that Wilson did not allow his machismo to be impugned. Viewers, seeing the country's leaders on the screen, expect their masters never to be tired! The following event is both trivial and ridiculous but still symptomatic.

A few days before the 1987 general election two senior Conservative cabinet members, who were authorized to plan the daily strategy, found it necessary to discuss the harmful impact of Nigel Lawson's long hair upon potential voters for the Conservative candidates. The Chancellor of the Exchequer was then the most prominent departmental member of the Thatcher cabinet and his policies seemed to be appreciated by large segments of the electorate. But of course his looks on the TV were apparently deplorable. He was so powerful that the two men did not dare to tell him this, lest he be offended. Though her schedules were very tight, and toothache caused her much pain, there was no alternative but to approach Thatcher in person and ask her to rule whether the chancellor ought to be informed what he must do for the party he loved. The prime minister affirmed that this was necessary and related that when she had appointed him chancellor of the exchequer in 1983 she had already then told him to have his hair trimmed. She instructed one of the two ministers who had pleaded with her, Lord Young, to speak to him about the length of his hair on her behalf. After his retirement Young confessed that he refused to carry out this important mission: 'No, Prime Minister, you've got to tell him.' She did and the chancellor immediately had his hair cut. This fact is unchallenged and remains the salient point of this episode though controversy still rages as to who had induced him to do so. In his autobiography Lawson found it necessary to deny that he went to the barber because Thatcher demanded it. He insists that he did so due to an unprompted intercession by his wife.

The loyal hagiographers of Lloyd George and Ramsay Macdonald, of Arthur Balfour and Henry Palmerston — to cite but four British prime ministers — did not include in their accounts the unpalatable sexual features in the lives of these politicians. In those days few breached the convention, that so long as politicians were alive, the electors were not to be apprised of their unorthodox and/or improper sexual conduct. On the whole newspaper editors and other cognoscenti, *including political adversaries,* chose not to make such disclosures. Such reticence is today a thing of the past; journalists and political enemies are no longer restrained by the compunctions that once pricked the consciences of their predecessors. Nowadays, newspapers give prominence to sordid carnal affairs relating to both humdrum parliamentarians and the most illustrious members of the cabinet. Bishops, trade union bosses and judges are also no longer protected by the erstwhile reluctance of the media to become responsible for the downfall of political (and other) personalities through the reporting of unwholesome matters in their private lives. Divorce, adulterous relationships, the parenthood of illegitimate children, (openly) living with an unmarried partner, avowed homosexuality — once these things become known to the electors — do even today cause substantive harm to the 'guilty' politician. The prime minister cannot remain indifferent when unorthodox aspects of the private life of one of his ministers are being publicised. If a large segment of the population is likely to be outraged by the non-political sins of a prominent politician, this rubs off on to the party which he leads. Even when the prime minister would have liked to retain a capable individual, who is hounded by the tabloids for raffish behaviour, he usually has no choice but to succumb to populist clamour. It is therefore wrong to assert that the social mores have been transformed so fundamentally that politicians can shrug off with impunity strictures on their personal behaviour. When the media debunk politicians because of proven sexual peccadilloes, they do leave scars. But, there is joyful news for sinning politicians. Unlike in the past, the scars are sometimes allowed to heal. No longer does a sexual exposure in the tabloids automatically kill off for ever the political career of an errant. A minister, forced to leave the cabinet, can nowadays look forward to being recalled to office after a lapse of some time if he is able, penitent and has behaved wisely while in exile. There are also already instances where homosexuals — who informed the selection committees of the constituency party of their sexual proclivity — were selected as candidates and subsequently became MPs. There are several other hurdles too which have to be cleared before an individual can become a full-time politician in contemporary Britain. The aspiration of interfering do-gooders, to bring it about that the social composition of the HoC *mirrors* British society, has gained many adherents. To be wealthy is already a debilitating element — almost as bad as not having been educated at a state school — if an ambitious individual seeks to be a member of the HoC. Thus, in several respects, being an MP is more onerous today than in the past.

The Whimsical Electorate

The Swinish Multitude

'The swinish multitude' — this is how Edmund Burke described them. Today's *active* politicians laud them as the salt of the earth. Only in their memoirs do some of them denounce their former constituents, whom they used to idealize with mock humility, for lacking intelligence, altruism and integrity. Harold Wilson's chief whip related — after he had become Baron Glenamara and sat in the House of Lords where one is not in need of populist approbation — how he once advised the leader of his party to ignore colleagues who asserted that the electors 'were all high-minded citizens who would gladly accept rationing, wage restraints and higher taxes for the long-term good of all. In fact they are mainly just ordinary, decent folks whose first thought about every government is how it will affect them. Cynical, maybe — but Harold agreed.' What Edward Short really meant was that the prime minister had concurred in *private*. As I am under no restraint, I can afford to say in this book that the majority of voters are cowardly, fickle, inconsistent, myopic, mendacious, sanctimonious, selfish, stupid and ungrateful. This is of course not a secret and provides the benevolent liars in the HoC with sound alibis.

Walter Bagehot warned in the second half of the nineteenth century that English democracy could not be transplanted to societies where 'every man thinks he is as good as every other'. Countries in which the 'classes at the bottom feel that they are equal to or better than the delicate classes at the top' are not suitable for representative democracy. He furnished us with an adoring description of bygone England as a deferential nation. 'Deferential' described the contentment with which voters entrusted collective decision-making to intermediaries, 'an educated minority, superior persons, who are fit to choose a good government . . . in the English constitution the mass of the people yield obedience to a select few'. More than a century later David Marquand sat on the Labour benches in the HoC where he represented the people of Ashfield. When he left parliament in 1977 (and afterwards the Labour Party) to do academic work, he was free to ignore the activists of his constituency association. He went so far as to mention the possibility of a 'collapse of the political order' because of the current defects of British democracy. His students were referred to the views of certain political scientists who opined that only until 1960 was the UK electorate 'held in check by traditional values, a traditional system of authority and traditional methods of social control'. Thereafter, however, egalitarian attitudes have become more general and this, in his view, undermines all forms of authority and thereby has made it more difficult for a government to govern:

> In its struggles to carry it, government expanded public spending. The imbalanced growth of public expenditure exacerbated inflation. Thus the dynamics of the democratic process produced a surfeit of democracy.

> By implication, at any rate, democracy is to adults what chocolate is to children: endlessly tempting; harmless in small doses; sickening in excess.

The jewel in Marquand's prognosis was his cryptic declaration that at the end of the twentieth century 'some of the spectators have begun to descend on to the field'. What did he seek to convey? I assume he was concerned with the increasing tendency of football fans to regard themselves not just as spectators but also as experts who are competent to teach the players how to score better and also entitled to express forcefully their opinions about the decisions of referees. I am not so excited about this because quite a number of the spectators may well be knowledgeable enough to utter informed judgements *on football*. What I fear is the analogy appertaining to politics. The growth of extra-parliamentary activities and the expanding influence of the electronic media, which are emasculating the importance of elected parliaments, have become a fact of modern life. More important is the false belief of the 'players', i.e. the population at large, that they have enough intelligence and wisdom to comprehend the complexities of modern governance and therefore are qualified to determine the contents of legislation before parliament. The apex of our representative democracy is not the obsessive zeal of politicians to ascertain the views of the ignoramuses who elect them but rather their capitulation to vox populi: they are showing deference to the voters.

Myopia

Canada's Pierre Trudeau opined that the essential ingredient of politics is timing. Because of the electors' myopia, the time element has precipitated many of the deceptions practised by well-intentioned politicians. It is a crude, but true, axiom that the vast majority of our fellow citizens prefer consumption today to consumption tomorrow. This tendency to discount heavily the future has aroused the wrath of economists who describe it, as Pigou did, as a 'faulty telescopic faculty'. Roy Harrod, with astonishing acerbity, has denounced the culpability of the masses as the

> conquest of the reason by passion. We may all be dead at the future date and not rate the welfare of our heirs as highly as our own. The desire to use the money now is

reinforced by animal appetite. Greed may be thought to be as appropriate a name for this attitude as time preference, though less dignified. Time preference in this sense is a human infirmity.

Only an academic, aloof from real life, can suggest as Harrod did that governments should 'pay no attention to pure time preferences when planning what is best for its subjects'. Of course politicians would like to act in this spirit but they know of the plebeian obstacles in the way. Shortly before he died, Aneurin Bevan, Labour's leftist leader, spoke of this as the central problem facing representative governments. But he was knowledgeable enough to question whether it is possible to persuade the 'ordinary man and women' that it is worthwhile to make sacrifices in their present standards of living in order to expand the scope of fixed capital investment which would ultimately lead to their being better off. Chancellor Denis Healey annoyed the comrades when he addressed the party's annual conference in 1975 and proclaimed that 'investment is not a soft option. The most difficult thing in a democracy is to persuade people to consume less now. But, unless we are prepared to do that, all we say about industrial regeneration is claptrap.' In 1976 several cuts in public expenditure had to be made and he convinced the cabinet that this must be done at once. He forgot about the relevant speech which he had made in the previous year and behaved as politicians, deferential to the voters, feel obliged to behave: he curtailed the capital spending of the government, leaving largely untouched the current expenditure on subsidies and welfare benefits. When Chrysler sought to close down with immediate effect its Scottish subsidiary, Prime Minister Harold Wilson asked the US corporation to at least defer this decision for a short time; if they did so, they would be rewarded with hefty monetary aid. It was expected that the most extreme socialist in his cabinet, Michael Foot, would fulminate against the government spending taxpayers' money to subsidize a hated US multi. In her indiscreet *Diaries,* where she revealed cabinet secrets, Barbara Castle disclosed that Michael Foot actually supported shoring up this economically unviable automobile plant. He is quoted as having said: 'I do not think it is reprehensible for this cabinet to take some short-term views as well as long-term ones. I am all in favour of the long-term reorganization of British industry but I am [also] in favour of the survival of this government.' Of course he did not share this reasoning with the public.

In authoritarian regimes there is a high rate of capital accumulation. Because of the inherent inclination of the public to eat two apples today rather than three tomorrow, democratic regimes are by their very nature inimical to the investment ambitions of their altruistic politicians. Furthermore, it is inequitable to force old people to sacrifice some of their present consumption in order to help create capital projects from which they will benefit little or not at all. Hence, on both these grounds, some state-promoting investments are being made by stealth. In the jargon of economists, 'involuntary investments' are automatically financed by 'forced savings'. Once again, this is only feasible if the astute politicians do not enlighten the public. Politicians of all species are guilty of a momentous (related) crime: having financed infrastructure schemes and capital projects within the orbit of the state sector, they frequently allow these after completion to deteriorate structurally. The functional values are eroded because sufficient funds are not made available for regular (albeit costly) servicing on the same scale as capital investments are maintained in the private sector.

The Obtuse Electorate

Stupidity is not a sin and does not tell us whether a person is good-hearted or not; it also has only little bearing on the conduct of conceited individuals who think themselves competent to express considered views but in fact utter outrageous rubbish. Stupidity refers to the behaviour of persons who are not deemed sensible in that they are unable to form meaningful opinions and cannot draw rational conclusions from given facts. If the majority of the citizens in the Anglo-Saxon countries believe, as apparently they do, that viruses can be fought with antibiotics, this denotes scientific ignorance but has no impact on their voting inclinations. Sensitive politicians ought, however, to be distressed when large sections of the electorate accept antediluvian tales about the causes of inflation. However stupidity is defined, one may conclude that many of 'the common people' are not best suited to judge what is or is not in the national interest. The following snippets exemplify non-political and political fatuity.

No interest is paid on the billions of a British government security, the Premium Bond, but each month small and mammoth prizes are drawn by a gigantic computer, answering to the name of Ernie. A number of civil servants are engaged solely to answer questions, raised in the media or in letters, concerning the probity of this mechanical monster. There is a pervasive feeling that his brain favours those bonds which are designated with certain letters and numbers. It is also widely believed that the wicked Ernie discriminates against the owners of Premium Bonds who are female and/or reside in the southern counties of England.

Nature has published a survey which evinced that only 34% of Britons and 46% of Americans know that the earth went round the sun once a year.

Coins, weighing one ounce of 22-carat gold, are traded widely in Asia, not for religious or aesthetic reasons but as a store of value. Because of the putative inferiority of women, coins engraved with the face of male kings are priced higher than those which bear the portrait of our dear Queen Victoria.

In 1974 Khrushchev introduced a purely technical currency reform which divided the then current rouble by ten. This had no economic significance and was done merely for administrative convenience. The public, however, was convinced that this was a trick; they suspected that the exercise was meant to raise prices surreptitiously. In his memoirs the Russian leader relates how he tried to dispel this ridiculous notion by adducing simple logical arguments but ultimately he had to concede that he had no success. Khrushchev, despite the pervasive resentment, was of course in a position to execute what he had planned because he had no reason to fear his cowed, stupid subjects. At the same time the politicians of democratic Japan told their people of the even more urgent need to re-base the current yen; they wanted to divide it by one hundred. There, the populist opposition to this purely organizational change proved, however, too clamorous to be ignored. The government was subdued by the muddled preconceptions of its citizens.

The UK's RPI rose by 57% in the 1971-4 period. According to several public opinion surveys, 63% of the respondents opined that two causes, 'Britain joining the Common Market' and 'decimalization' had brought about the rising prices. In February 1971 the anachronistic £1 = 240 pence currency had been replaced by one in which £1 = 100 pence. This led to the rounding-up of some prices to the nearest (new) penny and caused a tiny upward movement of the RPI. To regard this one-off adjustment — at most in the order of one or two percentage points — as a serious factor in the then inflationary spiral was factually no more sound than the myth that witches were alive in London's Epping Forest. The fable was not buried even six years after decimalization was introduced. A London newspaper explained that since sterling had been 'debased by the disastrous switchover to decimal currency the RPI has since risen by 120% and decimalization was a major element in the soaring rate of price increases'. The widespread belief, that the UK's joining the Common Market in January 1973 was a decisive cause of Britain's soaring price level, was even more absurd. If sceptics had augured that joining the Common Market would bring about vital price increases in the future, they would have made a very plausible point. But at the time when Gallup and National Opinion Polls arranged these surveys — between October 1973 and June 1974 — membership of the Common Market was at worst a minor quantitative element. This was underlined by the fact that though the UK had joined in 1973, a five-year transitional arrangement betokened that the Community rules would come into effect only by stages and thus could have had only a gradual impact upon Britain's taxes and domestic prices.

When electors are in a state of personal euphoria, their 'feeling good' makes them more likely to cast their votes for the incumbent politicians. In the past the birth of a child to a leading member of the royal family was an event to which psephologists paid attention. Spectacular international accomplishments or defeats by the national football, tennis, rugby teams could also sway some voters. In June 1970 England's football team was beaten by Germany in the World Cup tournament. Prime Minister Harold Wilson surmised that the resultant mental depression in the UK was in part the reason for the Labour Party losing the general election which took place in the same month. The weather can also make the electorate 'feel good' (or 'worse off') with concomitant repercussions at the polls. At the September 1987 general election in Denmark, the Social Democrats had the ambition to topple the Liberal-led coalition government. The opposition found it unrewarding to try to persuade the electorate that the incumbent government's policies were bad. They were, however, on a good wicket when they associated their adversaries with the horrible summer weather that had just been visited upon that unhappy country. Perhaps academics will be aghast but this line of attack hurt — and was efficacious. In response, the major government party called a press conference to parry this blow which the Social Democrats were delivering with such good effect. The former, in power since 1982, presented their defence along two parallel tracks. The minister for foreign affairs demonstrated statistically and with the help of illustrated graphs that in the three-year period before they had taken office, and during which the Social Democrats had been in charge of the government, the weather had been wetter, colder and foggier than was the case in the years of the current Liberal-led coalition. The pragmatic Liberal prime minister recognized that this impressive achievement, which favoured his party, might not perhaps be as strikingly impressive as it deserved to be. Hence, his second line of defence was to concede that during the current election campaign the weather was indeed not as good as one might have wished. But, he stressed, that 'the Danish national soccer team has never played better'. There is nothing wrong with a society, the citizens of which become elated or dejected in relation to the weather or football. The charges of stupidity and flippancy must, however, stick when many voters admit to have been under the influence of these factors as they entered the polling-booths.

'We Are Not Better Off'

In 1957, when *real* disposable incomes had risen in prosperous Germany, the opinion polls showed that only 24% of the respondents testified to this; 45% said there was no change and 30% actually averred that they were worse off. According to a Roper survey in 1978, the majority of the US public regarded itself worse off than in 1973. In fact inflation-adjusted disposable income had risen in the relevant period by 8.4%. During the 1980 presidential campaign Reagan cunningly intimated to the voters that their standard of living had dropped — which was not the case — during the rule of Carter, the incumbent president: 'It might be well if you would ask yourself whether you are better off than you were four years ago.' The American electorate deluded itself that the answer was in the negative and Reagan triumphed. During his eight years in the White House the material living standards continued to go up but Reagan faced, already two years after his accession, an electorate, not all of whom were agreed that things had generally been improving. Though inflation was lower than at any time in the previous ten years, 44% of the interviewed citizens opined that prices were rising faster than had been the case two years previously. Reagan's pièce de résistance, a radical lowering of taxes, was conceived by many not to have taken place; only 6% acknowledged that it had while 34% believed that there had been no change and 42% asserted that federal taxes were higher since he became president. By 1986 Reagan had no longer a personal electoral reason to study the findings of the pollsters. Had he done so, then — contrary to the actual statistical evidence — he would have found that only 40% considered themselves better off while 60% of all respondents declared that during Reagan's incumbency they were worse off or had experienced no change in their situation. Carter had cause to smile with Schadenfreude. In 1972 the British Market Research Bureau organized polls, asking 'Are you better or worse off financially than a year ago?' 29% replied that they were better off; 51% claimed to be worse off; 20% said 'the same or not sure'. The facts: in that year inflation had risen by 7.8% while wages were up by 11.7% and consumers' expenditure by 11.3%. Two UK academics chose the town of Nottingham to investigate 'subjective welfare' in 1984. Only 14% of its residents said that they were better off, compared with the preceding year while 54% claimed to be worse off. During the relevant period disposable income had risen by 8.3% while the RPI was up by only 4.9%. Most bizarre was the reaction by disgruntled citizens of the former DDR. Fifteen years after the communist German state had been absorbed at tremendous financial cost by capitalist West Germany, a sample interviewed by the *FT* complained that 'all subsidies have gone; we have to beg for money; we are much worse off than we were in the DDR'.

The cited incongruities have been replicated in many democratic countries in hundreds of surveys during the whole of the second half of the twentieth century. Those who gave answers, which were factually incorrect, are not necessarily liars and nor are the respondents blatantly stupid. They are individuals who do not base their views on objective evidence but on their personal perceptions of well-being which, mentally, they do not measure by increases in wages and the lowering of taxes. In quantitative terms they do not, for example, calculate the personal benefits which they have obtained from enhanced communal services provided by the state. If asked, they will sincerely acknowledge the desirability of infrastructure investments which furnish, say, cleaner water and better roads. The reduction in the size of school classes is not priced, nor are the ameliorated services of the NHS. The higher fringe benefits from employers are of course welcomed but frequently not taken into account. There are also other factors which cast a dark shadow over the numerous erroneous reports that real incomes have gone down. Hilde Behrend has found that in the British Isles many of those interviewed by the pollsters do not compare present prices with present incomes (and past prices with past incomes). The images of relatively low prices in the past dominate their current thinking. These misguided people do not recognize that today's higher prices are accompanied by higher incomes. Psychologists can probably explain best why being 'better off' has a connotation which is not linked to the fluctuations of the real GDP. Thus, individuals, who had hoped to receive a 5% increase in their real emoluments but were awarded only 3%, may not consider themselves better off. Unhappy employees, whose anticipation of being upgraded to a loftier status did not materialize, will feel dejected enough to blurt out that they are not really better off.

Before professional economists scorn the many flawed answers to these questions by public opinion pollsters, they ought to read the prominently displayed feature of Dr Tony Smith in the *British Medical Journal,* of which he was an associate editor. Published in 1990, and based on official statistics, he referred to the 20% rise in the average income for the whole UK population during the 1980s. He highlighted, however, that 'the bottom 10% saw their real income rise by only half the average'. What demagogic inference did Dr Smith draw? He felt accredited to propose a political strategy: 'a determined effort will be needed to reverse the *progressive impoverishment* of the poorest people in Britain' (my italics). How can this nonsense be made compatible with an increase in real incomes by half of 20%? If such a confused statistical assertion can appear in a journal which is directed exclusively at readers who are thought to be among Britain's intellectual elitists, one should not be too impatient with the arithmetically incorrect opinions that are conveyed in all sincerity to the pollsters by less educated persons.

Why Do They Lie?

Democratic politicians are desperately eager to discover what the public thinks. Dictators are no different but they are rarely in a position to know. Their citizens, when questioned, are too frightened to tell the truth and, in any case, the senior adjutants of the dictators would not pass on surveys which demonstrate the unpopularity of the regime. Through public opinion polls, media interviews with the 'common people', TV and radio programmes where audiences are encouraged to participate vocally, democratic politicians have access to independent indicators but these are frequently distorted by mendacious responses. UK Gallup abandoned in 1997 its long-standing face-to-face interviewing, replacing it with random telephone dialling; the new methodology was intended to induce greater honesty from 'shy' individuals. All polling organizations are of course very conscious of the dishonest answers that are given to the pollsters; hence, the raw results are adjusted in-house by cutting out the guestimated bias. The main reasons for not telling the truth are fourfold.

(1) A large segment — some say, the majority — of the interviewees do not have a considered opinion on the political subjects on which they are questioned. They are of course flattered that somebody is actually writing down what they are saying and they do not want to admit their ignorance. So they just nod their agreement with one of the options mentioned by the interviewers.

(2) Certain questions are put to adduce whether the respondent has cultured tastes and/or is sophisticated. Stirred by vanity, interviewees give answers which demonstrate their modern taste and urbanity. It is possible to document this quantitatively. The electronic media have highly accurate data on the number of persons who watch given programmes. When these facts are compared with the

answers, given in response to the question as to what programmes they watch mostly, huge disparities come to light. While most men actually favour football, soap operas and other lowbrow features, they declare their favourites to be the news, the natural world and other putatively cultured programmes.

(3) Multifarious lying is common when the questioned person wants to prove that he is a progressive, caring, decent individual with a social conscience who would like nothing better than to see a huge increase in the governmental contribution to the Third World. When teachers on strike appear on TV, they will shamefacedly argue that the reason why they closed down the schools is not to improve their own material position but in order to help children get a better education. Striking railway personnel will similarly deny that the havoc they cause is to better themselves materially — they do it to make travelling more safe for the public. For decades pollsters in Western Europe have reported that the man-in-the-street has displayed extraordinary concern about the national unemployment figures. Robert Waller, a perceptive observer of British politics viewed this particular mendacity as a 'curious phenomenon'. He opined that if someone is asked to name the most pressing social problem, 'it has become the respected and moral thing to reply: "unemployment". It is now seen as the correct answer.' Research and the autobiographies of socialist cabinet ministers have attested that these declarations were mostly bogus.

Another outrageous instance of disingenuous mendacity, prevalent in Britain, is the assertion, shouted from the rooftops by so many: 'we are happy to pay more taxes for . . .'. It has taken a long time before most, though not all UK politicians, ceased believing this sanctimonious lie. Genuine altruists may welcome the imposition of additional taxes even though it means a lower living standard for them. There are selfish individuals who do not pay taxes themselves and shamelessly advocate that others should be taxed more severely. These two groups constitute a small minority and, by definition, should not be categorized as liars. As for the rest of the population, even a leftist MP, such as Ian Mikardo who thought taxes ought to be raised, finally had to conclude that this is not what Labour voters (and others) want: 'It's true that there may be a difference between what a man says to a pollster and what he is prepared to do in practice.' Before the 1992 general election Gallup published bad news for the Conservatives who were deemed to be the tax-cutting party: only 11% of the population were for tax cuts, 13% for the status quo and no less than 72% of the respondents had said that they wanted tax increases. The distinguished professor of government at Essex University, Anthony King, had enough professional wisdom not to take too seriously these numbers; he said that 'people undoubtedly exaggerate their willingness to pay extra taxes'. He forecast that the coming general election might well prove decisively the notion that high-tax political parties lose elections. The Liberal Party actually promised explicitly to raise the standard income tax rate. The Labour politicians, encouraged by the above mentioned poll and similar indicators, shrugged off the Conservatives' accusation that, if they won and formed a government, they would be raising taxes as indeed they intended to do. As Labour believed that public opinion was indeed in favour of higher taxes, they did not find it necessary to lie and therefore did not deny that they were a high-tax party. The election result was clear-cut. The Liberals lost votes and were humiliated. Labour, for the fourth time running, had to concede victory to the Conservatives who scored an overall majority. With hindsight most commentators conceded that the single most important reason for the Conservative victory was embedded in the dread of the electorate that Labour may raise direct taxes. When, subsequently, Blair and Brown took over the leadership of New Labour they laid down a sacred rule, to wit that never again shall responsible party leaders hint that the Labour Party would raise income tax. They have since won three general elections. (Chancellor of the Exchequer Brown covertly raised other taxes but as it was done surreptitiously many of the public were not fully conscious that they had been subjected to partly disguised tax increases.)

(4) Elisabeth Nolle-Neumann, one of the famous German psephologists, has produced voluminous evidence that the German public, when questioned by the pollsters, is no less mendaciously-minded than the British electorate. She highlights in *The Spiral of Silence* a reason for the widespread lying which has universal application. She argues that individuals avoid expressing unorthodox minority opinions due to the

fear of isolating themselves from the run of the mill. It is not always pleasant to be known as an eccentric, one who professes novel or nonconformist loyalties. Speaking to pollsters or journalists, many respondents do not necessarily wish to ventilate their views when these infringe the, often undefined, bonds of the peer groups to which they belong. In the UK few trade unionists have acknowledged publicly that they are voting for the class enemy, i.e. the Conservatives. In fact large numbers have done so — but in silence.

Personal Selfishness

Apart from a few dissenting voices, the *American Journal of Political Science* has for decades borne witness that the — real or perceived — state of the economy is the greatest of the public's concerns. Excluding the Vietnam and Iraq periods, one Gallup poll after another has recorded that some 70% of US electors treat economic issues as 'the most important problem facing this country today'. Ian Gilmour echoed the views of the major UK parties who believe that 'economic issues are paramount' in the British body politic. (Strictly speaking, the voters are not really interested in the movements of the national economic indicators; they care only about those elements which they think impact directly upon their personal material well-being). The English economist James Meade praised the already cited Virginia professors for their models that are 'based on the assumption that the individual citizen is wholly selfish in his behaviour in the voting booth'. Gordon Tullock faced excommunication from the Virginia School — of which he had been a founding father — when he refused to push this ridiculous axiom to its ultimate limit. Charles Rowley has recorded Tullock's sad encounter which ensued after he had formulated a theory according to which individuals are only 95% self-centred, a retreat from the orthodox postulate of 100%. Some academics wanted Tullock to be penalized for conceding that individuals can be unselfish up to 5% (sic) of their actions. This sweeping dogmatic assertion, that there are no altruists in our society and consequently only personal, material considerations are cardinal, is unsound. It is, however, correct that adults in the years after 1951 seem to have become progressively more motivated by personal material considerations than those who lived in the nineteenth century and the first half of the twentieth century. It is astonishing that while post-1951 material living standards have continuously risen, the intensity of public concern with idealistic causes and political affairs, unless very obviously linked to personal material welfare, has diminished . Exemplifying this by the British experience, I have heard it conjectured that in the past a larger proportion of residents in given parliamentary constituencies knew who their MP was than is now the case. Portraits of Gladstone, Wesley, Lloyd George, Churchill, inventors, colonial governors and successful entrepreneurs could be found in palaces as well as in humble abodes where the Bible was the only book. They have since been replaced by other pictures, not those of current political leaders but of film stars, football heroes and TV comedians. Even during the Iraq wars, the tabloids in the UK frequently gave them less prominence than football news, gambling competitions and sexual incidents. Leaving aside life during the two world wars, I mention below a few of the *personally non-material and non-selfish* issues which, when debated in parliament and elsewhere, aroused deep passions in the country; they motivated citizens, eligible to vote, to elect politicians in accordance with their differing standpoints on these matters. Patriotism was certainly not a dirty word in the pre-1951 period.

Today's politicians must pay serious attention to people who question them on 'what's in it for me?' Though cynics in the twenty-first century may sneer, in the past large numbers of people seriously asked aloud 'what's in it for the country?' For several years the British public was divided along party lines on the vexed issue of Turkey. The contrasting policies of the Tories and Liberals both demanded hefty government expenditure but money did not play a decisive role; the determinant factors were moral values. The poor and the rich in the last quarter of the nineteenth century were outraged by what they thought was the wickedness of Turkey and, particularly, their wholesale massacres of Bulgarians in 1876. Gladstone attacked Turkey which, because of its Moslem faith, was 'radically incapable of establishing a good and tolerant government over civilized and Christian races'; he called the Koran an 'accursed book' and for electoral purposes published a pamphlet, *The Bulgarian Horrors,* which underlined the popular perception of Islam as 'an antihuman specimen of humanity'. Gladstone hoped to persuade the electors to vote for the Liberals because the Tories, under the leadership of Disraeli and Lord Salisbury, were disparaged as supporters of the Turkish cause. The Queen was more sympathetic to Muslim sensibilities and denounced the 'impolitic half-mad attitude of Gladstone'; she also opined that going to war to destroy the Turkish empire, an idea fostered by the Liberals, was not commendable. It was the main theme at parliamentary elections. The Liberals' bitter attacks on the Tories, who were accused of condoning the Turkish carnage of Bulgarian Christians, were applauded by large segments of the electorate. If we exclude the feelings of many recent immigrants, we can safely assert that, at the beginning of the twenty-first century, Britain's indigenous voters were not as passionately divided *on moral grounds* with reference to the Iraq wars as their ancestors had been on the Boer war. Home Rule for Ireland created deep fissures in the Liberal Party while present-day voters in Great Britain are largely apathetic on whether Northern Ireland is annexed by the Republic of Ireland or not. In the aftermath of WWII, the UK's armed forces were gradually emasculated by both the major parties. It is perhaps not easily comprehended by today's youngsters how, at the beginning of the last century, Britain's poor and rich were emotionally involved appertaining to the building of naval vessels. In 1906 the newly launched Dreadnought was a battleship that outclassed the warship of any country. By 1909 the UK had six and intended to build four new ones every year. When the British people heard that Germany planned to build fourteen similar ships, a lobbying organization, the Navy League, rallied the people to demand of their politicians that Britain must accelerate its own programme and indeed Asquith was pressured to announce that eight more would at once be constructed. The Treasury supplied huge funds to finance this operation and there was no outcry, as there would be today, that it was preferable to spend the money on health and better pensions.

As drunkenness was a serious social problem, the Salvation Army's fame was enhanced by its advocacy of total abstinence. Particularly among the manual working class, it was fashionable to 'take the pledge'. It was a hot political potato when the state and the municipalities were charged to intervene by introducing ordinances that regulated the opening times of pubs, especially on Sundays. In the twenty-first century there are not many who feel ardently either way about the plans to abolish altogether the existing restrictions on the opening times of public houses and inns. Politics used to play a more decisive role in religious matters than it does today. Hard-fought battles were engaged until all infidels — Catholics, dissident Protestants, Jews, atheists — were allowed to study in the Oxbridge universities, take their seats in parliament and other forms of discrimination against them were removed. Currently, there are deliberations on whether the law should be changed so that a non-adherent of the Church of England can become the sovereign of the UK. Most people are disinterested and there have so far been no massive demonstrations for and against. It is not easy to persuade people today that once upon a time capitalists and exploited workers felt personally involved when parliament debated whether a widower should have the right to marry a sister of his late wife.

The educated and the non-educated citizens of a past age were bitterly and clamorously embroiled in the lengthy parliamentary processes that led to the disestablishment of religious communions in Ireland, Wales and Scotland which had a special status by favour of the state. Whatever the outcome from the present deliberations about the possible disestablishment of the Church of England, one can predict with near-certainty that if the HoC has to resolve this issue, the MPs will be doing so in the knowledge that the majority of the electorate does not behold this legislative proposal with the same fervour as the pre-1951 public would have done. The (authorized English-language) *Holy Bible,* the King James Version, was first published in 1611, prepared by His Majesty's special command and 'appointed to be read in churches'. For a variety of reasons its replacement in 1881–5 by a *revised version*, aroused scepticism among some sections of Christian believers and had a political dimension. The disputatious controversy dragged on for years. The country was divided and the debate was sometimes conducted in bad temper. In 1961 *The New English Bible,* and in 1989 *The Revised English Bible,* came out under the auspices of the Oxford University Press; they constituted a radical departure from previous English translations. In theological journals various opinions were expressed about the respective merits and demerits but among the electorate at large only very few thought it a matter of great consequence that aroused their great interest and called for favourable or unfavourable endorsement. What had once been vital controversial bones of contention for their ancestors were now insouciant stuff.

The following contemporary national narratives illustrate how material personal selfishness can clash substantively with wider non-material objectives. The intent to secede from the UK and establish a wholly independent Scottish state is not a novel idea though its proponents were only relatively recently represented in the HoC. The early promoters were genuine nationalists to whom Scottish sovereignty was so desirable that they were willing to attain it even at the cost of lowering the material living standards of the people residing in Scotland. While the notion was cheered by many, very few actually abandoned their loyalties to the towering UK parties in order to vote for candidates espousing independence. Things changed radically when North Sea oil was discovered in large quantities in the Scottish province. When appealing to the electorate, the (reformed) Scottish National Party ceased to emphasise the traditional idealistic grounds for independence, connected with religion, culture and history, but instead highlighted the personal material benefits which would accrue to the holders of Scottish passports if, inter alia, the oil revenues were to accrue to the new state and no longer flow to the Treasury in London. The argumentation was not wholly plausible but it had the immediate effect of rallying many selfishly-minded voters to its banner.

Prime Minister Edward Heath and all his successors (with the exception of Margaret Thatcher) set themselves the task of selling to the British electorate the personal material blessings which they would enjoy if the UK became a full member of the Common Market and, at a later stage, the EU. Intellectually, this was not the core of the issue and ought not to have divided the 'yes' and 'no' voters. If there was an honest historical reason for joining, it was the belief that the notion of independent nation-states had become obsolete and that therefore all European countries would benefit if they gave up their national sovereignties in order to become citizens of the United States of Europe. The substantive argument of the opponents was their creed that Britain's sovereignty should be retained. The promoters of the 'yes' campaign realized that this philosophical reason for becoming a member of the EU would only bore the British public. They knew, however, that if the reason for joining was presented as something which would enhance the personal material welfare of Britain's citizens, this selfish consideration would convert many to the idea that the UK should join up. And so it was. The frightened population of the UK were warned that the country would not be able to export any longer to the EU countries, three million would consequently become unemployed, taxes would have to be increased, foreigners would no longer invest in an isolated UK, etc. This is not the place to discuss the verisimilitude of these (false) economic forebodings except to say that the majority of the British publish was swayed by the material argumentation something that might not have played a decisive role in the years preceding 1951.

Following WWII two German states came into being. Subsequently public opinion pollsters regularly asked the citizens of West Germany what, in their opinion, was the most important issue which their country should concern itself with. A very large segment mentioned 'reunification'; in some years this answer was even more weighty than 'economic problems'. Few foreign observers doubted that West Germany would do all it could to bring this about. But only when the USSR agreed in 1990 to reunification was it feasible. Shortly before the union was legally consummated, the ENMID organization polled the West Germans, questioning them on whether this step would bring 'more or less advantages for West Germany'. No less than 63% expressed their displeasure at what was about to happen, saying that it would be to the detriment of West Germany. No less than 86% of the respondents were convinced that, in order to subsidize the newly-joined territories of East Germany, tax increases would have to be imposed. No less than 61% of the respondents were not ashamed to say that they, personally, did not like the idea of being made to pay more taxes to help their brethren in the former communist Germany. German commentators believed — and subsequent events have tended to confirm this — that among the 39% of West Germans, who said that they would happily pay the expected higher taxes, there were many who did not tell the truth; they merely averred what patriots are expected to say.

Laziness

The costs of voting intelligently are mirrored by the manner in which urban housewives make their buying decisions. In our main street, all within a short walking distance, there are five supermarkets which sell more or less the same kind of products. But for promotion purposes each store selects periodically a few items — 'on special offer' — which are priced distinctly lower than the identical ones sold by the competitors. Such loss-leaders usually have a short shelf-life. Two weeks ago store A offered Danish bacon at very reduced prices but this bargain was no longer available last week. By then Danish bacon had, however, become the chief merchandising attraction of store B. If a housewife, aiming to purchase a pre-determined collection of goods at the least cost, is indifferent to the time spent and does not mind trudging along miles of aisles, how will she organize her shopping expedition? At the beginning she will make an inspection visit to all the five stores, buy nothing but merely write down the diverse prices of the items she planned to acquire. Only after this information has been collated, does she start making the actual purchases; she will probably have to call on all the five supermarkets in order to acquire their respective bargains of the week. Marketing managers are adamant that such rational buyers may flourish on the moon but constitute an insignificantly tiny minority on earth. They maintain that not all wives are mentally and/or physically *capable or willing* to exert themselves in the required fashion. A large number could not afford the time needed to carry out the described exercise. But, above all, the majority is too lazy to operate efficiently and this is not stated in a carping pejorative spirit.

Let me now return to the real McCoy, the average man-in-the-street who is eligible to vote and wishes to carry out this civic duty. We have already noted that most citizens are stupid, uneducated, fickle-minded persons who are not capable of being knowledgeable on most political matters. But we must also record that there are intelligent and educated people, capable of assembling the relevant facts and thus in a position to arrive at logical inferences — many of these may nevertheless choose not to become informed on given subjects and will remain therefore ignorant by default. A PhD in chemistry is not relevant for understanding the intricacies of politics and economics. As Downs made the point: 'rational men will be informed to different degrees ... even if men received the same amount of data, not all could use it with equal efficiency'. To research political issues, the layman must make strenuous, expensive and time-absorbing efforts. As these are continually changing processes, the information must be regularly up-dated. When intelligent voters are not prepared to pay this high price, one can of course just condemn them as being lazy. There is surely a more gratifying explanation: the investment needed to become a rational and erudite voter is proving to be too costly.

No Gratitude

The capricious voters in Western democracies rarely feel grateful to their political masters even if these have done something which pleases them. If they do show their appreciation, it will often be muted. When politicians are seen to transfer resources from one section of the population to another, making the former worse off and the latter better off, the clamorous bitterness of the aggrieved citizens will be more vexatious than the pronounced thanksgiving by the beneficiaries. There are 30m deposit accounts in UK banks and building societies and about 10m outstanding mortgages; most of these two financial instruments fluctuate in the UK in accordance with the interest rate set periodically by the state-owned central bank. If the price of money is put up by government action, the voters whose mortgage payments in consequence go up will scream their denunciation of the government party in much shriller voices than the more numerous owners of deposit accounts say 'thank you' for having been made better off. That asymmetric effect has been studied by two Conservative politicians, Bruce-Gardyne and Lawson. They confirm that 'while bad economic times appear to erode popular support for political leaders, good times may be doing little to boost it. Voters are primarily concerned with the negative side of economic performance. They punish failure but do not reward success.' Some politicians may feel offended, while others may rejoice to learn, that the ungrateful voters do not appraise at a general election the incumbent administration by what it has done during the whole of its four-five year term of office. There is convincing evidence that they will only remember with sufficient vividness the good or bad things that were done in the most recent months before the election.

Chapter V

The Furtive Saviours

There is no such thing as a painless tax but next to it is a tax that only experts understand. The victims may never know what hurt them. Or by the time they find out it will be too late   *Christopher Fildes*

Four Prescriptions

Margaret Thatcher reputedly stormed into the Conservative Central Office in 1975, banged one of Hayek's books on the table and said sternly: 'This is what we believe.' The revered and famous Friedrich August von Hayek and his equally appreciated colleague Joseph Schumpeter had indeed much to say about economic freedom which was pertinent to Thatcher and her supporters. However, it is doubtful whether she would have wanted to be associated with their pronounced views on the decadence of British democracy. Schumpeter was highly critical of the postulate that 'the people' were the best judges of their own welfare. This, he regarded as a fallacious assumption: voters, when participating in the democratic process, prove themselves 'base and corrupt'. He sneered at private citizens musing on national affairs and described the average voter as one who yields to irrational prejudices and impulses. In Schumpeter's books, the typical citizen is said to be on a low mental plateau who is transformed into an infantile creature when he steps into the political minefield: 'he becomes a primitive again'. In his invectives, the extremist Hayek strove to outdo Schumpeter's abuses of Britain's political system. Hayek would have it that it 'gave the world the pernicious principle of parliamentary sovereignty'; the HoC was a single omnipotent legislature which necessarily led to corruption and proved unable to resist pressures from the component groups. The dreaded repercussions of unbridled democracy on liberty and economic growth were aired in the comfort of London's exclusive clubs for some two hundred years. Until 1951 there were still British luminaries, including active politicians, who felt unrestrained to say openly that the extension of the franchise had had undesirable consequences because the uneducated masses could not be trusted. Since 1951 British politicians, employers and most academics have felt that it was not 'correct' to voice publicly such sentiments, particularly as they conceded that universal franchise had in any case come to stay. Privately, however, the British establishment did not disguise its deep anxiety about the spread of the 'English disease'. Panic stations were manned when it was thought that the country was slipping fast down the hill and — a common phrase in those days — 'the country was being turned into a banana republic'. In this atmosphere of self-flagellation, many business executives of a despondent British society were ready to clutch at every available straw. Hence, those who had heard of Schumpeter and Hayek saluted them for their prescriptive messages which were deemed to be relevant for the British predicament. They were also impressed by the then guru of Wall Street, Henry Kaufman, who in moderate language, propagated the view that a 'democracy oriented toward an unaffordable egalitarian sharing of production ... makes it virtually impossible to impose the ongoing discipline required for long-term stability and growth'. At a time when Howard Davies was still in a position to utter freely unorthodox views, he publicly went on record to say that if Britain's parliament did not ratify UK's membership of the EU, 'we would be left as a kind of North Atlantic Cuba'.[1] When Norman Lamont had to resign as chancellor, he defended his policies, which had many critics in the HoC, by using mild words to convey his unarticulated strong sentiments: 'Since the war only two Conservative chancellors have been responsible for bringing inflation below 2%. Both of them were sacked. In my view, that tells us a great deal about the difficulties of reducing inflation in a democracy as lively and disputatious as ours.'

To manifest that anti-democratic notions were widely and enthusiastically subscribed to by many of the Great-and-Good, one would have to rely upon anecdotal stories told at

---

[1] 'Thoughts from a Dangerous Man', *The Spectator*, London, September 5 1992.

private luncheons. This, however, would not be sufficiently convincing to prove to subsequent generations that people like Schumpeter and Hayek had indeed once been the unsung heroes of numerous leading British decision-makers who anxiously sought to resolve the twin-edged crux of representative democracy. While many senior executives firmly believed that the masses were not intelligent enough to apprehend what is good for them, they also noted that the MPs, even when they did know the right remedies for Britain's ailing economy, were unable to prescribe the needed bitter medicine lest it alienate their voters. For an outright view of the thinking that prevailed during much of the second half of the twentieth century, I am bringing into play two erudite and influential economic commentators who were also associated with political affairs. They did not abuse their fellow-citizens in the language of Hayek-Schumpeter but set out most of their radical messages clearly and unambiguously. I believe that, by default, their opinions mirrored soundly the perceptions of many important leaders of the British establishment who, however, did not think it expedient to articulate them publicly. Sam Brittan was known throughout the financial world as the UK's most celebrated economic analyst; he wrote regularly in the *FT*. Peter Jay had a chequered career. (He was the son of Douglas Jay, a member of the Attlee and Wilson governments. His first wife was a daughter of James Callaghan, the chancellor of the Wilson administration who was to become prime minister.) After a stint in the Treasury, Peter Jay was appointed economic editor of *The Times* and later of the BBC. For a time he was Britain's ambassador in the US.

Though disagreeing on details, Brittan and Jay recognized the same flaws of Britain's democracy: if the stupid voters were not so feared by the elected politicians, the GDPs of the UK could have been much bigger and consequently would have engendered higher living standards. Both commentators underlined that the non-deferential voters were deluded by excessive expectations, nurtured during the competitive bidding by the towering political parties which asked for their support. The two, as behoves altruistic paternalists, differentiated between the true interests and the expressed wishes of the masses. Brittan and Jay wanted to rein in the decision-making powers of the HoC. For this purpose they sought ways and means of imposing *discipline* upon the British electorate. This is a coded word that surfaces frequently in ominous declarations. Though the two of them prepared scenarios which depicted Britain as a society which is about to disintegrate, they refuted charges that they were yearning for some kind of dictatorship. There were indeed a few prominent members of the British establishment who toyed with the idea that Britain should be governed, temporarily, by an authoritarian regime. In the post-Thatcher days Charles Moore acerbically characterized Prime Minister John Major as the spokesmen of politicians, civil servants and bankers 'who are bored with parliamentary democracy and want to construct a form of government impervious to the wishes of the people'. Brittan felt obliged to issue an explicit disclaimer lest his advocacy of 'limited government' led his readers to arrive at a wrong conclusion: 'The last thing I should favour is a preventive authoritarian regime ... a dictatorship can hardly be a remedy.' Some murmured that he did protest too much but they were doing him an injustice. Jay and he did not advocate a dictatorship but planned to change the governance of the country by instituting inbuilt external constraints. If these were in place — some are outlined in the next section — politicians could then wring their hands insincerely when the country suffered temporarily deflation, high unemployment and lowered living standards. The representatives in the HoC would have the good fortune to be able to justify their 'inactions' by referring to the existence of legal hindrances. The electorate would be told by their representatives that much as they would have liked to pursue populist policies, existing contractual undertakings fettering the government prevented parliament from doing so. They would be like the boy who, having murdered his parents, asked the judge for mercy because he was an orphan. The Blair government has frequently employed such apologias when they had to defend unpopular actions.

Brittan spurned 'the contemporary belief that no constraints should stand in the way of an elected government, a belief sometimes given a traditionalist coat in Britain by expressions such as the "sovereignty of parliament" or "the Queen in parliament"'. For a long time he was engrossed in the dangers to democracy which are created by inflation. But he would have it that even if the threat of a runaway inflation receded, the tensions between democracy and excessive expectations would then assume other 'more dangerous and more serious forms'. He developed this argument in a paper, the title of which *The Economic Contradictions of Democracy* reveals his disputatious thesis: 'Liberal representative democracy suffers from internal contradictions, which are likely to increase in time, and on present indications the system is likely to pass away within the lifetime of people now adult.' Brittan predicted that the then prevailing trends would bring into being a situation 'where nothing much remained of liberal democracy but its label'. As to what had caused him to arrive at such pessimistic inferences, Brittan referred his readers to Bagehot's gloomy forebodings about the effects of enfranchising an ignorant and greedy electorate. His conjecture, that the 'system' (i.e. liberal democracy) might disappear, was not attended by an explanation as to when and how this would happen. He maintained that putting forward the opinion, that the 'present situation is unsustainable', did not oblige him to spell out the nature of the new system. Brittan did mention vaguely the off-chance of an 'overnight coup . . . the army becoming a political agency'. While he regarded such conjectures as possibilities, he thought it more realistic to assume that there will not be 'an overnight coup' and the process of disintegration would be gradual. In defence of Brittan's doomsday script it is right to point out that it was penned in 1974. At that time both Jay and he attributed many of the UK's evils to the nefarious conduct of the trade unions. (Margaret Thatcher and her close ally, Norman Tebbit, were later instrumental in weakening the unions' stranglehold over the UK economy). In the cited paper there are no prescriptions beyond some trite remarks about the virtues of a 'Government of National Unity'. In later years Brittan did propose concrete (anti-democratic) remedies. Originally, he had opposed the UK joining the Common Market, but he changed his mind when he was converted to the notion that membership would act as a desirable weighty constraint on the legislative powers of the UK's parliament. Hence, in 1995, Brittan announced that he had become a pro-EU supporter because 'British inflation is likely to be lower if monetary policy is run by a European central bank than if it is decided by Westminster politicians'.

In the same year that Brittan's crucial article appeared, Peter Jay was also speculating on the imminent breakdown of democratic governance in the UK. At a London seminar he confronted Milton Friedman who had lectured on the implications for a hypothetical country where trade unions were so powerful as to bring about 'either a runaway inflation or an authoritarian society ruled by force'. The eminent American economist, having explored the possibility that an economic clash of interests could lead to violent political confrontations, maintained that the US and the UK did not face such a predicament. Jay agreed that this was true of the US but, with regard to the UK, 'inflation accelerating to an infinite rate with grave political and social consequences is [already] happening here [and] in most of the Western European countries'. His employer, *The Times,* furnished Jay with ample space to frighten its readers as he outlined 'British democracy's last chance before extinction'. Jay claimed that it was unrealistic to rely on the citizens of the UK doing the right things once they were made aware of his doom-laden prognosis that pointed to a looming debacle. He censured British politicians for seeking to achieve *simultaneously* stable prices, free collective bargaining and full employment. In Jay's prognosis these were unattainable targets unless the form of Britain's government, which rested on renewable popular consent, was radically changed. He called it the 'irreconcilable quadrilateral'. Jay's panacea called for unemployment in the millions during several years and a statutory incomes policy. He also proposed that monetary policy should be devised and executed by an autonomous Currency Commission which alone would regulate the supply of money; neither the BoE nor the government would be allowed to interfere. As Jay was convinced that people would not voluntarily agree to his three economic objectives, he hypothesized that democracy would collapse. An article of his in 1974 commenced: 'When, in 1980 or so, democracy as we know it has been suspended . . . ' He conceded that 'it is as futile to predict exactly when this moment will be reached as it is to try to describe the exact chain of political events which will show the eventual breakdown of a government depending on popular consent. My own guess is that we may stagger round one more economic cycle, perhaps two, and that something should be allowed also for the tendency of

logic always to take rather longer to work itself out in Britain than one expects. But 1980, give or take a couple of years, seems to be a cautious-to-middle view.' Peter Jay was still at it in 1987 when he co-authored a book, titled: *Apocalypse 2000: Economic Breakdown and the Suicide of Democracy*. Against the background of major defects in the UK's democratic governance four panaceas were debated by the country's elitists:
  (a) opting for some kind of dictatorship;
  (b) appealing to the wisdom of the electorate and retaining the status quo;
  (c) making greater use of externally imposed disciplines;
  (d) relying on the mendacious tools at the disposal of politicians.
When these alternatives are aired in public, the elected parliamentary representative feel obliged to advocate (b), arguing that, notwithstanding the obvious blemishes in the present system, the will of the people must remain paramount and that 'politics is the art of the possible'. This pragmatic prescription of 'no change' is expected to be well received by the majority of the electorate. It is however, a cowardly solution in that it debars politicians from espousing the needed but unpopular remedies. If (a) and (b) are rejected and, instead, the highly effective options of (c) and (d) are chosen, this heralds the application of unpalatable tactics. Politicians would have to be prepared to engage in active and passive lying to execute the wilful deception of the electorate. W.F. Deedes, a former Conservative minister, boasted that democracy never flourished on a strict diet of truth: 'It is impossible to govern a democracy without *occasionally* resorting to deception.' I maintain that the gist of the word, which I have italicized, is specious.

I shall concretize (c) and (d) with illustrations, mostly drawn from the UK. There have been a number of cases in which MPs were guilty of deceiving their fellow parliamentarians in order to cover-up personal non-material misdemeanours or egotistical acts of self-aggrandizement. Very few British politicians have lied for personal commercial rewards. I am not writing about any of these. The American theologian Reinhold Niebuhr maintained that the 'whole act of politics consists in directing rationally the irrationalities of men'. I think he meant us to forgive in the spirit of charity the sinful, but well-intentioned, politicians who lie when they are engaged on such tasks. Plato, no lover of democracy, insisted strongly that individuals, who utter 'pernicious' or 'subversive' lies for private ends, must be punished. The rulers of the state were to be the only ones with the privilege of lying at home and abroad: 'they were allowed to lie for the good of the state' which I interpret to be 'the public good' or 'the national interest'. Deceiving the electorate is only holy if it is benevolent lying, i.e. if it is an auxiliary instrument in the hands of democratic politicians which helps them to carry out good policies that, because of the character of the electorate, have to be introduced by stealth. But, as will be seen, well-intentioned ministers may also feel justified to lie to the MPs of their own party if it is necessary to prevent them blocking good deeds. As the British prime minister is only primus-inter-pares in the cabinet, he consequently owes accountability in major affairs of state to his ministers. In the last resort he may have to deceive them with passive lying by withholding vital information or even go to the extreme of actually telling untruths. British prime ministers must also be able to retain the express loyalty of a majority of MPs in the HoC. In order to secure their votes for the enactment of legislative proposals considered to be in the national interest, prime ministers have been known to exert their influence by not adhering to the truth. Of course, withholding the truth from the ignorant public is a much easier task than deceiving one's political colleagues .

Of Britain's ten post-war prime ministers who are no longer in office, the champion of deviousness and passive lying is the man who, according to the memoirs of his PR adviser, boasted: 'we politicians are trained in the art of evasion'. None of the ten was a saint but in my estimation Harold Macmillan was the most skilled and unscrupulous master in the manipulation of public opinion — and, at times, of his colleagues in the Conservative Party. This outstanding opportunist was a magnificent actor who wore well the populist mask of an upright, high-minded, paternalistic leader. The deceptive languor of his speeches and his wily duplicity helped him earn this unwarranted accolade. His great talent was so to camouflage his misdeeds that most were discovered only years afterwards, when they could no longer damage his career prospects. An admittedly hostile narrator of

Macmillan's life story has reported that 'both his political and personal life rested on his talent as a concealer . . . the suppression of truth and facts were necessary and habitual to him'. His parliamentary activities were saturated with reticences, evasions, expedients and palliations. In 1958 Macmillan's Treasury team (Nigel Birch, Enoch Powell and Thorneycroft) resigned from the government on a matter of principle: 'With an outward show of cheery aplomb, he spoke to reporters in his usual avuncular style', describing the resignations as 'little local difficulties' which did not bother him greatly and he was not going to spend much time pondering about them. This consummate piece of active lying was impressive. The public, admiring their unperturbed leader, were led to believe that the cause of the resignations was not of substance. It can now be proved that he had been an accomplished liar and that the impression he created was a sham one. In fact he was deeply worried that the cabinet over which he presided would disintegrate; he attached great significance to the resignations because they might leave his party 'in a hopeless and even ridiculous position, without policy or honour'. These are the very words he penned in his diary which of course was not published till his own political life had come to an end. His official biographer also exposed this mendaciousness. Macmillan told the BBC thirteen years after he had made the comment, cited above, that it was a 'throwaway remark made with the utmost casualness . . . I just thought of it'. This was wholly untrue: 'He had thought it out most carefully, worrying about it throughout most of the previous night.' Macmillan would not have become prime minister if he had not demonstrated superbly his beguiling skills when he was minister of housing and chancellor of the exchequer, respectively. More about him later.

External Disciplines

The Craving for Dictates

The craving for dictates emanates from either a renunciation of the democratic process or from a wish to persuade colleagues, by means of an external constraint, to accept a policy they disagree with. Disciplinary swords wielded by foreign institutions are more efficacious than domestic ones: 'the EU has ordered us', 'the IMF is threatening', 'the rules of the UN make it obligatory'. The constraints we are dealing with are neither God-given nor are they irreversible. The British body politic has not been chained by force; it is shackled today because domestic schemers — many of them benevolent politicians — took the initiative to have the chains imposed for reasons that were not always disclosed to, or understood by, the public at large. Furthermore, politicians deceive the public when the electorate is not informed that a sovereign country, which is a participant in an international association, nevertheless remains free to negotiate improved terms of membership; if these are not granted, the country can consider withdrawing from it. Such cancellations are not likely to be amicable and, initially, may even be costly. But until the governmental authorities feel compelled to take such a drastic step — as John Major did when he unilaterally took the UK out of the ERM — constraints are marvellous techniques which silence critics and, incidentally, show up the impotence of emasculated parliaments. The rulers of a country who wish to introduce some unpopular measure are sometimes sustained when they can produce a real or contrived force majeure as an alibi. Anti-democratic decision-makers find it particularly propitious if foreign institutions or governments intervene or are depicted to be the villains. The rulers can then beat their breasts and lament: 'we are being coerced'. Contemporary history records that there are many instances where the alleged coercions were spurious. By the last quarter of the twentieth century, the British establishment had lost faith in its native representative democracy where the non-deferential voters had the upper hand. In an ugly temperament they denied the possibility of repairing the blemished economy by domestic endeavours and sought ways and means of inflicting external disciplines upon the electors, parliamentarians and cabinet ministers. Margaret Thatcher somewhat weakened these depressive tendencies. She fulminated continuously against those who opined that only foreign associations can help crush the ravages of British inflation. But at the end of the day she too was driven to give in to the powerful voices of the British establishment which urged that the UK's economy be reined in by external monetary constraints that were controlled from abroad. At the dawn of the twenty-first century a decisive volte face had occurred. While the ruling Labour Party was now relying strongly upon external constraints, many in the UK's pro-capitalist camp were viewing with distaste the disciplines they had once promoted.

The Panacea of the EU

The panacea of the EU was sold to the electorate by a disingenuous prime minister. Originally, it was backed by an overwhelming majority of the country's elitists and in particular by the luminaries of the City of London. They followed in the footsteps of the anti-democratic Keynes who had propounded that economics should be outside the bounds of politics. His concomitant belief was that experts — he described them as disinterested individuals who are qualified because of their scientific expertise — manage public affairs better than elected politicians. In the absence of a written constitution, all laws enacted by the UK parliament, can be rescinded or amended at any time when the parliamentary representatives choose to do so. Hence, general elections used to be very meaningful. A change of government betokened a new set of policies; the victorious party had the powers which enabled it to rescind the laws brought in by the party which had previously been in office. Membership of the EU has already enervated the fundamental character of British democracy and Brussels is preparing further far-reaching encroachments upon the sovereignty of the member-states. Edicts from Brussels automatically supersede national laws. The judiciary in the UK must automatically obey what has been determined by the top echelons of the EU.

The HoC still likes to think of itself as omnipotent in accordance with the erstwhile sovereignty of Britain but this is a chimera. The UK can leave the EU but, unless it does, its parliament can only rubber-stamp the laws promulgated in Brussels. Chancellor Brown submits, as did his predecessors, an annual budget for approval by the HoC. But the HoC has now no longer the sole right to determine what should or should not be in the budget. There are already revenue items in the British budgets which the chancellor has been compelled to insert, whether he likes them or not; they have been dictated to him by the lawmakers in Brussels and the HoC cannot show its disapproval by voting against them. The HoC has ceased to be the UK's absolute decision-maker which it once was and this is of course greeted with relish by those who treat democracy with disdain and are jubilant about external restraints. A.R. Prest, a professor at LSE, was once invited by a banking group to formulate certain fiscal legislative proposals. Having done so, he added despondently, that even if these were adopted by the current British administration, a successor government might well turn them upside down. He deplored this situation in which legislation, enacted by the HoC, is subject to the 'impermanence of any remedies'. As far back as 1973 the professor had expressed the hope that things would change radically as a result of the UK's membership of the European Community. Brussels, so Prest would have it, would then 'impose some constraints on governmental freedom in the tax field, as in others. But, once needed changes are introduced, they may have a better chance of survival'.

We have already mentioned the florid language with which Howard Davies described the bitter fate that awaited the UK if it did not become a full member of the EU. In 1975, as a young man, he had been a very junior civil servant in the Paris embassy. In the referendum of that year he voted 'no' to Britain joining the Common Market because he regarded the proposed membership of the Community as a 'conspiracy to sell our birthright'. In time he changed his mind and raced up the ladder to occupy exalted positions. He became the Director General of the CBI, a senior civil servant in the Treasury, deputy governor of the BoE and chairman of the FSA. The pronouncements of this high-flier are interesting because of the reasons he has since given to justify his U-turn. Davies persuaded himself that neither he nor his confreres 'could really be trusted with a currency' and also bemoaned the fact that Britain was making a mess of controlling inflation because of the *'domestic* approach'. (The italicized word should really be replaced by 'democratic'). As a result, so he argued, 'we are drifting hopelessly'. Why? It is the absence of a 'firm anchor'. Davies admits that he is now impatient with those of the British people who deplore the loss of national sovereignty and sneers at the 'peculiar fiction about the unfettered dominion of parliament which flies in the face of reality'. With refreshing honesty he has affirmed that he no longer cares whether decisions affecting the UK are made in Brussels rather than in the HoC.

Chancellor Kohl contemplated financing the costs of the reunification of Germany by raising the sales tax from 13% to 15%. The very idea was obnoxious to the German electorate and in any case he had a few years previously promised not to do such a thing. His party, the Christian Democrats, held him to this promise but he found an oblique way to circumvent it. Egged on by influential Germany, the EU issued a new directive, according to which all member-states were now compelled to introduce a sales tax with a minimum rate of 15%. Kohl, with the tongue in his cheek, explained to his loyal supporters that he had not really intended to bring about such an unpopular tax increase. Yet, what could he do but obey the directive sent out by Brussels?

Monetary Policy

Monetary policy is a supreme function of a sovereign government which administers the controls that regulate the interest rates, the quantity of money in circulation, the foreign exchange rate and the bailiwick of the central bank. In 1976 Nigel Lawson was an MP but not yet a minister and could therefore ventilate publicly his doctrinal precepts: 'The question is whether the government are prepared to accept any external constraints on their actions in monetary matters.' He expressed his displeasure that the dimensions of the money supply were fixed at the discretion of the politicians in office. Between 1979 and 1989 Lawson was a member of the Thatcher administration and therefore had to guard his tongue in public and could not spell out what constraints he had in mind. He did, however, privately pressure the prime minister and, on his own admission, tried to sell her sweeping policies that were intended to weaken the decision-making powers of the HoC. In his extensive memoirs he confessed to several sins which included his striving, in which he ultimately succeeded, to transfer certain statutory prerogatives, hitherto within the domain of British governments, from London to Brussels. When he was chancellor, Lawson launched a vital anti-democratic initiative in a secret memorandum to the prime minister. He had been unhappy with a situation in which chancellors and economic ministers were constantly held to account by parliament. Lawson was impatient with the need to explain to the parliamentary representatives his monetary policies — and seek their approbation. He wanted to change the status of the BoE so that it would no longer be effectively under the control of a democratic government and parliament. By changing the character of the central bank, he would 'depoliticise interest rate changes' and in this important sphere the politicians in office would be freed from the tiresome task of appeasing the electorate. Thatcher fully understood the reason for Lawson's plan which she rejected outright. She saw in his proposition a public acknowledgement that democratic politicians are unable to curb inflation. Her chancellor produced a tempting bait to induce her to agree to the immediate grant of political independence to the BoE. In his scheme, so Lawson proudly emphasised, counter-inflationary policies would be entrenched and any populist monetarist aspirations of a new government would thus come to naught. Thatcher was not enticed by Lawson's entreaty because she held that every new government was entitled to carry out its own partisan policies and this included the determination of interest rates. Thatcher held out against her hero Hayek who had also wanted to abolish 'governmental monetary monopoly' and she thereby turned her back on Keynes's anti-democratic vision in which central banking would be 'utterly removed from popular controversy'. The very first act of Gordon Brown, when he was appointed chancellor of the exchequer in the 1997 Blair government, was to implement what Thatcher had refused to do.

The leaders of the EU arrived at the logical conclusion that the impending formation of the United States of Europe called for all member-states to abjure the foreign exchange workings of the free market and to give up the right of their governments and parliaments to set the price of the national currencies. Initially, they installed the Exchange Rate Mechanism [ERM] and thus resuscitated the discredited fixed exchange rates of the Bretton Woods system. This decreed the minimum value of the currency of each EU member (except for Greece and the UK) against each other, though for practical purposes all the participating EU currencies were tied to the DM. When the comparative economic situation in an EU country deteriorated, the fixed parities were not adjusted. In order to remain within the framework of the Brussels-administered ERM, the weakening economies had to hike their interest rates which caused domestic unemployment. Lawson who, passionately, sought to bring the UK into the ERM relates in his autobiography that the external financial discipline of the ERM 'would enable us to get inflation down ... it would [also] be helpful in future arguments about spending and borrowing in the HoC if our backbenchers in effect faced a discipline of their own choice [and] would make it clear to industry that they could not look to exchange rate depreciation so solve their difficulties.' Margaret Thatcher's three chancellors all bullied her to join until, against her conviction, she gave in at the end of the tenure of her prime ministerial office. John Major, her successor and fervent believer in this disciplinary system, told the public that being a member of the ERM was good for British business. This, however, was not the main reason. He and many in the City of London were happy to give the Bundesbank an indirect say over the UK economy. They believed in this anti-democratic step for they did not trust the British parliament to pass tough legislation. According to a perceptive analyst, the true intent of the British supporters of the ERM was to harness the domestic economy: this would relentlessly squeeze out inflation and make it impossible for the government to print money to bribe voters before an election. Can this devious intent by leading Conservative politicians be proved? Fortunately, some have gone on record to say so and may thus be quoted verbatim. In his retirement the unrepentant Lawson hypothesized that had the UK joined the ERM earlier than it did, this would have put a damper on pay and price increases and moderated the credit expansion. But revealingly he also suggested another advantage that would have accrued: 'Margaret would not have been able to prevent me from raising interest rates ... Margaret was right in arguing that what I was advocating would constrain the freedom of government to do whatever they like. But a constraint of this kind should be welcomed.' While the electorate knew of course nothing about the implications of the ERM for democratic governance, Thatcher and Lawson clearly did.

Since those days things have moved fast in Brussels. They buried the ERM and created instead the euro, the designated future currency of the United States of Europe. The important countries of the EU have already abandoned their own currencies and now use only the inflexible euro. They have transferred in toto the right of national governments to determine interest rates and thereby the price of money affecting their economies. The buildings of the national central banks are empty; most of their employees have found employment elsewhere and these once powerful institutions are left with very little to do. The parliaments of these countries still talk and make laws but in the most instrumental economic spheres they have no role to play. I agree with Prime Minister Tony Blair and the many other politicians in Britain who share his view that full membership of the EU would sooner or later compel the UK government to abandon the sterling currency in favour of the euro and consequently abrogate the monthly interest rate announcements by the BoE. If Britain should adopt the euro, Keynes will be able to smile in his grave when he learns that the British electorate are no longer able to have a meaningful say in the formulation of the UK's most important economic policies.

The Indexation of State Benefits

The indexation of state benefits, pensions and personal income tax allowances — originally introduced as a means of neutralizing the effects of inflation — provides for *automatic* adjustments. While this is not the most outstanding instance of a built-in constraint, it is nevertheless a weighty infringement of democratic governance. Those who enacted the apposite laws put all subsequently elected parliamentary representatives into a straitjacket. When Australia passed such legislation in 1976, the responsible minister stated openly and explicitly that this was done for the express purpose of laying down 'a desirable discipline upon future governments'. Indexation laws are bad for democracy when newly elected governments might wish to rearrange public expenditure according to their notions and reverse those of their predecessors. Why should *all* inflation-adjusted state benefits remain tied to the *same* extent, commensurate with the rise of consumer prices? Governments ought to have the opportunity to change, uninhibitedly, the priorities of their social expenditure. Indexation laws can admittedly be repealed or amended but in reality — as the governments of the US, UK, France and Germany have learnt to their distress — it is politically very embarrassing to abrogate or lower the indexation statutes even when there is a parliamentary majority to do so. Politicians strive to avoid public odium. It is for that reason that ingrained indexation formulae are retained long after they should have been abolished or amended.

Concorde

Concorde was a marvellous technological achievement. Alas, it also demonstrated how the purveyors of public funds were led astray by legal niceties, secretly devised by altruistic and non-altruistic enthusiasts who were infatuated with this august venture. The latter did not disclose the - burdens that were surreptitiously heaped upon the electorate and, more remarkably, their injudicious, disloyal behaviour was aimed at queering the pitch of colleagues with whom they were serving in the same government. It is astounding that in their published reminiscences the deceivers actually registered boastfully the details of their improper interventions.

In 1962 the aviation minister Julian Amery persuaded the Conservative cabinet to support the Concorde project. Thirty years later he wrote with pride how he had frustrated the intention of the 1964 Wilson government to cancel the project: 'It was unable to do so because I had tied up the treaty so tightly that the human and physical resources involved could not risk a cancellation from either the French or the British side.' He did not tell his colleagues at the time how and why he devised an unbreakable hindrance which would fetter future French and British politicians. During the first Wilson government (1964–70) there were endless committee meetings aimed at finding ways to cut the already incurred losses and halting any further expenditure of British public funds on the nascent Concorde. We know from the indiscretions of the cabinet minister Richard Crossman that most Labour ministers were in favour of cancellation and cursed the Conservatives for having initiated it: 'this confounded, awful, absurd thing . . . a scandal . . . it is a nightmare'. Notwithstanding these strong feelings, Wilson was ready to pay some small compensation to the French. Little did the opponents of Concorde appreciate Amery's foresight. They also discovered that senior civil servants and interested parties in the aircraft industry had anticipated such a contingency and with stealth had slipped in preventive clauses that would frustrate any attempts to slaughter the extravagant white elephant: 'We found it impossible to scrap Concorde without tearing up not merely a commercial contract but a treaty, so possibly making ourselves liable to pay bigger compensation to the French than the cost of going ahead.' The Edward Heath government (1970-74), which followed Wilson's reign, concluded immediately that it was desirable to put an end to Concorde. The Solicitor General Geoffrey Howe has related that one of his first assignments was to check the legality of the contract: 'Were we entitled to terminate our joint venture? I had to attend at Number 10 to give Ted Heath the same advice that our Labour predecessors had given Wilson in 1964.' The contract was unbreakable. Julian Amery, who was at this meeting, confirmed with a smile that that had indeed been his intention when he struck the deal as minister of aviation: 'We wanted to be sure with the French.' Amery thus claimed, as an English patriot, to have introduced the constraint to stop the perfidious French from cancelling. In his confession shortly before his death, he made it clear that he had been just as concerned with those perfidious British who might not like Concorde. Indeed, most of the time it were not the French but the British politicians who wanted to renege on the Concorde project.

In 1974 Wilson returned to Downing Street and appointed the leftist Tony Benn as the minister of aviation. He, at least made no bones, about his intention to fight by fair and foul means those of his party comrades who screamed that the UK must get out of its Concorde obligations. His *Diaries* reveal a great deal. Civil servants informed him that 'there was now unanimous official advice throughout Whitehall for the cancellation of Concorde, and they had agreed that it was unsaleable in it present form'. Tony Benn was not impressed and pledged himself to work against his ministerial colleagues. On this subject he made one of the frankest and personally most damaging entries in the *Diaries* which he later published. He was in a quandary. While enamoured of this innovative aeroplane, he also had a personal reason for championing it: much of the UK work for the production of Concorde was destined to be carried out in factories which were located in his constituency. Benn set out to fight for Concorde 'with tremendous care because it could be a disaster' for him politically and personally. How could he best undermine his colleagues' wish to halt the manufacture of the aeroplane? He concluded that this was best and most effectively done if he organized a collusion that would stiffen French resistance to a British cancellation. Benn has revealed that he started the process by being 'candid' with a Rolls-Royce delegation that called on him to discuss Concorde: 'At the end I took the [trade union] convener aside and said: Just one word — very important and don't ever say it came from me, but everything depends on the French government standing firm. I am going to fight Healey [the chancellor] like a tiger to see he doesn't get rid of Concorde.' A few days later Benn met George Edwards, the chairman of British Aircraft Corporation, in charge of the UK end of the joint venture. As was the custom, Benn's private secretary, a civil servant, was in attendance and took notes. He was ordered by his minister 'to put down his pencil because we are having a private talk'. The *Diaries* disclosed:

> I told him the whole story. The cabinet have told me to go forward and suggest that we discontinue but if the French insist on producing sixteen planes we shall go ahead. Therefore, without breathing a word that you have heard this from me, your job is to persuade the French to make such a demand and then we shall have to build them. It is not very reputable but I have reached the point where I shall fight any way I can to keep it going because I know that it is right, and there is a complete collapse of morale in the top leadership of this country. I know that you don't agree with my ideology, George, but unless we pull ourselves up by the bootstraps we are finished.

The plot succeeded. The original estimate, put forward to persuade the politicians to finance Concorde, had put the cost at £160m. The final direct burden borne by the British and French taxpayers was £2b. When London and Paris were still deliberating, unrealistic sales figures were bandied about to induce the politicians to give the go-ahead. It was said that there existed commercial buyers for 150 Concordes. In fact not a single plane was ever sold. Two of the 16 built planes were kept for testing. The state-owned British Airways and Air France were each compelled to take delivery of seven planes. The costs of the indirect subventions from the public purse have never been divulged.

Not A Genuine Doomsday

If politicians are unable to depend on weighty constraints to implement necessary but unpopular policies, they may have to make use of subterfuges. The lies they employ are not falsehoods which describe things which have happened. They are apocalyptic mendacities which dwell on the dismal future which is certain to come unless drastic measures are taken immediately. It is known as the Doomsday agenda. The truth about the first of my two episodes has filtered out haphazardly years after the event. There is no concrete evidence which describes how this conspiracy actually worked but strong hints, dropped by two highly knowledgeable witnesses Joel Barnett and Bernard Donoughue (and other sources), have hinted at what seems to have occurred in the privacy of the cabinet room. Harold Wilson found it difficult to square Labour's electoral promises with the UK's stern economic reality. The tabled tax increases and some mild expenditure cuts in the April 1975 budget did not resolve his dilemma. In the summer of that year Chancellor of the Exchequer Denis Healey requested that he be allowed to present an emergency budget which would incorporate a hefty package of expenditure cuts. A majority of the cabinet rebuffed him. In the subsequent twelve months — James Callaghan had meanwhile replaced Harold Wilson as prime minister — the agony deepened. Inflation rose to above 24% and there was a run on sterling which exhausted the foreign exchange reserves. In mid-1976 Healey again had a message of gloom for the cabinet, this time asserting that salvation could now only come from the IMF. Its loans, however, would be conditional on a massive curtailment of public expenditure. Confidential Treasury documents were circulated which forecast that the balance of payments would show a deficit in the first half of 1976 and other bad news was in the offing. Healey and his Treasury ministers let it be known that the only way out was to sign the harsh IMF loan conditions. The cabinet was pressured to agree on the ground that if the draconian expenditure cuts were not made, the economy would collapse and with it the Labour government. Though several ministers remained strongly opposed to the IMF conditions, not one of them resigned when the majority of the cabinet gave Healey carte blanche.

It had been clear from the outset that if the government, on its own volition, had proposed to the HoC a mammoth reduction in public expenditure, it would have suffered a defeat because Labour's leftist MPs would not have given their approval. However, now Labour ministers maintained that substantive assistance from the IMF was available but only if drastic cuts were made. This was spelt out in detail to the Labour parliamentarians who were sufficiently impressed to give their (reluctant) assent. As soon as the cuts were agreed upon, Britain's economic fortunes improved with astonishing speed. Inflation dropped to 8%, monetary growth was curbed, the value of sterling rose and the BoE's interest rate was lowered from 14% to 5%. An inflow of foreign capital enabled Healey to repay, before the agreed dates, all the IMF loans. Labour's critics naturally highlighted the sordid humiliations which the Callaghan government had to endure when it was being bailed out by the IMF. But could there have been more to it than that? In the memoirs of the Chief Secretary of the Treasury Joel Barnett there is to be found the cryptic remark that the IMF medicine had not been unwelcome; he asserted that Callaghan and Healey had used it to 'soften up the potential opponents in the cabinet'. The influential senior policy adviser of two Labour prime ministers (Wilson and Callaghan) also voiced his suspicions. Lord, as he now is, Donoughue told the House of Lords in 1991 that when the 1976 balance of payment data were revised, they indicated that the UK had been in surplus and not in deficit which is contrary to what the cabinet had been told during its deliberations on the IMF loans. He opined that it could have been a 'statistical cock-up' or a 'Treasury plot, as some thought'. Whatever the truth, without Healey threatening his colleagues with the IMF conditions, the expenditure cuts would almost certainly not have been confirmed. A curious editorial in the *FT* in January 1993 remarked that in the mid-1970s the UK was said to have had an appalling balance of payments problem: 'yet, with hindsight the gloom was hopelessly overdone'. Comparing the situation in the 1990s with those of the 1970s, it remarked that 'the IMF was [then] there to impose a tight fiscal embrace on the Labour government. Today . . . the IMF is absent. This matters . . .'

I have already referred to the Anglo-French Suez expedition in 1956. Prime Minister Anthony Eden had originally deceived not only the country but also the Conservative Party and its MPs in relation to the British and French collusion with Israel. The ambitious Chancellor of the Exchequer, Harold Macmillan had good reason to think that if Eden were deposed, he would be his likely successor. Macmillan did not hesitate to further his career by turning the majority of the cabinet against Eden by means of sophisticated deceptions. When, militarily, things were going badly in Egypt, the chancellor conveyed to the cabinet reports, which in part were untrue and at best very exaggerated, about a run on sterling and fatal losses in the UK's currency reserves that, so it was implied, threatened to turn into a disaster if hostilities did not cease immediately. The US was admittedly displeased with the Anglo-French operation but, according to US sources, Macmillan's disastrous forebodings about the terrible punishments to its erstwhile ally that Washington was preparing if hostilities were not halted at once, were certainly not proven. The size of the foreign currency losses that the UK allegedly suffered, turned out to have been inaccurate but at the time no one in the cabinet had the authority or knowledge to challenge the chancellor. Macmillan, who had gently put a knife into a discredited Eden and wounded him politically, took up residence in 10 Downing Street. When this happened, few in the Conservative Party were inclined to rake up the inaccuracies in those Treasury figures which helped to bring it about.

Dishonesty To Do Good

The phrase *ad captandum vulgus* is used to describe policies which are advocated 'in order to win over the masses'. E. Ehrlich, a Latin scholar, maintains that it refers to those politicians whose actions were meant to please the common people; they were aware that what they were doing was not really in the best interests of the community — their intention was to achieve popularity. Some contemporary altruistic politicians vote for legislative proposals of which they disapprove because only by doing so can they remain prominent leaders of their party and this, hopefully, will enable them to do in the future many unselfish things. My unsavoury examples illustrate how opportunistic lying and representative democracy are entwined. Conor Cruise O'Brien was not opposed to Ireland becoming a member of the Common Market. He was however sufficiently astute to recognize that if he did not support publicly the Irish Labour Party's opposition to joining, he would be removed from his position as the party's spokesman on foreign affairs; this included dealing with Northern Ireland, a task he relished very much. 'To be able to go on telling the truth [about Northern Ireland] I told a whopping great lie', to wit he argued against entry. According to his biographer, 'in trimming his political beliefs, Conor was doing what any politician has to do but it bothered him. He reflected on Burke's words "we must practice an economy of truth so that we may live to tell it longer".'

The governments of Wilson, Callaghan and Heath imposed price and wage controls — and simultaneously also dividend controls. In reality the latter were not aimed at curbing the profits of successful companies though the electorate was given the false impression that this was the purpose of the exercise. The wage controls were unpopular and to counter this the politicians of all the parties, some of whom even invoked patriotism, were happy to use the dividend stick with which, so they claimed, the wicked rich could be beaten. Chancellor Callaghan knew that this was nonsense but as he was eager to be applauded by the ignorant, he referred contemptuously to shareholders as people 'who sit in their nests squawking for higher dividends and waiting to be fed'. When Harold Macmillan had been chancellor, he was of course also fully conversant with the fact that the paying of dividends had nothing to do with profit-making. But as a devout populist, he was concerned with what the electorate perceived to be true. Hence he praised the directors of companies who declared low dividends; they were said to be doing 'the right thing for the country'. Macmillan at least conceded that the economic significance was minimal but he affirmed that it 'counted psychologically'. Not surprisingly, the Conservative Party under Heath favoured statutory dividend controls. Amidst the clamour to pacify the country's employees, whose emoluments were being regulated by the state, it was an attractive PR proposition to make it appear as if the rich were also being pounded. But, clearly beyond the comprehension of most voters, it was an illusion that dividend controls would hurt the shareholders. The opposite was true: they enriched the wealthy. The Inland Revenue had long been conscious that astronomically high personal tax rates and a relatively modest capital gains tax combined to create an inducement for the rich to invest in companies that either paid no or only very low dividends. To counter this anomaly the tax authorities used to compel companies to pay out high dividends but the statutory dividend controls put an end to this. The populist dividend restrictions were a perverse gift by the HoC to the rich in that they legitimatized tax-avoidance. When the top marginal tax rate on investment income hovered between 89% and 98%,[2] realized capital gains were assessed at a flat rate of only 30%. Had politicians really wanted to soak-the-rich, they would have enacted a law that made mandatory a 99% distribution of all corporate profits. Though a few erudite parliamentarians knew about this, they did not act upon their knowledge for they feared that it would endanger the public's passive acceptance of the wage and price controls.

Fiscal policies are generally discussed within the purview of the economic discipline but soak-the-rich policies are more appropriately evaluated within the compass of political science. The 98% rate was certainly not instituted to raise additional revenue — it actually achieved the very opposite. But, until Lawson became chancellor, all parties were devotees of such high rates. Even Conservative decision-makers, who privately thought it was unjust and counter-productive, aped their socialist adversaries. They had convinced themselves that if they did not advocate punitive taxation for the better-off, their party would be defeated ignominiously at the polls. There were some in the Labour Party who even advocated a 100% rate; the renowned chief of one of the UK's most powerful unions actually went on TV to urge this. Neil Kinnock, who almost became prime minister, also played with this populist toy. Hoping to impress the leftists in his party that he was a true man-of-the-people, he tabled in the

---

[2] While Labour was in office between 1964 and 1970 the top marginal income tax rate did not exceed 91.25%. When the Conservatives replaced them at 10 Downing Street, they reduced the top rate to 90%. In 1974 Labour returned to power and Chancellor of the Exchequer Healey was able to boast of two top rates: 83% on earned income and 98% on investment incomes. (Playing to the gallery, investment earnings were described as 'unearned' incomes.) Mrs Thatcher's first chancellor lowered the two Healey rates to 60% and 75%, respectively. Her second chancellor, Nigel Lawson, brought in a unified top rate of 40% in 1988.

HoC a foreboding question: 'What revenue would be raised by imposing 100% taxation on those with [annual] incomes above £10,000?' Clearly, not everyone thought that this was a hare-brained notion. Something ominous apparently took place at a cabinet meeting in May 1975 at which Chancellor Denis Healey found it necessary to castigate the advocates of 100%. He tried to persuade his colleagues that even if all annual incomes above £6,000 were confiscated, only tiny additional amounts of money would flow into the Treasury. In her *Diaries*, the leftist Barbara Castle confessed that to her this was a 'startling revelation'. Harold Lever was an influential and erudite MP, a faithful colleague of Wilson and Callaghan. Since his schooldays he had been a devout socialist which, however, did not impede his urge to become also wealthy. He was the eccentric guru of the Labour governments who was listened to in awe when he spoke about the City, cross-border finance and the psychology of the well-off. Between 1974 and 1978 he was a member of the cabinet and was frequently used as a trouble-shooter when the Labour politicians needed an expert to woo international bankers. From several sources — and most explicitly from the *Diaries* of Barbara Castle who respected his expertise though she treated his prescriptions with disdain — we learn that he complained to his cabinet colleagues about 'confiscatory' taxation. He opined that this upset the City and could produce repercussions that the Labour government would find difficult to handle. He begged them to adopt a more diplomatic approach. It is known that shortly before Healey's 1978 budget, he had almost convinced the cabinet that the ludicrous 98% marginal rate should be lowered — at least symbolically. Initially, the prime minister was sympathetic but then changed his mind because he feared that it would provoke a backlash from the left of his party and the militant trade union bosses. Harold Lever did not resign. It is said that he recognized the merits of Callaghan's over-riding political objective which was to keep the party united, however much this would damage the British economy. Lever concurred that expediency should dictate the retention of the 98% rate.

Stafford Cripps was Britain's first post-WWII chancellor of the exchequer. Unlike many of the other socialist stalwarts in the Attlee cabinet, he was in the good books of *The Economist*.

Yet, when his budget included a top marginal tax of 147.5%,[3] they described it as a 'blot on what is otherwise a sound budget'. It was not introduced to raise money but to give off loud political bangs. Nevertheless, *The Economist* exculpated the chancellor; it admonished its readers not to be too harsh with Cripps. It argued that Cripps knew of course that what he was doing was injurious to the national economy but he was impelled to 'make some gesture to those of his colleagues who are less objective'. Angry readers were asked to recognize that draconian taxes on the rich were unavoidable because: 'The trade unions had made it clear that one of their conditions for reluctant agreement to the policy of wage stabilization was that something should be done to capital and this [i.e. the confiscatory retrospective levy on investment incomes] was probably the only thing that could be done that was sufficiently spectacular.' Other commentators were not so forgiving and described it as fiscal lunacy but Stafford Cripps was probably jubilant that he was attacked by Labour's opponents. Perversely, these were helpful to the Attlee administration in general and the chancellor in particular. Cripps's desperate prescription was pigeon-holed for twenty years when it was revived by another socialist chancellor. Plus ça change, plus c'est la même chose. It was a one-year tax in excess of 100% upon investment incomes and like Cripps's precedent was applied retroactively on past incomes.

The chancellor in the Wilson government, like Cripps, was not motivated to gather more revenues. He wanted to endear himself to the 99.9% of the electorate who were not affected by this tax. The fiscal artifice by both chancellors was identical. They wanted to improve their standing within the Labour Party. They wanted to be loved by all the comrades.

---

[3] *The Economist*, April 10 1948 was unjustifiably kind to the chancellor — though at one stage it had described his doings as 'lunacy'. The editors praised the budget's indirect impact on the economy. They even maintained that the 147.5% tax of Cripps would not have been such a bad thing if it were really a once-for-all expedient. 'But surely it is childish to suppose that it will be non-recurring. Any tax which is administratively easy and brings in revenue without costing many votes will always be repeated. Investors have been put upon notice that they should so arrange their affairs as to avoid having any income, and the whole national economy will inevitably be the sufferer.' Jenkins in 1968 prided himself upon emulating Cripps. The above quoted stricture applied even more strongly to his misdeed.

Like Cripps, Roy Jenkins did not wear a cloth cap. But, unlike Cripps, he did not conceal his liking for claret and the pleasing things of life that could be bought for money. The leftists in his party denounced him as a reactionary. Many of them were openly suspicious of his loyalty to the cause of socialism. He did many things to try to prove them wrong. The 1968 budget was his greatest 'achievement'; in it was this measure which he appreciated would harm Britain but, hopefully, would be beneficial to him and his party. He placed a 10–45% levy on distributed investment income earned in 1967. As, at the time, the top marginal personal tax rate was 91.25%, the joint top rate was therefore 136.25%. It was pointed out to the chancellor that this did not penalize the ownership of capital but only punished the recipients of rent, interest and dividends; undistributed company profits again escaped the net. There was an indignant chorus in the City of London about the 'unfairness' of the tax. He could not have cared less. His critics missed the point: for Jenkins, the exercise yielded political profits precisely because he was being denounced by the class enemy. *The Economist*, pointing out the damage Jenkins had caused followed this by praising his opportunism: 'the real and good economic effects [were] a crafty political move on the part of the chancellor . . . he successfully fed blood to his baying party . . . the spectacle of people purposelessly enjoying the despoiling of somebody else is very nasty . . . the Labour backbenchers looked extraordinarily loutish'. But the distinguished journal implored its readers to be compassionate in their evaluation of the performance of this socialist chancellor. It implied that Jenkins's heart was really bleeding because — for populist purposes — he had felt compelled to resort to such demagogic trickery. The editors conveyed the impression that he did not really like what he was doing but what, politically, he thought he ought to do: 'Roy Jenkins does not ride well in front of a roused tiger of class hate.' It is untrue to say of him that he was not happy doing that sort of thing.

Were the outrageous tax rates helpful in promoting the political and personal objectives at the back of his mind? Apparently, only to some extent. In the HoC a leftist MP, John Lee, praised the chancellor for the levy on the previous year's investment incomes. No doubt this was music to his ears but it was followed by a discordant punch-line. Lee explained that he did not regard these high tax rates, welcome as they were, 'as a sufficient sop to ward off the objections we have to statutory control of wages.' In his *Diaries* Tony Benn, one of his leftist cabinet colleagues, described Jenkins's budget as reactionary. But he was perceptive enough to understand why the chancellor inflicted such heavy penalties on investment incomes. This was done 'to keep the Left quiet . . . it is a clever budget from Roy's point of view'. History records that ultimately Jenkins failed to pacify Labour's left — though not for lack of trying. His adversaries knew what he was up to and their hunches were proved correct when Jenkins left the Labour Party in 1981 and merged the group of his supporters with the Liberal Party. In his huge autobiographical tome, the 136.25% rate is only mentioned en passant but not a word about its injurious consequences.

The unquantifiable damage to the public interest, which may be caused when politicians play to the gallery, can be enormous and soak-the-rich taxation furnishes an unhappy illustration. Hundreds of thousands of young and middle-aged British entrepreneurs, inventors and outstanding professionals emigrated to escape the tax penalties that were exacted in the UK from the successful. They mostly left the country quietly because the reason for their leaving clashed with the then prevailing ethos in Britain. Few were prepared to expose themselves to derision by expounding what caused them to emigrate. Rejecting the creed of egalitarianism, they wanted to be rewarded financially with higher post-tax incomes than most of the politicians thought 'socially acceptable'. Only with the passage of time has it become apparent that many of them managed to establish profitable enterprises in their host countries. The comprehensive economic loss, caused by the departure of numerous technicians, scientists and doctors who had been educated at public expense, can be measured in billions of pounds. They were denounced for their putative lack of patriotism and occasional attempts were made by the authorities to stop them leaving though most of these failed. Not all the individuals, who escaped from the high-tax Labour and Conservative regimes, were already subject to the outrageous marginal tax rates. What, in part, impelled them to emigrate was the apprehension that if and when they did reach the top of the ladder in their home country, they would not be allowed to enjoy fully the material fruits of their success. Their decision to leave the UK to reside in more tax-friendly environments was lawful though it undoubtedly damaged the home country while the US and other countries, which received them with open arms, benefited from their skills and capital. But even larger numbers of similarly aggrieved Britons remained at home. Among them were older persons, particularly those in senor managerial positions, and individuals who had already reached the summit of their professions. However, the manner in which many of them expressed their disgust for Labour's soak-the-rich populism was no less harmful to the UK's national interest.

The emigrants had removed themselves physically from the claws of the British legislators. The majority, however, of those who could or would not leave the country attempted actively to escape from the current despotic tax afflictions by (lawful and unlawful) devious stratagems. In that heyday of prosperity for tax lawyers and clever accountants fat fees were charged for the formulation of subterfuges that transformed incomes into capital. At the time the taxation yardstick also played a decisive role in the profit evaluation of investments. Why acquire machinery to manufacture machine tools when politicians confiscated 'for the common good' most of the resultant profits? Far better to invest in antiques, properties, gold, jewels, pictures. Businesses, which were too large and prestigious to pay wages and salaries in black money, furnished their employees, particularly the executives, with non-monetary rewards that were outside the orbit of personal taxation. Though one cannot measure its ensuing effects, mention must also be made of the ethical debasement engendered by the punitive taxes. Many citizen, who were formerly law-abiding, concluded that they had become morally justified to smuggle funds out of Britain — exchange controls were then still in existence — in order to avoid paying UK taxes. Tens of thousands of illegal bank accounts were opened by British residents in foreign tax havens. Others evaded taxes at home by making fraudulent declarations to the Inland Revenue. Surely Jenkins was not unaware how, in the wake of his retrospective levy on investment incomes, capital was being taken out of the country. One of his victims said: 'I have been caught out but now I have taken steps to protect myself from future swinish conduct by politicians who are out to please the mob.' Jenkins would certainly have disapproved of such immoderate language and brushed aside reactions of this kind with contempt. Yet, the encouragement of illegalities, which his 136.25% tax rate had nurtured, must be treated as a crucially injurious fall-out from the populist games that he had been playing as chancellor.

Chapter VI

The Tools of Their Trade

> Nowadays ministers lie not only to get away with the wrong policies but even more to get away with the right policies.
> *Peregrine Worsthorne*

Après Nous le Déluge

In Cardinal Newman's famous hymn, believers are encouraged to take pride in myopic faith: 'Lead, kindly light, lead thou me on . . . I do not ask to see the distant scene; one step enough for me'. Politicians fear that they would be highly unpopular if they made the electorate pay pari passu the costs of all the state's current and capital expenditure. The astute members of the political tribe therefore aim to earn kudos by so arranging it that the tax payments for many items of this expenditure are deferred or spread over many years. When the final payments become due at some stage in the future, the politicians, who have already cashed in their brownie points, will no longer be in office and their successors are the ones who will be blamed for collecting the money from the public. Politicians live recklessly and rarely suffer pangs of conscience when thinking of their successors. Consequently, though pay-as-you-go guidelines are frequently wholesome prescriptions, politicians do not find them salutary. To make the public bear the costs of all public expenditure concurrently is actually very often in the comprehensive national interest. This is not immediately apparent for it brings about initially a relatively lower standard of living which, in turn, affects adversely the survival of the politicians who are held responsible. To finance large chunks of state expenditure through borrowings is therefore a temptation that politicians tend to succumb to, especially as the majority of the voters are not cognizant of the side effects they will have to put up with. When the Bundesbank was still a central bank with immense powers and influence, it launched in 1992 a savage attack on the German government which it accused of using borrowed funds to finance current state expenditure. It said that by applying borrowed money for the purpose of funding welfare benefits, it gave the impression to the German electorate that this state munificence was 'free', i.e. painless, an impression that would not have been conveyed if taxes had been put up instead. The features of the drawbacks, ensuing from state borrowing, are not always easily recognized to be detrimental. (a) The interest, that has to be defrayed to finance state expenditure through borrowing, can be an onerous albatross. (b) State borrowing leads to crowding out investments in the private sector. As the state's credit rating is higher than that of private sector borrowers, it follows that lenders will prefer to lend to the state or its agencies which leads to a transfer of funds from the private sector to the public sector. (c) Alternatively, if the state's appetite for increased borrowings is compelling, it can satisfy its financial needs, without starving the private sector, by raising the level of interest rates. This will attract new, local and foreign, funds to the domestic money market. Both the public and the private sectors then have to pay more interest and among the painful macro-economic repercussions are higher consumer prices plus more expensive consumer credit charges plus higher mortgage payments.

Ministers of finance all over the world defend borrowing, instead of taxation, by promising that the funds obtained by borrowing are spent exclusively on large capital projects in the state sector. Even if this were true, it would not necessarily be a convincing defence for failing to finance the costs of some state investments through taxation. But, in real life, those politicians who are able to manipulate the budgets can mercilessly ignore this homiletic compartmentalization and spend some of the borrowed funds on current expenditure. The German constitution has actually laid down that the state and the municipalities shall only be allowed to use long-term borrowed money to fund large projects which can be shown to be economically sound. Yet, German politicians have paid little attention to this meticulously formulated prohibition. In practice they have denoted purchases of, for example, bicycles and personal computers for their civil servants as capital investments. In the 1990s the unlawful use of borrowed money was so widely exposed in the press that the German parliament debated the issue and legalized some of the current practices by abating the statutory restrictions: it widened the legal scope of what, in this context, is a capital investment. Not only in Germany but also in the rest of the world, do borrowings, destined in theory for infrastructure projects only, finance indiscriminately all kinds of other state expenditure.

We have already mentioned that the guru of the Wilson and Callaghan governments, the MP Harold Lever, had been lobbying that Labour reduce the draconian tax rates; he also pleaded that the government should rely more on borrowing than on taxation. Fully aware of the high interest rates in the UK money market and the deleterious effects upon the economy when the state increases its domestic borrowings, he came up with a wretched 'wheeze' for which he was much admired. He advocated borrowing abroad *dollar-denominated* funds. There would be two seemingly attractive advantages. By borrowing abroad, the UK Treasury would have access to a lower interest rate than that which prevailed in the domestic money market. In addition, money borrowed from foreign lenders would obviate the mentioned negative consequences which would have ensued from increased borrowings in the domestic money market. The British government followed his politically convenient advice though they must have known, as Lever knew, that it was a cunning but dangerous scheme. As the sterling exchange rate was unrealistically high, it was obvious that sooner or later the British currency would have to be devalued. When this happened, as it did, the budgetary costs in devalued sterling of servicing these past loans, and ultimately repaying them, were very much higher than if the government had borrowed at home sterling-denominated funds. The somewhat lower interest rate advantage was more than swamped by the repercussions of the (anticipated) devaluation. What had once been praised as a sharp-witted expedient, opportune for incumbent politicians, proved to be an expensive calamity.

In the aftermath of WWII, the rationing of consumer goods and other war-time controls were progressively repealed. There was one supreme exception: housing remained the single tightly controlled section of the British economy.

Apart from rent controls and Inland Revenue provisions for subsidizing mortgages, it was subject to two important features of state intervention: the authorities had to grant permission for the construction of new dwellings; the distribution of building materials, which were in very short supply, was governed strictly by Ministry of Housing allocations. The minister's powers of discretion enabled him to decide upon the proportion in which the available materials were assigned to temporary housing, the repair of the existing housing stock and the construction of new dwellings, respectively. A politician, eager to be loved by the thoughtless majority of the electorate, earned applause by formulating the banality: 'housing is not a question of Conservatism or Socialism; it is a question of humanity'. At the 1950 Conservative Party conference the Labour government was criticized heavily for building only 200,000 housing units per annum. When a motion, demanding more houses but mentioning no figure, was put to the vote there was orchestrated shouting from the floor that a target of 300,000 should be proclaimed. The chairman thought this a 'magnificent idea' and acted upon it. The 300,000 figure was also highlighted in the party's manifesto for the 1951 general election and was an important factor in the victory of the Conservatives. Prime Minister Winston Churchill offered Harold Macmillan — the author of the cited claptrap — the housing portfolio. This was not to his liking because he had hoped to be given a more prestigious post. Churchill comforted him, saying that this assignment 'would make or mar your political career'. Macmillan resolved to make the best of a difficult job and achieved what few thought could be achieved. In 1954 — the year when he was deemed to have earned his promotion and was appointed first minister of defence and then chancellor of the exchequer — 354,000 new dwellings were completed. The true cost of this success was to become apparent only when Macmillan no longer had reason to worry about the negative aspects of his housing record; he had calculated correctly that they would only surface belatedly. By 1954 Macmillan, a little known politician, had become famous and was adored as a 'doer'. It is generally accepted today that without his acclaimed housing halo, he would never have been in a position to grab the prime ministerial prize in January 1957.

When the vaults of the statistical offices of the DDR were opened after unification, a host of collated, but unpublished, data were found. The German communist statisticians had rarely invented figures but they did play around with raw data and dressed them up in suitably propagandist dresses. The housing achievements were among those statistics which were released with fanfares. Shortly before the collapse of the DDR, a great victory was celebrated: in the 1971–88 period 3,059,792 *newly-built* dwellings were said to have been constructed. Truly, a tribute to socialist planning! The secret archives revealed the truth. Instead of more than 3m, less than 2m, new housing units had been built. The communist loyalists of the DDR had simply added to the number of genuine new constructions those existing houses which had been improved.

Such crude falsifications were of course never perpetrated under the supervision of the UK's housing ministers. They are however guilty of other statistical sins. When evaluating the state's interventions in the building industry, it is misleading to refer only to the total number of new permanent units. Quality matters greatly and so does size and the provision of auxiliary facilities. In the UK it was of decisive importance *who* received most of the allocated building materials for new constructions. Almost invariably they were developers, mainly in the public sector, who were prepared to build in accordance with the edicts issued by the Ministry of Housing. When the two major British parties vied with one another, each claiming to have achieved more than the other, little mention was made of the *type* of dwellings for which they claimed credit. 'Clever' Macmillan (and those who later aped him) knew what really mattered for PR purposes. It is a fair historical judgement to say that the electorate was deliberately cheated by him. Britain's first housing minister had been the leftist Aneurin Bevan. He pointedly set high standards, opting to build fewer, but high-quality, dwellings. Hence, he attained the annual construction of only 200,000 units and, for this allegedly poor performance, was abused not only by the PR-oriented Conservatives but also by members of his own party. Bevan's biographer quotes his apologia: 'While we shall be judged for a year or two by the number of houses we build, we shall be judged in ten years' time by the type of houses we built.' He maintained that it was cowardly to play the numbers game: 'It would be a cruel thing. If we have to wait a little longer, that will be far better than doing ugly things now and regretting them for the rest of our lives.' He was replaced by the opportunistic Hugh Dalton who, when he penned his memoirs, sneered at his predecessor's passion for high-standard houses. He surmised accurately that Bevan had damaged Labour's electoral prospects. Dalton relates with pride how he had at once countermanded Bevan's minimum standards for municipally-owned flats. His tenure was cut short when Labour was defeated and Macmillan took over.

Unashamedly, this ambitious but competent Conservative went full steam ahead with the anti-Bevan strategy that Dalton had initiated. In Macmillan's autobiography he concedes with amazing frankness that he had no interest in long-term considerations. In his vaunted ruthless style, the civil servants were told that the performance of the ministry was to be gauged by 'a simple test: the figure of houses and flats actually completed'. The direction of this policy could be realized thanks to his absolute control over the allocations of building materials. To maximize the number of new dwellings, he laid down that the average house under construction should be allotted only 90% of the materials that were allowed in Bevan's days. Savings were introduced by, for instance, designing houses with minimum passages. Above all, Macmillan gleefully announced that the size of the new units would be smaller than hitherto. Until he became the national housing boss, three-bedroom dwellings accounted for a considerable proportion of the total built. Macmillan saw to it that this proportion should decline sharply — and it did under his tutelage. When he was no longer in office, politicians of the Conservative Party disparaged Macmillan's dubious record. One such critic would have it that 'some of the meanest council houses were built during the l950s', the Macmillan years, by cutting down on standards. When Dalton had retired from public life and was then no longer constrained by party loyalties, he wrote kindly of the Macmillan-built dwellings. Admittedly, he pointed to the decline in the quality but brushed this aside as a 'secondary debating point'. Full of praise for the political acumen of his successor as minister of housing, Dalton stressed that it was 'the total of new houses which counted with public opinion and public comfort'. Macmillan's adroit manipulation of statistics was also admired by Richard Crossman, the shifty academic who had the housing portfolio in Wilson's first administration. Twenty years after the war had ended and when there were no longer any physical shortages, Crossman still thought it was vital for Labour to emulate Macmillan and play the numbers game. He implored the leader of the Greater London Council to persuade his socialist colleagues

> to reduce the minimum floor-to-ceiling height [of the new houses built by the municipalities] from eight feet to seven feet six inches. I know it sounds trivial [he wrote in his *Diaries*] but it is a matter of the very greatest importance in terms of speedy house-building.

Crossman was happy to be told that if his ministry issues the apt orders, London's socialist councillors 'would be brought into line'.

Macmillan's political heirs have sometimes voiced their acerbic feelings about the erstwhile hero of their party. Peter Walker, a Conservative in the Macmillan mould, was minister of housing in the 1970s when he found it appropriate to distance himself gently from the Macmillan folly: 'It is cheaper and more economical to modernize the existing housing stock than to build afresh'. He pointed to the accomplishments of the Conservative government in 1973: 'We *improved* a total of 453,000 houses ... the campaign was a success and made an even greater impact on Britain's housing then the famous Harold Macmillan campaign.' The misjudgement of the Conservative conference in 1950 still rankled with some veterans in the 1990s. The retired cabinet minister Kenneth Baker wrote disparagingly about the 300,000 debacle: 'It led to the building of the great social disasters of high-rise tower blocks and low-cost estates.' In principle it applies to all capital goods. The manufacturers of turbines recommend to their customers that they should institute yearly checks and heed the repair-and-maintenance instructions. If this advice is not followed, mechanical breakdowns are soon bound to occur. The buyers are also told that if they defer the overhaul for three years, the costs of the maintenance work will definitely be more expensive than the combined costs of three annual routine scrutinies. If no maintenance has been carried out for, say, five years it is near-certain that the turbine with a planned operational life of 15 years will cease to be functional and is destined for immediate delivery to the scrap heap. Entrepreneurs in the private sector have a profit-incentive to safeguard the maximum operational life of capital goods. They will scrape together their last pennies to retain them as long as possible in good working order. In the public sector the same guidelines ought to prevail but this has frequently not happened. The housing policies of successive British post-war ministers of housing illustrate this copiously.

Macmillan won in the numbers game by deliberately pursuing a strategy which inevitably led to the unnecessarily early destruction of many existing dwellings. This came about because he only made symbolic allocations of building materials for the maintenance of existing houses. He was thus directly and personally responsible for turning part of the building stock, constructed before the war, into uninhabitable slum properties which his successors had to pull down. That which was so promising for his immediate political advancement harmed the national economy. He succeeded because the British electorate could not have been expected to appreciate the gulf between 'gross' and 'net'. If, in one year, two million new houses are built while simultaneously one million dwellings become uninhabitable, the net accretion to the housing stock is one million units. In order to maintain (and sometimes to improve) three to four average pre-war dwellings, the financial resources and building materials equalled those that were needed to construct one new unit. However, from a PR standpoint, the political kudos, earned from building 100 new houses, were greater than repairing 400 old houses which transformed them into usable dwellings for many years to come. Even at this distance in time it can be appreciated why an ambitious politician had to reckon with the populist imagery which considered it more laudable to build new houses at the expense of saving a much larger number of old houses. In terms of social welfare and economic optimization, it is now clear where Macmillan went wrong. But is this merely wisdom with hindsight? Did Macmillan know at the time how damaging was his housing policy when evaluated on a net basis? Amazingly, his autobiography reveals that he had been fully conscious of how his positive housing attainments were being offset — if not outweighed — by the rapid dilapidation of the existing housing stock. Macmillan noted that 'millions of houses [are] falling down because the landlords cannot do the repairs . . . A great many houses, whose life might have been prolonged by reasonable repairs, were continually falling below standard.' Macmillan, in his own words, confessed that, when he was minister of housing, he had received a warning from people whom he regarded as experts. They indicated to him that his ministry was in effect responsible for the unnecessary destruction of wealth. He cites the report of the Sanitary Inspectors' Association, according to which 'the annual wastage of houses was equal to and perhaps even exceeded the new accommodation likely to be made available. This was due partly to the deterioration into slums of some of the older houses, but even more to the lack of repairs.' No further proof is required though one may still conjecture as to why Macmillan introduced such devastating evidence into the autobiographical account of his life.

The Inflation Gadget

In J. Alt's considered view

> the perceptions of inflation are not worth investigating because popular perceptions of price rises are wildly inaccurate and idiosyncratic and public knowledge of the term 'inflation' is low. Whenever people have been asked, it appears they believe that, even though income goes up, prices go up faster.

I regard this generalization as only partly correct. I have found that it only applies to moderate doses of inflation but not to the public's responses to run-away inflations. I do not regard inflation per se as a cataclysmic evil and consequently treat with some scepticism Keynes's prognosis, written in 1919 when much of Europe was in ruins:

> Lenin is said to have declared that the best way to destroy the capitalist system was to debauch the currency. By a continuing process of inflation, governments can confiscate, secretly and unobserved, an important part of the wealth of their citizens . . . Lenin was certainly right. There is no subtler, no surer way of overturning the existing basis of society. By this method they not only confiscate but confiscate arbi-

trarily. The process engages all the hidden forces of economic law on the side of destruction.

There are many more effective ways of destroying capitalism than through inflation. Lenin destroyed by non-inflationary means what there was of a Russian market economy. The British Labour Party (from Attlee to Callaghan) emasculated successfully much of British free enterprise; the unbridled power of the unions, punitive taxes and nationalizations were more weighty instruments of destruction than the debauching of sterling. Keynes did not foresee that many of the iniquitous aspects of a tenacious inflation can be nullified by ingenious legal and illegal techniques. Several countries in Latin America and Asia have successfully demonstrated this to be so and, as a result, many economies with hyperinflation have registered larger increases in their real GDPs than Western democracies with very low rates of inflation. Chancellor Macmillan discovered to his delight that Keynes did not intend his sweeping statement to refer to the kind of inflation which the UK has had to endure.

Macmillan described himself as an apostle of Keynes and cites his observations on the subject to exonerate himself and other devious democratic politicians who made use of inflation for nefarious reasons. His friendly biographer refers to a taped interview in which Macmillan affirms his philosophy according to which it is salubrious for Western politicians to run a country with some kind of inflation: 'A permanent inflation that's too high, it's not fair to the saver, the creditor who is normally in the saving classes . . . So Keynes always said, between 2.5% and 3% — then nobody would notice . . . and this we achieved.' Macmillan was jubilant in his retirement when he held forth on this kind of 'mild' deception. He justified it by leaning on Keynes's sacred authority. If you cheat the public just a little, people will not notice it and it is therefore also politically painless. Alan Booth has unearthed a pertinent document, which was prepared by a group of Treasury officials as WWII was coming to an end. Disingenuously, these senior civil servants advised their political masters how much better off they would be politically if in the post-war period, they created a moderate inflation: 'A rise in prices and incomes, sufficiently slow to avoid a violent disturbance of the expectations of the recipients of fixed income, yet sufficiently perceptible gradually to unloose the dead hand of debt, has much to be said in its favour.' These pearls of wisdom were not written for the enlightenment of the masses; they were penned to enlighten naïve politicians how they can dupe the public. At the same time, as this British plot was hatched, Milton Friedman — then a civil servant in the US Treasury — was asked to compose a speech for his political boss, Henry Morgenthau. The purpose was to exhort the American public to buy saving bonds issued by the government. 'I found it impossible to write an honest speech. I believe it is absolutely disgraceful that a democracy should demand of its high public officials that they lie to the people they are talking to, and knowingly lie.'

Whatever else they are, mild inflations are disguised taxes which, without explicit parliamentary consent, transfer *gratuitously* certain resources from the private sector to the state. Milton Friedman — perhaps facetiously — has pointed out that they are the sort of taxes which obviate the necessity to employ additional tax collectors. (It is only right to mention that while the state is clearly the main beneficiary, there are also other inflation winners, such as the banks and corporations with outstanding non-indexed debt.) That Western governments have on the whole gained from inflation is an historical fact. It is, however, more difficult to ascertain whether politicians have brought this about inadvertently or with deceit aforethought. If we are to believe his cabinet colleagues, President Johnson knew what he was doing when he rejected the advice of economists who urged him to raise taxes and/or curtail domestic spending in order to finance the galloping costs of the Vietnam war. The President turned out to have been a superb political strategist in that he opted for inflation instead. He was rewarded because, for a considerable time, he managed to make the US public believe that they were eating free lunches. Indeed, it was only after a span of three years that the chickens came home to roost; his monetary engineering had resulted in the doubling of the annual inflation rate.

The people of the US were more backward than the wise and experienced citizens of Brazil who have too often had their fingers burnt by their politicians' inflation tactics. In Brazil, an unheralded inflation strategy of the kind which President Johnson pursued, would already have shown up in the national price levels within three months, if not within three weeks.

(a) When governments increase the money supply, they are effectively levying a tax on all who have monetary cash balances and/or current bank deposits. There is a time lag before the victims pay the whole amount of the levy but, finally — however much they squirm — they cannot prevent the state from collecting it. (b) When embarking on inflation, the full consequences are rarely transparent at the beginning of the process. Inflation generates an effective demand for goods and services that exceeds supplies at the, initially unchanged, prices. Only after some time, during which the augmented money supply works itself through the system, do the price levels go up (but it would be a fluke if a doubling of the money supply were to raise automatically the price level by 100%). (c) Among other inimical consequences is the adverse impact upon those who were net lenders, ie those who had invested in bonds or extended credit to suppliers and others. (d) Inflation does not reduce either the nominal value of the National Debt or the size of personal and corporate borrowings. The state, as a borrower, does however benefit indirectly and in time because, *measured in real terms,* the National Debt and the costs of servicing it are effectively curtailed. Pari passu this also applies to individual and corporate net borrowers and thus this — for some — beneficial feature of inflation causes the suffering of the borrowers, referred to in (c).

There was a period in the 1970s when lenders, for example those who had bought UK government securities, lost every year 7% of the *real* value of their holdings. More poignant is the case of individuals who invested in 1951 £100 in British treasury bonds with a life of 40 years. There are governments, many governments, which have at one time or another reneged on the repayment of state bonds. British governments of all complexions would never do such a dastardly thing. Honour-bound, they have always repaid their debts in full. Hence, the mentioned patriotic lenders were in 1991 promptly repaid the whole of the £100 they had invested in 1951. The RPI had jumped from 100 in the month in which the bonds were acquired to 1,514 in the month in which they were redeemed. Apart from the inflation-levy that the investors suffered periodically on their annual interest, the 1991 repayment of their £100 investment consisted of 100 nominal pounds sterling. While in 1951 the funds they lent to the Treasury could have purchased £100 of a given basket of British goods, in 1991 the nominal £100 could only buy a basket with £7 of identical British goods.

Personal income tax allowances, state pensions and welfare benefits are nowadays index-linked but these adjustments are made only once a year; the same applies to most wages and salaries. In the years following WWI, Germany was ravaged by a runaway inflation of such dimensions that the nominal wages and salaries were modified every few days. In the years following WWII, several countries in Asia and Latin America with runaway inflation also had to make the wage/salary adjustments monthly or at least quarterly. But in most Western countries, even in the days of relatively high inflation, index-linked emoluments were and are usually adjusted only annually. This gives rise to what economists call a 'financial drag' that makes inflation a blessing for the Treasury because the inflation-induced rises in the price level, which are reported upon monthly, are ignored and taken account of only — in those cases where the government is the payer — on the first day of each financial year. The inflation-victims lose out because the indexing does not occur simultaneously with the increases registered in the RPI. The Inland Revenue also comes into its own because — until the tax thresholds are changed — many employees, who receive their annual wage increases in the middle of the financial year, are lifted (temporarily) from the lower to the higher tax bands and individuals, hitherto exempt from personal taxation, are thus dragged into the fiscal net.

Modest inflation — more likely than a runaway inflation — is a capricious fiscal weapon which can cause havoc, particularly in the private manufacturing sector. To arrive at corporate profits, the Revenue allows manufacturers to deduct from their gross profits the depreciation on capital assets. The permissible annual deductions, formulated in percentages of the acquisition price, are laid down irrespective of the pending rate of inflation even though the rise in the price levels determines largely the genuine replacement costs. The revenue authorities are professionally indifferent and as a result assess companies to corporation tax on illusory gains made in the past accountancy year. Inflation can even bring it about that unrealistically-calculated net nominal profits are assessed to tax though the companies are actually operating at a loss if their accounts were prepared realistically by incorporating the government-induced rise in the price levels.

Inflation-engendered index-linking is a concept unknown to our grandparents.[1] In countries with hyperinflation this is an absolute necessity for without it their economies cannot function smoothly. It is a clumsy but comprehensive instrument. No medium- or long-term contract is entered into unless it is index-linked, from alimony payments laid down by a judge to renting a flat to borrowing or lending money. The consequences have proved to be phenomenal: the pains of inflation are temperate and there are few serious victims. The state, however, is in large part deprived of the many benefits which it could have obtained had the inflation rates been low and index-linking would therefore not have been practised so intensely. In economics, where inflation is not so rampant as to produce total index-linking, the state does gain more at the expense of law-abiding citizens and companies.

In the 1960s and 1970s UK's politicians were busy 'printing money', the figurative term which the man-in-the-street uses to describe the main cause of inflation. The government tried to have the best of both worlds: they wanted to avoid imposing visible tax increases and simultaneously aimed to stem the inevitable rise in the national price levels. Strict statutory wage controls were imposed. (Corporations which broke the letter of this edict were penalized with a battery of sanctions. Ford which, to settle a bitter strike, paid its manual workers in the UK higher wages than the authorities thought it should, was punished.) For two main reasons price controls were introduced at the same time. Politicians instituted them as a ploy which sought to convince the labour force that these were an appropriate quid pro quo for wage controls. The second, more prosaic, target was to curb the upward trend of prices for the politicians had to assuage the feelings of the aggrieved population that measured its well-being by the

---

[1] Index-linking in this book refers exclusively to the movements of the RPI, the retail prices index. In some countries index-linking is geared to the movements of the national currency against, say, the US dollar and/or other monetary barometers.

rise in the prices of consumer goods. This in turn gave rise to the surreptitious manipulations of the RPI.

In certain countries this was not an urgent issue because the statisticians were willing to produce false data when ordered to do so. (Official figures for inflation in the DDR, from 1980 to 1989, registered a total increase of 0.1%. The statistical office of the West German government has calculated that the true DDR inflation figure was 12.3%.) In the UK the government statisticians were never ordered to produce misleading data — this was done circuitously by their scheming political masters.

In 2005 the British government had only a general interest that the official measurements of the price level should be relatively low in so far as this influences the payment of emoluments in the private sector where now practically no indexing prevails. The government, however, has a strong specific budgetary reason for keeping the index as low as possible because much of its expenditure is statutorily index-linked. British chancellors, from Nigel Lawson to Gordon Brown, and also the finance ministers of other countries, have shamelessly thrown overboard the consumer price index in use and substituted for it another index when this promised to record a lower inflation rate than the former. (Gordon Brown's choice of a new index in 2004 was derided because it excluded all housing costs and municipal taxes.) Astute politicians have rarely hesitated to construct a new, to wit 'favourable', index that then became the authoritative guide to inflation.

In 2006 there co-exist in the UK six official national comprehensive indexes, each of which reports a different figure for the rise of inflation during the preceding twelve months. In the year 2000, Tony Blair, Britain's prime minister, formally accorded the government's Office for National Statistics 'political independence' — except when it was engaged on measuring inflation; Britain's chancellor of the exchequer was to retain control over the 'scope and definition' of the chosen index 'because of its importance'. When the Royal Statistical Society expressed its displeasure, the chancellor's office issued a statement which said that 'any attempt to talk it up into something is misleading'.

In Franco's days the Spanish authorities had enough clout to arrange for the publication of mendacious statistics. These were distrusted by educated and non-educated Spaniards. After the dictator's demise, a new director, Ricardo Torron, was appointed to head the National Statistical Institute and the government could no longer take for granted the servility of the statisticians. In 1976 Torron arranged for a new index to be constructed, one which contained 389 items as against the existing one which covered only 244 products. When Torron announced that in future Spain's inflation data would be based on the new index, the government vetoed it as Torron's more accurate index showed Spain to be experiencing a higher rate of inflation than that measured by the old one. The cabinet accepted Torron's resignation. His staff could not afford to resign but at least they were no longer afraid of being punished for open defiance as they would have been under Franco. They released to the press a letter in which they protested at being compelled to work with an obsolete index that would affect adversely the accuracy of the Institute's published inflation figures. Democratic governments, that manipulate the inflation data by opting for a 'favourable' index and are also guilty of the cheating outlined below, risk that their index-linking is no longer regarded as genuine. This is bound to induce interested parties to construct an index that serves their own partisan purpose.

France, which used to have a great many indexed wage contracts, discovered this when the CGT, the largest union federation, denounced the official index as a flawed measuring rod. The unions created an index of their own which at times reported inflation to be three percentage points above that of the government index. The CGT insisted that, in future, employers signing labour contracts with an escalation clause must use its index. The Renault company was the first which was compelled to concede. This alarmed the authorities. It was like a shot across the bows, warning the incumbent government not to cheat too blatantly if it wanted their official index to be treated as an acceptable measurement of inflation. Even in the US the government, in November 1981, had no compunction in proposing to change the weighty 'housing cost' component in the national consumer price index. Critics pointed out that Washington would be the main beneficiary from the new index as it would now denote that inflation had risen less than under the existing index. This betokened higher revenues from the index-linked income taxes and lower social security pension payments. The unions which had medium-term indexed labour contracts were also up in arms. The president of the AFL-CIO federation, Lane Kirkland, denounced the changes in the RPI and sneered: 'If you don't like the measurements of inflation, invent a new yardstick.'

Large segments of the public display an intense interest in the periodic measurements of inflation even if they are not directly affected by index-linking. All over the world, behind closed doors, governments have cooked the indexes in one way or another. It is a universal truism that when democratic politicians introduced legislation, enabling them to control prices in order to halt large wage hikes, they centred their attention on those goods represented in the basket of the relevant indexes. The selection of which items are to be components of the index is to some extent a political decision and so is the exclusion of certain sensitive products and services. The manipulators are concerned mainly with the weighty items but even in that sphere a caveat must be brought in. To collect periodically the prices of, say, the article 'marmalades', the statistical researchers do not bother to examine the prices of the many brands on the market. They choose, in great secrecy of course, one of the brands, the prices of which are then taken to indicate the average for all 'marmalades'. This presents the deceivers with an easy task. With a given amount of money, intended to lower statistically the price of the item 'marmalades', they need not spread it to cover all brands but can concentrate on the trademark which matters. Australia seems to have been the country where we have bona fide evidence that such deceptions first took place. We owe this knowledge to Colin Clark who, however, only disclosed it after he had become a recognized academic personality in England. As a young man he had worked for the government of Queensland where, already before WWII, wages were linked to an RPI:

> I remember myself receiving an urgent query from a price-fixing official as to which particular kind of jam was included in the index number so that he could take special steps to keep its price down. This tampering with the index by selective price control constitutes plain dishonesty.

Retrospectively, Clark makes the salient point that at the time not many people comprehended how indexes were constructed and the financial consequences thereof. Even the few who knew were therefore not worried about this tactical cheating of the ignorant public.

Three decades after this venture, an honest and loyal member of the British cabinet spoke openly about the merits of selective tampering with the RPI. The discerning Peter Shore, an economist and ally of Prime Minister Harold Wilson, had concluded that the control of *all* UK prices should be abandoned. It ought to be replaced, so he said, by specific interventions in which only those prices were kept down 'which needed to be kept down'. If Short's prescription had been candidly implemented, it would have made transparent the clandestine sham game that dishonest politicians were and are playing. Richard Crossman claims credit for having torpedoed the proposal. There exist of course several other opaque tricks. Price controllers have readily acquiesced in the overt and covert downgrading of the quality of weighty items in the index. Almost without exception, they do not take into account the black market however large its size. 'Ingenious' double-dealing also proved helpful when multi-product firms were encouraged to charge unsustainably low prices for their index-vital goods. As a reward ways were found to compensate the companies for their resultant losses by allowing them to increase considerably the prices of those of their goods which were not represented, or not represented heavily, in the RPI. When Edward Heath followed in the footsteps of his socialist predecessors and set up price and wage controls, he found this kind of cross-subsidization to be a constructive technique. Bakers were ordered to freeze the price of the standard loaf of bread even though the needed inputs had become dearer. To prevent bakers going bankrupt, the controllers accompanied this draconian edict, relating to bread which had a very heavy weight in the index, with a compensatory gesture: they allowed the prices of buns and rolls to be lawfully raised by 25%. The Conservative government could now bask in the glory of having provided the population with low-priced bread, rescued the bakers from economic extinction and contorted the official measuring rod of inflation.

The RPI obsession accounts, in part, for the UK's high income taxes for these are of course not a component of the RPI. Chancellors Callaghan and Healey complained that they had little fiscal room to manoeuvre and sincerely wanted to raise more revenue through increased indirect taxes. Both relate that they were frustrated by their colleagues who would not let them bring in higher indirect taxes because this would raise the inflation rate as measured by the RPI. When Callaghan hatched his 1966 budget, he encountered strong objections from his cabinet colleague George Brown, who was in charge of RPI manipulations, when — as an alternative to increasing the already high income taxes rates — he proposed to increase the duties on cigarettes and spirits. George Brown won of course. Margaret Thatcher was bold enough to reduce the income tax rates and as a counteract raised the rates of VAT; this caused a spectacular rise in the index. The Conservative prime minister had toyed with the proposition, implemented by the ministers in several countries, to eliminate VAT altogether from the index; she did not do so after she was advised that the resultant distortion of the RPI would have been so visible as to create an unpleasant public outcry.

While such a radical step did not therefore prove feasible, post-war UK budgets have been framed with the specific aim of discouraging price rises that bear upon the RPI, and in particular to spare the items with a heavy weight. UK's nationalized industries used to be run with enormous losses because the managers were told to charge below-cost prices; these governmental orders distorted the RPI without any hocus-pocus though they were millstones which impelled the Treasury to augment the National Debt. Richard Crossman relates that in the spring of 1967 the economic ministers in the Wilson government were resolved to curtail the growing deficits of the public utilities by raising their prices. As the managers of the state-owned corporations were preparing to carry out those instructions from the cabinet, they were told to stop doing so. The back room boys in 10 Downing Street had convinced the prime minister that the ensuing increases in the RPI would grievously undermine the prices-and-wages policy. The minister of transport who had already instructed the railway authorities to put up the fares also had to rescind his order. Almost at the last moment the railway bosses were told 'to keep the price of tickets down'. A ridiculous, but true, story is told relating to Tony Barber, the chancellor in Heath's administration. Jock Bruce-Gardyne, later himself to become a Treasury minister in a Thatcher government, described how Barber initiated the VAT from which, however, he had exempted most food products — but not sweets. These details were announced in 1971. A year later Barber changed his mind; he chose to exempt also sweets. Bruce-Gardyne reproached him for this volte-face:

> I protested vigorously. Having at that time two small children of the sweet-consuming age, I told the chancellor that I found it crazy that we should thus encourage our offspring to wreck their teeth. Tony Barber was sympathetic but unyielding. 'It's worth a whole point off the RPI', he explained.

How deeply does politics tinge the RPI? The mentioned manipulations are sometimes so finely tuned that they can influence the reporting of inflation on the eve of a general election. Lord Donoughue, after he had left his post in 10 Downing Street, told the House of Lords about the

> wicked fiddling of the numbers by the government. If it happens, it happens through subtle political and departmental pressures which can never be documented. We should be aware that honourable people in the fields of poverty and unemployment have alleged that the statistics in those areas are manipulated for political reasons.

To back up his accusation he quoted the Royal Statistical Society which had published its 'own devastating critique of the state of government statistics'. Lord Donoughue also relied on the Public Accounts Committee which had

> reported on the retail prices index and savagely criticised both its collection of data and the construction of the index ... Many other doubts have been expressed about the quantity, the accuracy and the timeliness of our statistics ... The RPI certainly matters.[2]

Lord Donoughue should know.

During Carter's re-election campaign the prices of some important items in the indexes, which had been expected to

---

[2] House of Lords *Hansard*, London, March 13 1991.

rise, actually dropped. Whether with justification or not, the Republican candidate Ronald Reagan charged that the incumbent administration had played with the statistics for PR reasons. He used strong language when he claimed that the price indexes had been rigged to create a 'cruel hoax on the American people'. Valery Giscard d'Estaing may have made French history when, in February 1973, on the eve of important national elections, the public learnt that the January index had remained unchanged. This zero rate of inflation was not a fluke but had been engineered. At a massive cost of foregone revenues, VAT had been lowered as from the first of January. In his memoirs Harold Wilson denounced the Conservatives who had defeated him at the polls in June 1974 for callously exploiting the vagaries of the RPI. Shortly before the elections, the April data were released. They showed an astonishing jump of 1.53% in a single month. Wilson, long after the event, polemicized that his overall economic record should not be blemished because the month of April was 'in any case, almost invariably one of the worst months of the year because of seasonal facts'. Furthermore, he blamed the Conservative-controlled municipalities for raising local taxes and putting up the rents of the dwellings which they owned. (This was a derisory factor but Wilson apparently felt that he must enumerate it in his defence.) Wilson also lamented that the escalation of the RPI could be explained by bad luck. In April potato prices had gone up 'following the previous year's poor crop — more an Act of God than a machination of Her Majesty's government'. Wilson's pitiful alibi is detailed here to illustrate the electoral importance which an erstwhile prime minister attached to one monthly RPI figure that he treated as a vital cause for his party's defeat. In any case it was puerile and disingenuous for the leader of the Labour Party, under whose tutelage the RPI had been warped so frequently and effectively, to write in anger about his opponents who merely highlighted facts which the voters regarded as illuminating.

Esoteric Contrivances

When elected parliamentary representatives are cunning enough, they can ward off those of the public who demand to be active players in political decision-making. Shrewd ministers are sometimes in a position to implement policies that they consider to be in the national interest but which would be rejected by the voters if their drift was fully understood. Dominic Lawson formulated the dictum that 'those in power dare not speak the truth'. On the whole he is right. Politicians can accomplish many noble things if they do not have to explain exactly what it is they are doing. If they are able to frustrate opportunistic populism, they can retain much of their idealism and freedom of action. But they have to operate by stealth. It often suffices that they keep quiet about the purport of their good, but unpopular, plans. Alternatively, their aims can be achieved by dressing up their policies in esoteric language which only the initiated can understand. It is also helpful if their propositions are so complex that they frighten off people who might seek to investigate them. If the manipulators perform successfully, many of their adversaries will then have been silenced. People do not like to admit that they have not understood something because it was too difficult to understand. Individuals do not want to lay themselves open to the implicit charge that they lacked the erudition needed to digest the veiled sense of ambiguous and seemingly incomprehensible legislation.

Scheming politicians can, but do not necessarily always have to, lie actively. If the manipulators are able to bridle the truth, obscure the facts and are good at fudging, then only in extreme cases need they utter downright lies. A lack of clarity is of great assistance. One of the tools of their trade is to envelop in fog the edicts which the voters are not supposed to comprehend. Hugh Gaitskell thought that in politics vagueness and complexity are advantages. In his view lack of clarity can be a meritorious device to mask the facts. I am not seated on a high moral stool and hence do not make a virtue out of a necessity as Sam Brittan did when he published his controversial article: *The overwhelming case for paying stealth taxes:*[3] 'I am not defending the deliberate cheating of the public ... We might rather not have a cough and have to take medicine for it. But if we do, why not give the medicine a sweet strawberry flavour?' In his autobiography Denis Healey proudly relates how he, as chancellor of the exchequer, and three close associates, deceived the public by pas-

---

[3] *FT*, London, November 25 1999.

sive lying and were thus able to reach painlessly some desirable goals, which they could not have achieved without their dexterous tricks. The already mentioned Harold Lever, a master in obfuscation and cynicism, was one the four conspirators; Healey wrote that he 'had a supply of what I used to call "Leverettes" or "Lever's ripping wheezes" with which to bamboozle the financial markets; this I regarded as a legitimate objective'. The others were Joel Barnett, the Chief Secretary of the Treasury who was an expert at 'juggling' the budget deficit, and Leo Pliatzky, a Treasury mandarin who, since his youth, had been an avowed socialist. Reading the post-retirement books of Barnett, Healey, and Pliatzky, that contain shockingly frank admissions, one cannot help conjecturing what would have been their political fate if the public had previously had the slightest idea of their innermost thoughts. Barnett confessed that as an active politician he had to suffer the

> inability to speak freely . . . That one learns to accept as part of the job. Clearly it would be rapidly self-fulfilling prophecy, if I, as Chief Secretary, were to express my darker thoughts freely and publicly. No, 'speaking freely' and 'Open Government' are fine aspirations . . . But truly Open Government, even with the most ardent advocate in charge, can never be more than a myth.

In the 1970s British governments were criticized sharply on two germane counts, both of which Healey's team managed to deal with: (a) the large budget deficits which had to be covered by state borrowings and (b) the frighteningly high proportion of the public sector within the GDP. The conspirators were able to make immediate changes which, in the public perception, constituted laudable achievements. Without falsifying figures or uttering an untrue syllable, these miraculous feats were accomplished though they did not deliver any substantive improvements. They were PR exercises. What Healey's Treasury did was on the whole positive but it was presented — and that was the deception — as if something real had happened and this was wholly untrue. One of the major items, explaining the huge budget deficits, was the state financing of housing. The money went either to the municipalities or to housing associations. In the national accounts the subsidization of housing was of course a component of the growing Public Sector expenditure about the size of which there were so many complaints. The Treasury disbursements on housing swelled the budget deficits for the finance was not procured through taxation but by borrowing. Joel Barnett congratulated himself on putting into practice one of Lever's 'ripping wheezes'. A supposedly private sector limited company — which in fact was indirectly owned and controlled by the Treasury — was registered to borrow money on the open money market; these funds were then channelled to the housing associations. This obviated the need for the government to provide the money directly. The private company's borrowings were now no longer considered to be state debts and the whole exercise, i.e. the financing of the housing associations, was no longer recorded in the GDP as a public expenditure. What was the trick? The banks happily subscribed as much capital as was requested and at relatively low rates of interest because the debts were effectively guaranteed by the government. 'By this sleight of hand' — I am quoting from Joel Barnett's memoirs — 'the housing associations received, as before, their money and I got my cut'. (Barnett meant that he could tell his critics that he had cut the budget deficit.)

There is not the slightest reason why the public or members of the government or the MPs should have been knowledgeable enough to comprehend that a country's national accounts can be presented in different garbs without changing any of their contents. Healey was later to write of Pliatzky as an expert in the 'presentation of our public accounts'. When the former chancellor paid him this compliment, he did not intend to convey the impression that this civil servant (or for that matter the UK Treasury) had increased the national wealth, as measured by the GDP. He made it clear that Pliatzky's talents lay in the field of 'presentation'. For our purpose it is enough to point to two modi operandi which are most commonly used to display the national accounts: the GDP at factor cost and the GDP at market prices. Although, numerately, the two differ greatly — the latter is considerably more voluminous than the former — the actual contents are identical. If you switch from one to the other, as happened in the UK when the four conspirators played their games in the 1970s, it is only the presentation of the national product which has changed. But the public at large was allowed to conclude that, thanks to the endeavours of Denis Healey, the UK's GDP had risen considerably from one year to the next. It looked fatter. If one had not studied rudimentary economics, one could be forgiven for thinking that the UK was now governed more efficiently and the average citizen had thereby become more prosperous. Before the decision was made to recalculate the data in the national accounts, the Treasury had released figures which showed that the 'ratio of total public expenditure to the GDP at factor cost, had grown from 50% in 1971 to 60% in 1975'. These numbers frightened many who regarded this as a dangerous development in dirigisme; they also made foreign investors shudder. After the UK had adopted the 'GDP at market prices' formula, Healey proclaimed a victory on two fronts. The GDP was now on a statistically higher plateau and as to public expenditure, this had been reduced 'at a stroke' by £8bn. (Healey did not dare to assert that public expenditure had been cut because the dramatic statistical reduction was due to several 'wheezes' like the mentioned housing expenditure.) Healey went on to illustrate the joint impact of these two determinants: the ratio of public spending to GDP had suddenly fallen from 60% to 46%. In December 1978 Joel Barnett could boast that the victory had been even more impressive. In the budgetary year of 1977-8 the ratio of public expenditure to GDP at market prices was down to 41%. It is only right to acknowledge that these strenuous games had injured nobody and must surely have made a lot of ignorant people a great deal happier.

My next instance also illustrates how ignoramuses were deceived but this time the people who were targeted by the Treasury team were the politicians and activists of Labour's left. Introducing the March 1974 budget, Denis Healey remarked that companies were doing very well and they ought therefore to bear with equanimity the increased taxes he was imposing upon them. His judgement turned out to be abysmally flawed. In November of that year he was compelled to make a U-turn and submit an emergency budget to parliament. He now had to rescue the corporate sector which was being ravished by inflation and clobbered by his March tax increases. Two decades later Healey acknowledged his original mistake, blaming it on the civil servants: 'The Treasury greatly overestimated company liquidity, so that the increases I made in corporate taxes [in my March budget] brought many companies close to bankruptcy.' No year in post-war Britain brought such misery to the private sector as 1974. In the parliamentary debate Liberal MPs spoke of the 'collapse that now faces us'. Edward Heath, the Conservative leader, referred to the 'gravest situation that we have had since the war . . . the real task [of the emergency budget] is to prevent the immediate collapse of a large part of industry'. On this occasion nobody accused the bloody-minded union bosses for it was obvious that they were not responsible for the threat of insolvency which now menaced solid, world-renowned British corporations. Ostensibly, Healey had been right in March when he spoke of healthy company profits but in fact they gave a false impression: the phoney profit statements, prepared as the law demanded it, were meaningless for they ignored the inflationary impact. The taxes were assessed on the basis of putatively healthy profits though in economic reality the companies had earned no profits but made losses when inflation was taken into account to gauge their true financial performance. The liquidity outlook was even more grim. Chancellor Healey had no choice but to be the saviour of the private sector. Had he failed to do so, it would have brought about mass unemployment and the Labour Party would have been seen to be culpable.

British industrialists wanted him to reduce the rate of corporation tax and provide state credits but Healey could not oblige. His boss, Harold Wilson, was rightly fearful that such measures would provoke a backlash from the leftists in their party. Charles Fletcher-Cooke spelt out why the Labour government could not apply orthodox cures:

> Straight [tax] reductions across the board would have been easier to understand, to administer and to work but they are ruled out because of the domestic objections by the chancellor's honourable friends below the gangway [Labour's leftist backbenchers].

The Conservative MP William Clark also said aloud that 'Healey was doing a tightrope act. He had to satisfy his left wing'. In order to furnish clandestine aid to the class enemy, Healey opted for a cryptic, covert policy, the implications of which would not be widely understood. Designedly, he delivered the salient message in convoluted language that baffled all but the experts. He succeeded. Though his plan constituted the most radical pro-capitalist policy of any Labour chancellor, it was greeted with relative apathy not only by the uninformed voters but also by his parliamentary critics. Having recently re-read the verbatim report of the two-day budget debate in the HoC, I found it remarkable how little the MPs referred to his esoteric plan. My impression is that the vast majority did not appreciate how far-reaching it was. This is particularly so when one examines the speeches of Labour's leftists. Only one of their MPs, John Lee, attacked Healey and reproached him for his rescue operation. Unlike his accordant comrades, he depicted correctly the central strategy of the budget which, he said, was intended 'to shore up a reluctant and mutinous private industry'. He advised Healey that as good socialists they should not be concerned if private companies go to the wall. The other leftists did not talk along these lines. Seemingly, they did not comprehend, as Lee did, what a momentous policy was being initiated by Healey.

When the chancellor rose to speak, he did not of course unfold his non-socialist strategy in a scrupulous manner. He devoted only a few dry paragraphs to the new statutory instrument which he was selling to the HoC. In a didactic style he told his, presumably bored, audience how company profits are prepared for submission to the Inland Revenue. Having established the amount by which receipts exceed outlays, accountants deduct from it the value of the opening stock [inventory] and then add the value of the closing stock. Healey went on to say that in inflationary times this produces distortions:

> The cost value of the closing stock becomes much larger than that of the opening stock because the stock is replaced at higher prices. This causes an acute liquidity problem . . . I am persuaded the industry needs a substantial immediate improvement of its liquidity through the deferment of tax on that part of the profit which corresponds to the abnormal increase in the value of the stock . . . I therefore propose that companies should have the right to reduce the closing valuation of their stocks . . . by an amount for which the increase in the book value of stocks exceeds 10% of the trading profits of the business.

This passage is quoted verbatim because it demonstrates the astuteness and competence of Healey, who knew how to bewilder the uninitiated. Who, listening to him, could have guessed that this innocuous stock relief led to virtually no corporation tax being paid in 1976? Voters, who understood what it means to raise or lower duties on petrol and beer, would have been displeased with a Labour government that lowered the existing rates of the corporation tax. Yet, this ominous stock relief did not make them angry for they did not, and were not meant to, understand its consequences. When asked in the HoC whether it would not have been better to reduce corporation tax from 52% to 45%, Lever did not reply. He was of course fully aware that, in terms of PR, the chosen rough-edged instrument of stock relief was politically superior to reductions in the tax rates. Furthermore, he did not dare to say openly that the proposed stock relief would be of much greater assistance to companies beset by cash flow problems. His Conservative critics had to wait years before they learnt that the modest tax reductions which they had advocated would have given only puny aid to the besieged company sector while the enigmatic stock relief proved a more rewarding godsend. According to Joel Barnett, the stock relief at once reduced corporation tax receipts by £800m and the cumulative volume in subsequent years represented tax deferments 'by thousands of millions of pounds'. The chief economist of the CBI, Donald Macdougall, also confirmed that the stock relief 'was worth billions of pounds to business and may well have saved many from financial disaster'. In his retirement Healey wrote with pride that his measure had made 'British companies the most lightly taxed in the developed world'. It is of course highly relevant that there is no record of his having uttered such a boast when he was still in office or hoped to become a minister again. An American business journal explained why a British socialist government resorted to the Healey subterfuge after refusing pleas to lower the rates of the corporation tax:

> To have accepted this proposal would have had an adverse public relations impact on the trade unions which were urged to stick with wage restraint. Healey clearly thought it politically propitious to understate in public the relatively large concession he had made to aid companies in the private sector.

When he had no longer any ambitions to hold elective political office, Barnett let the cat out of the bag. Initially, the architects of stock relief had been unsure of how it would be received by the voters at large. Comparing this measure with past Treasury debacles, Barnett noted with relish that this time the Treasury ministers were not at the receiving end of any 'outcry'.

The Attractions of Capital Goods

> Democracy makes it more difficult for governments to hold down the level of consumption in the degree necessary for rapid development. There is no other road to economic development than a compulsory rise in the share of the national income which is withheld from consumption and devoted to investment.

G. Myrdal, the author, is indeed a celebrated economic *theorist*, for otherwise he would have taken account of the fact that in a democratic society politicians do find it difficult to generate investments at the expense of consumption, even by *compulsion*. What he regards as so vital can usually only be achieved by stealth so that the people are unaware what is happening. Voters may indeed applaud preachers who propagate the blessings to be derived from increased capital investments; frequently this is the case because they fail to comprehend that they are expected to play their role by lowering their own current consumption. State support for investments has to be sustained by higher taxes or other hurtful means. (Private sector investments are often financed through lowered dividends.) Furthermore, Myrdal is guilty of exaggeration when he suggests that 'there is no other road to economic development' than investments. While these are obviously a significant factor, there are many other things that can be done to bring about meaningful economic development; some investments, financing huge capital projects, are even detrimental to the well-being of a national economy.

Myrdal's obsession with the investment fetish is not unique. His semi-religious proposition accords with the ethos of both capitalist and communist societies where the investment cult is nurtured with deep-seated fervour. It is worshipped as something virtuous per se because, allegedly, by its very nature it is deemed to be a positive feature propelling the growth of the GNP. The Treasury mandarin Leo

Pliatzky has confirmed that this approach conditioned the Labour Party's thinking and ushered in the Wilson government's investment incentives; the most luscious grants and fiscal benefits were reserved for large manufacturing plants as in those days politicians thought it preferable to support one huge project rather than a number of smaller ones.[4]

Joel Barnett was a member of a government which idolized new-fangled ideas that it was prepared to back with money from the public purse. A National Enterprise Board was formed, charged with funding all manner of glorious ventures, most of which had this in common: they either crashed or had to be sold at a loss. Barnett suffered from a severe handicap. Before he became a full-time politician, he had been a chartered accountant. He sneered at his colleagues who wanted the world to share their conviction that the UK's future was linked with 'new enterprises like microprocessors'. He recalled that whenever a related investment proposition was aired in the government — together with the demand that money be made available in large doses — most ministers 'wanted to show how up-to-date and forward-looking they were by supporting it with or without evidence of viability'. Barnett, the loyal Labour politician, could not shake off easily his professional past. He had the awkward habit of examining the numerate aspects of projects which the state was urged to support. Without bitterness, he disclosed in his retirement what he experienced when one particularly curious proposition was made the subject of deliberations at the highest government level.

---

[4] These flawed criteria were also widely applied when aid was provided to the Third World during the first three decades after the end of WWII. Quick and effective help for the Indian peasants would have been forthcoming if, say, one million hand-operated water pumps had been supplied. Instead, aid funds were used to finance huge irrigation dams that took many years to become operational. The proportion of the agricultural output in the developing countries, that was fit to be consumed, could have been enhanced substantially if more of their (own and donated) investment resources had been directed to build sound storage facilities. But ameliorated protection against dampness and pests is an unromantic political target. At one time one third of India's food production was badly contaminated or destroyed by rodents. Had the dirigiste politicians of India and the foreign donors been less imbued with the glory of grandiose schemes, they would have given priority to mundane, but wholesome, objectives. This would have brought more material welfare to the poor in Asia than the shipment of thousands of super-large tractors.

Barnett had done his home-work before the meeting and feared that a disastrous decision would be arrived at — as indeed it was. But already before the vote was taken, he felt intuitively that he would lose this battle and the country's economy would be saddled with a modern, loss-making, enterprise. The politician, overseeing the National Enterprise Board, won over the doubters in the cabinet, when 'like a magician, he produced a tiny silicon chip'. Barnett sarcastically concluded his narrative: 'I'm not sure what it proved but it had the desired effect.' Dirigiste- minded economists faithfully believe that politicians, assisted by their civil servants and planners, possess an investment expertise that is superior to that of rapacious entrepreneurs and wicked financiers. Keynes argued that the State — curiously, he used a capital letter — has the ability to 'calculate the marginal efficiency of capital goods on long views and on the basis of the general social advantage'. Keynes's pretentious portrayal of politicians as splendid investors rested on two linked premises. The first related to the unchallenged fact that private-sector investors are somehow disciplined by the economic calculus of the market; this, he seemed to imply, was a bad thing. The second premise surmised correctly that politicians are not subject to the same crippling constraints which apply to private entrepreneurs: backed by the authoritarian might of the state, politicians are in a better position to recruit investment funds. Keynes was certainly right in elucidating how politicians have opportunities to promote [non-profitable] enterprises that are shunned by the despised capitalists. But he was wrong in asserting that this was necessarily to 'the general social advantage'.

Altruistically-minded, dictatorial chairmen of private sector corporations are outside the scope of this book. A diversionary exception is made here because the views and actions of politicians, who were imperious investment enthusiasts, have at times been replicated by autocratic captains of mammoth companies. (I wrote on this at length in *The Ensnared Shareholder*.) Lord Harry Pilkington, head of a famous family firm, was elected president of the CBI. He preached sermons in which he held forth on how bright would be the prospects of the British economy if only greedy shareholders would desist from pressuring directors to pay-out a large proportion of corporate profits: 'We must persuade our shareholders to take a long view. If two companies in identical circumstances make £1,000 profit, the one that pays out £700 and reinvests £300 in the future is worth less, not more, than the one that pays out £300 and reinvests £700.' He scolded Britain's sinful shareholders who looked kindly upon companies which paid out a large proportion of the profits. In one homiletic address he suggested to his fellow-captains of industry that they should ignore the public's prejudices and finance new projects at the expense of current dividends. There was, however, one important snag. The directors of listed UK corporations depended on the goodwill of their shareholders. If the latter did not like what was being done, they could retaliate and either sell their shares or conspire to remove the directors. Many empire-building company chairmen, nevertheless, did take the risk and used retained profits to invest imprudently in uneconomic prestigious ventures. Some escaped punishment while others were penalized for following Pilkington's advice. He, himself, was in an advantageous position for he headed one of only five very large UK industrial companies that were exempt from the constraints that irked the majority of their confreres. Pilkington Brothers was then a private (family) company, not a public one; it was therefore not listed on the stock exchange and its shares could not be sold freely on the open market. (Most of the shareholders were family or the descendants of former senior executives.)

Pilkington exploited his position of strength and compelled them to accept minute dividends, thus freeing large amounts of money for a large project that was being hatched. Pilkington would otherwise not have been able to finance it unless he could draw on large subventions from the state which were not forthcoming. He was also sufficiently knowledgeable to recognize that tapping the money market by floating bonds or issuing shares, which could be freely traded, was not a smooth exercise and would have encroached upon his decision-making status. Above all, by brutally paying out only a small proportion of the profits, the retained profits were 'cheap' capital because no interest was due on them. He was in practice accountable to nobody and could thus afford legally to ride roughshod over the shareholders who were not in a position to revolt. He used the money on a risky research project which ate up large sums during a period of seven years when at any time the whole investment might have had to be abandoned. It did not and Pilkington Brothers became the owners of a floating glass patent that was highly profitable. The shareholders thought that at last they would now benefit from the profits by being paid high dividends. Lord Pilkington, who planned to invest in other projects, had other ideas. This produced a palace revolution on the board, interventions by City institutions and acerbic outbursts by the long-oppressed shareholders. The good man had little choice but to resign. The erstwhile private company was turned into a public company, listed in London, which enabled the shareholders to sell freely their equity — and at market value. Needless to say, the new Pilkington directors — not one of them is currently a member of the family — are highly sensitive to the paid-out profits which affect the price of their shares.

While the UK investment fetish affected the private and the public sectors, the biggest investment failures were those made by the state in the nationalized industries. In the year in which Margaret Thatcher took up residence in 10 Downing Street, Lloyds Bank gave space in its house organ to Walter Eltis, an Oxford don, who published a detailed financial analysis, covering the 17-years performance of the state corporations. His devastating conclusion centred on 'high investment which often has little economic purpose. [They operated] with a lavishment of investment and disregard of commercial considerations; the official presentation of their accounts was misleading.' He wrote disparagingly of the politicians who were guilty of misleading parliament and the voters. Eltis referred to 'hidden subsidies' and proved that the annual reports of the state companies did not convey a truthful picture; the investment performances were more dismal than the public was intended to know. Eltis was not the only critic. The all-party HoC Transport Committee struck a homiletic note when it urged that state industries 'should be above the suspicion of cooking the figures'. This was a prelude to their report which noted that even professional accountants were often baffled as to what story the official accounts were supposed to convey. The Committee submitted that there might be deliberate moves to obscure facts. The bosses of the nationalized industries were in a position where they could manipulate the financial statements. They could sow confusion so that one would not know what constitutes a 'loss' and what a 'profit'.

Nigel Lawson was Thatcher's second chancellor who was responsible for some cerebrally brilliant spectacles. As a politician in a representative democracy he did not hesitate to play by the same rules as his predecessors and, if need arose, he took care not to spell out the unpopular consequences. He had a penchant for swimming against the stream. Already in his first budget he declared war on investment-mania and dealt the ideological investment fetish a fatal blow in 1984. In cruel language he rejected unequivocally the notion that the set of existing incentives, which he was about to wipe out, had served any positive purpose. He argued that the UK had over-invested because much of the boosted investments had been 'low-yielding or even loss-making at the expense of jobs'. Lawson acknowledged that the majority of those firms which executed commercially sound investments would have done so in any case, even if taxpayers' money had not been showered upon them. Lawson did not hesitate to point out that some of the enterprises, propped artificially by state aid, finally collapsed. He scorned his predecessors for pursuing damaging policies:

> There is little evidence that these incentives have strengthened the economy or improved the quality of the investments. Quite the contrary. The evidence suggests that businesses have invested substantially in assets which yield a lower rate of return than the investments made by our principal competitors. Too much of British investment has been made because the tax allowances made it look profitable, rather than because it would be truly productive.

His successor, John Major, said that before the Lawson reforms UK investments could be made to look appear profitable though they were 'not profitable in any real commercial or economic sense'. In 1964 the Wilson government had hinted that 'Britain's investment incentives were the most generous in the world'. Before Lawson's 1984 budget, the UK had definitely no rival. The package of investment subsidies contained financial aid that consisted of various kinds of loans and outright grants, municipal infrastructure expenditure geared to a specific investment project and a host of non-budgetary aids. The height of absurdity had been reached in 1972 when the Conservative administration inaugurated 'free depreciation' for investments in all plant and machinery (but not cars). This unrestricted right to a 100% first-year depreciation was given in equal measure for capital goods with an operational life of one year to 100 years. Had the then prime minister, Edward Heath, increased the overt grants or decreased the corporation tax, there would have been an outcry about his depravity in 'making the rich richer'. The rewarding subsidy which he chose did not, however, meet with any populist resistance though its economic impact was considerable and the costs involved were appreciable. Gone were the days when corporation tax was charged on gross profits less the annual depreciation of assets according to diverse statutory schedules. Henceforth, the whole purchase could in one swoop be set against gross profits and thus wipe out altogether (in the year of buying the assets) any corporation tax liability or at least mark down substantially the appropriate tax payments. Being a deferred tax revenue, it did not need to be listed as government expenditure or capital subsidization.

In the budget which abolished the investment subsidies, Lawson in a drastic swoop — unparalleled in the history of British company taxation — reduced the corporation tax from 52% to 35%. He gave luscious goodies with his right hand which compensated the private sector for what he had taken with his left hand. The opposition parties and the industrialists were in a quandary as to whether his budget should be attacked because of his double-edged strategy. It would have been too much to demand of Lawson that he should tell the HoC 'I hate the investment mania' or 'I shall ensure that in future investments are no longer molly-coddled'. He said none of these things but acted as if he meant it. Lawson remained in office long enough to complete this portentous demolition work. He survived in large part due to his intuitive perception that the voters do not comprehend his 'boring' endeavours. Indeed they did not and this served him well.

So far I have argued that deceptions in general are the tools of the trade of altruistic politicians. I am now emphasising that, in the investment context, stealth bears fruit even more abundantly than in other spheres. When politicians make decisions — for good or for bad — on current expenditure items, they must be ready to face immediate opposition or in any case after a short period of time. It is so much more comfortable to be in charge of a long-term capital project, the merits or follies of which will only be demonstrated in the future and often only in the remote future. When a half-finished capital project, financed with capital raised in the private sector, is discovered to be a white elephant, construction is usually stopped and the losses written off. When a project, financed by the state, is discovered in midstream to be based on a fatal miscalculation, its construction will nevertheless proceed to the bitter end. The stealth so far cited in this book has dealt with the deception of the voters who are deemed to be ignoramuses. The stealth, that is an adjunct of the investment mania and relates to state-controlled investments, is frequently brought to bear on selling a non-viable project to political confreres. This demands specialized and more sophisticated lying.

In the UK a special section of the Treasury annually apportions funds to government departments, nationalized industries, municipalities and semi-autonomous state-owned bodies. The recipients are expected to submit separate claims for current and capital expenditure. It is as a rule much easier to persuade the Treasury ministers to support the latter than the whole gamut of the former. It is easier to obtain money to build a new school than to increase the salaries of teachers. Sadly, it must be noted — as we did in connection with the Macmillan housing debacle — that after the school edifice is erected, it is more difficult to receive annual subventions to make repairs and keep it up to scratch.

When the electorate has to be convinced of the need to spend large amounts on a given large project, the politicians may dupe the public by asserting that this does not lower their current standards of living because the money for the purpose is being borrowed. We have already pointed out why this argumentation is often unsound.

Both in duping the electorate and the Treasury, it is wholesome to present a case in which the anticipated £15m costs of a capital project are deceitfully estimated to be £5m. In some fields it is easier to obtain an approval calling for an expenditure of £5m rather than of £15m. Once the agreed sum is spent, the Treasury will find itself bullied by the ruling politicians to allocate additional amounts to help complete it. If the protagonists of nuclear power generation had submitted an honest and comprehensive cost analysis, the size of the total expenditure would then have been so much higher as to throw into doubt whether the government would have wanted to proceed with it. This is an extreme example which demonstrates that if politicians seek to sponsor a large and long-term capital project, they must lie and do so on a grand scale. The relatively low cost of nuclear power had been one of the attractive selling points put forward by its proponents. The submitted cost-benefit schedules, which vastly understated the commercial cleaning-up expenditure and the costs of ultimately decommissioning the plants, were not widely challenged for some thirty years. The nuclear cognoscenti were of course fully aware that not all the pertinent expenditure items had been included in the original submissions; they chose to treat the missing figures as an unfunded contingent liability. Of course neither the public nor the HoC knew about the mendacious calculations which had been dished up and swallowed by the governmental decision-makers. If Nigel Lawson is correct, all the Conservative and Labour ministers of energy were led astray: 'wittingly or unwittingly, a deceptive case had been made out in favour of the economics – the phoney economics – of nuclear power'. Lawson, an erstwhile secretary of state for energy, conceded frankly that he had been duped – not the sort of admission that he volunteered readily. Who was to blame? He replied that 'ministers can always be led astray by scientific experts' but failed to add that this is less true in the private sector. The real situation was discovered coincidentally in 1987 when the Thatcher government planned to privatize the electricity industry and the component companies. When the City of London attempted to put a price tag on the existing nuclear facilities, they came across the vague conjectures on the contingent liabilities. Some of them arrived at the dismal conclusion that the net worth of Britain's nuclear investment was negative. As a result, the prime minister privatized the non-nuclear parts of the electricity industry but had to retain the nuclear activities in the public sector. In 1997 the protagonists of Scottish nationalism were appeased when the Treasury in London agreed that all UK taxpayers should pay for a luxurious Scottish Parliament building. The cost was said to be about £40m. In the autumn of 2004, years later than planned, the building was finished at an estimated cost of £440m.

As exemplified above, capital investment projects are sometimes promoted with a misleading price label. There are also instances where, for a variety of reasons, the advocates of given projects or investment subsidizations do not state the costs involved which makes it easier to overcome any latent opposition. Being able to claim ignorance about the total costs and/or using esoteric language are efficacious tools. When we referred to the very exorbitant subsidization of investments through 100% first year depreciation, we said that because it was 'deferred tax revenue', the government could claim that it was not an item of state expenditure. What did this subsidy cost the Treasury and how much was it worth to the fortunate beneficiaries? There are no quantifiably accurate answers. This massive subsidy constituted a state expenditure which was so opaque that it could not be properly scrutinized. The politicians, responsible for this innovative financial instrument, were delighted that it was all shrouded in complicated mystery. To arrive at a meaningful calculation, one would have had to make arbitrary assumptions about a variety of factors, especially about the interest rates which were likely to prevail during the actual operational life of each group of assets. The recipients, the investors in machinery, could also only conjecture what was the financial worth of this gift. There were too many uncertainties for this subsidy to be concretely specified as being worth x, y or z pounds.

The most fertile field, where altruistic politicians can cheat splendidly in the public sector, revolves around 'capital consumption'. Keynes would have it that the entrepreneurs of the private sectors are not as ready to opt for investment projects with a long gestation period as are politicians in office. This is indeed correct though hardly for the commendable reason that Keynes cited. Unashamedly, I repeat myself and remind the readers that while incumbent politicians are sensitive about current state expenditure, they need not worry excessively about the accuracy of expenditure estimates of long-term investments. Altruistic politicians can safely issue bogus forecasts and prospectuses. It may be many years before the success or failure of the disbursed public funds is established. If things go wrong the then ministers will be able to blame any debacles on their retired predecessors. When the economic attraction of a capital investment is examined, it matters greatly whether the investment has a life of 50 or 30 years. The longer the period of amortization, the more attractive is the projected yield on the investment capital. Playing around with depreciation rates can be a rewarding game for political investment enthusiasts. As they are not individuals who falsify data relating to a *past* event, they escape being labelled as liars. The politician, who suggests that his proposed project has an operational life of 50 years, cannot be said to be telling a proven untruth — not even when respectable experts assert that 30 years is a more realistic estimate. After all the former may insist that the truth will finally be authoritatively established only after 30 years or more. Unless one knows with absolute certainty — like some Biblical prophets — what the future will bring, an outrageous prediction cannot be condemned outright as a misleading conjecture. This, at least, is the sort of convoluted apologia that is enunciated by political altruists who, expediently, obfuscate the truth appertaining to the likely rate of 'capital consumption'. Railway enthusiasts, who do not base their passion wholly on environmental grounds, are in deep trouble when they seek to bamboozle the Treasury and the public in order to obtain massive investment funds on economic grounds, to wit when they plead that travelling by train is cheaper than driving a car or coach. They have been known to make use of misleading assertions concerning the gestation period of new equipment. The planners of British Rail once forecast what would be the return on the finance needed to acquire new diesel trains. Their calculations assumed a working life of 40 years. If this were true, their proposed investments promised to be profitable. In other parts of the world such trains were projected to last only 25 years. Independent UK experts advised that British Rail's application for funds from the state should be judged in accordance with the more realistic assumption of a 20-year amortization.

Some Deplorable Obscurities

In democratic societies the annual budget and auxiliary documentation are presented to parliament for approval. In theory this is an accountability exercise in which the politicians in office set out the true and meaningful totality of the state's revenues, expenditures and the resultant budgetary deficits or surpluses of the past and coming years. My illustrations below are real in that they have all existed and/or still exist in some form or another in the Western capitalist world. They have this in common that they do not appear overtly, fully and specifically in the governmental budgets. When I support my argumentation by referring to old age pensions, export subsidies, protectionism, foreign aid, and other matters, I am in no way expressing a view on whether the expenditure on these items should be expanded or contracted. My critical observations dwell on the oblique manner in which they are honestly and dishonestly presented by politicians. The readers ought to join in my gratitude to Joel Barnett who was for many years in overall charge of the many papers which the British Treasury released for public scrutiny. Because he, later in life, enlightened us incisively on how some of them had been formulated, he should be forgiven for his ministerial sins: 'Finding ways of cutting the PSBR [i.e. the budget deficit] *without having any real effect* occupied our most fertile minds' (my italics). But this was not a game that only socialist politicians played in the UK. As far back as 1970, Edward Heath's administration was greatly worried for it faced a prospective overt budget deficit of £2b. To its aid came the government's chief economic adviser who was later to rejoice on how he had managed 'in 48 hours' to reduce the forecast deficit to just over £1b. But, he told us in his memoirs, this was not done by cutting expenditure. No, he boasted, I altered the PSBR in the offing *'without any changes in policy'*. Donald Macdougall was eager to let it be known that he arranged the hocus-pocus in a painless manner. He made his political bosses very happy.

The State Pensions

Since the end of WWII, UK citizens are statutorily obliged to pay, apart from income tax, National Insurance, which among other things provides the 'forced savers' with a state pension. Until today the majority of British people believe that it is a genuine insurance arrangement while in fact it is another, partly progressive, income tax. The premiums are not wholly related to the size of the pension; the National Insurance pensions are therefore only to some extent, but certainly not fully, geared to the premiums. If one buys a policy from a private insurance company, actuarial and not socio-political considerations determine the level of benefits. Thus, females, who are expected to live longer than males, pay higher premiums than males for identical pensions. Yet, the National Insurance acts on an obverse principle which has long been acknowledged to be nonsensical. Not only do British politicians not demand higher contributions from women but, moreover, females can draw the basic National Insurance pension from the age of 60 while men are only entitled to do so when they reach 65. Females must have worked only 39 years — while men need 44 years — to qualify for the maximum pension.

The statutory presentation of government aid to senior citizens is altogether in statistical shambles. The *overall* cost (per individual recipient) borne by the state is in part an enigma. Only the National Insurance payments are overt. The unspecified costs of free medical prescriptions for those over 60 are hidden in the budgetary provisions for the National Health Service. So is the free annual optical examination of elderly people made by private practitioners who are recompensed for this service. When the National Insurance pensions are not deemed to suffice because the recipients have no capital or other income, supplementary payments are made from the governmental welfare funds. Municipal councils compensate, under diverse conditions, bus and train companies for the free (or partly free) travel of old age pensioners; this concession is funded through council taxes. At year-end senior citizens receive from the state a flat-rate amount of cash, known as the 'fuel allowance'. Senior citizens, who are looked after at home by carers or are residents of special homes, are financially assisted by the local authorities and the central government. All owners of TV sets must pay a hefty annual fee to the state-owned BBC; senior citizens are exempt. Some additional benefits, the unspecified costs of which are paid out of the public purse, are furnished by various governmental departments.

Exports of Agricultural Product

Exports of agricultural product and natural resources are sometimes heavily taxed, especially in LDC countries. In some cases these taxes are meant to be punitive so as to discourage foreigners from buying them. The purpose of these (uncollected) export-taxes is to subsidize in a roundabout fashion the processing of the mentioned goods by indigenous manufacturers who are not as good at this job as the more efficient processors in other countries. For example, the export of fresh oranges from Latin America is sometimes curbed in order that the indigenous canners of orange slices and the bottlers of orange juice have an opportunity to buy the oranges relatively cheaply; the processed products are of course exported without export taxes. As an overt alternative to this covert circuitous subsidization, the state could of course have helped their inefficient processors with cash subsidies. These, however, would have appeared in the budget and might also have contravened international conventions on export subsidies. The British government once banned the export of scrap metal at the request of its steel-makers for whom this was a vital input. The reason why scrap metal was at that time no longer sold to British steel-makers was due to a sharp rise in the price of scrap metal in neighbouring France. The government could have pursued one of three policies. It could have forced the scrap metal merchants to sell to their traditional buyers at home or it could have entered into its budget an item 'subventions paid to the distressed steel industry' or it could have banned the exports. Politically, so much more expedient to choose the last mentioned covert avenue.

The Imposition of Import Controls

The imposition of import controls, either through high tariffs or outright prohibitions, has been and to some extent still is a beloved technique employed by politicians who want to reward surreptitiously their native inefficient manufacturers. By either the overt or the covert method, the local consumer pays for it — knowingly or not. Orthodox protectionism used to be the most important subsidy at the disposal of governments which chose to assist local producers by extra-budgetary means. In 1990 Sweden had very low tariffs; the customs duties totalled less than 5% of the value of all its imports. This seemingly admirable average excluded, however, the special protectionist imposts and restrictions which the Stockholm authorities operated to limit the import of farm products, textiles, clothing and footwear. Foreign institutions estimated that these hidden subsidies — to protect inefficient Swedish farmers and manufacturers — equalled a tax of 8% on the incomes of the average household. These hidden subsidies were of course not recorded in the Swedish budget. Most Swedish citizens had a vague idea that they existed but only when these findings, calculated by critical foreigners, were disseminated did they realise how onerous they were. The compilers of Washington's bulky budget books were also remiss in not informing the American voters how hefty were the implicit subsidies received by Chrysler, Ford and General Motors in the wake of the Washington-imposed 'voluntary' quota system that was intended to curb Japanese imports through hiking the price of Japanese cars in the US market. West European consumers suffered on the same score. Their governments subsidized the indigenous car producers by restricting the imports of Japanese cars. In the absence of this obscure state intervention, Japanese automobiles would have been priced 15% less. The EU (and its predecessors) have mollycoddled the European farmers by subsidizing them through cash payments for producing inefficiently but profitably. These and some other overt subsidies do appear in a sanitized form in the EU budgets. However, financial mist envelops the covert subsidies, the most important of which automatically lift domestic food prices: the EU imposes variable import levies on food imports. This is not done to generate revenues for the EU but to stop the physical inflow of many foodstuffs. EU consumers are thus in fact compelled to buy locally produced food at prices which are very much higher than they would have been if imports were not restrained in this manner. The non-cash techniques are very helpful to the decision-makers in Brussels. They protect them from the opprobrium which they would have had to endure if the *comprehensive* cost of the agricultural subsidization were ascertainable in a fashion that the man-in-the-street could grasp easily. According to the OECD, *only one half* of the total annual costs of the agricultural policy — which lowers the living standards of 95% of the citizens of the EU — is registered as such in the budget books of the EU.

Protectionism can be supplemented, or substituted for, by a less sharp but extremely devious weapon. My two UK illustrations were typical at a time when manufacturing was still an important activity of the public sector. Though the state-owned monopolist, the NCB, was the most pampered recipient of overt subsidies, the clamour for additional substantial aid from the taxpayers was vocal. If the politicians had granted this through visible budget allocations, it might have made the public think twice about the merits of keeping artificially alive an uneconomic monster. Most of the UK-produced coal was destined for the generation of electricity for which another nationalized corporation was responsible. 10 Downing Street issued a strict order to the latter, saying that it may not import better-quality and cheaper coal from abroad but must buy its supplies from the British coal monopolist. Obviously, there are no official figures to value this vast subsidization which hurt particularly hard Britain's fuel-intensive manufacturers. Only, when the English electricity monopoly was broken up and two private sector electricity generating companies came into being, did the public obtain some idea of the billions of pounds of covert subsidies which this clandestine technique had cost the British economy in the post-war years. It was estimated that the two private firms, thanks to Thatcher's privatization, could save £400m per year — equal to 10% of their total fuel bill — by the gained freedom to import coal; it compelled the NCB to adapt its formerly monopolistic prices to the new reality. Harold Wilson's government was very eager to ensure that a British-based, private sector, computer company should flourish but British corporate buyers preferred to acquire computers from one of the top four US manufacturers. As exchange controls then still prevailed, it was easily arranged that the BoE would refuse to allocate foreign currency for the acquisition of imported computers. To obviate this ban on their exports to the UK, three of the US firms established fully-fledged manufacturing facilities in the UK. This meant that it was unnecessary for British buyers of US computers to make an application for a foreign currency allocation. The UK manufacturing subsidiaries of foreign multis were and are treated by the British authorities for almost all purposes on par with UK-owned enterprises. As the sole British computer corporation was already heavily subsidized overtly, it did not suit the government to augment the visible state aid. Orders were therefore issued to all government departments, nationalized companies and institutions, such as universities which received state money for research, that they were not allowed to buy the computers made in the UK by the subsidiaries of US-owned firms.[5]

Exports Subsidized Candidly and Surreptitiously

Exports are subsidized candidly and surreptitiously in all countries of the world. Politicians and the public are agreed that exporting per se is economically meritorious. In the UK, Her Majesty the Queen, on the advice of her ministers, publicly honours each year the country's most outstanding exporters. Many a company chairman has received a knighthood because his firm excelled at selling abroad — no distinguished importer has received such an accolade. Economists ought not to join in this adoration of the export cult, particularly as the export-mania does not differentiate between sales abroad which benefit the country where they are made and those which do not deserve to be acclaimed. Governments hand out export subsidies irrespective of whether the foreign buyer is likely to pay for the goods which he has procured on credit. In few places in the world are the export subsidies given, not on the gross value of the sales but only on the value-added. Thus, to cite an extreme example, a UK exporter of $10m diamonds may receive subsidies and kudos commensurate with this large amount while in fact the true export which he has carried out is only $1m as the exporter, for this purpose, has imported unpolished diamonds from South Africa for $9m. If the subsidies are lavish enough, it may be profitable for firms to export at prices below production costs. When a state-owned enterprise exports, this is not difficult to organize. The erstwhile British state-owned NCB happily sold coal to France at two thirds of the price at which UK coal was sold at home. In this particular case the Treasury gave neither an overt nor a covert subsidy. The nationalized body, being a monopolist, could afford these loss-making exports by hiking the domestic price. Similarly, the EU has savaged farmers in the LDCs by dumping its agricultural exports at below-cost prices. Where is the support for these exports registered? The officials of

---

[5] While this circuitous subsidization proved initially helpful to the British-owned computer firm, its survival depended on the allocation of further massive subventions. The government therefore had to agree at a later stage that the company could be taken over by a Japanese firm.

the EU would laugh if such a question were put to them for these implicit subsidies are absorbed through higher consumer prices in the member-states. Two anomalies illustrate the ludicrous reality.

(a) Before Ireland and the UK entered the Common Market, the NCB found it difficult to market its output in Northern Ireland which was of course part of the UK. To overcome this, UK coal was exported at a loss to Ireland, a foreign market, where merchants then found it profitable to sell the subsidized British coal to Northern Ireland.

(b) The Amsterdam-based Royal Dutch Shell exploited the export subsidies offered by the German and British governments, respectively. Shell's German subsidiary had its ships constructed in the UK where the yards could offer lower prices to foreign buyers as the built ships qualified for export subventions. Shell's British subsidiary had its ships built in German shipyards which in turn could offer lower prices for the British orders as they were heavily subsidized by the German taxpayers.

In the distant past export subsidies were paid out overtly and were of course recorded in the annual budget. Because of Western cross-border agreements such an honest course is now outlawed. This means that practically all state subsidies are now either covert ones or overt ones, the costs of which are, however, are not disclosed to the public.

The most costly UK subsidies are those provided by the state agency, the ECGD, which provides guarantees and acts as an insurance company that underwrites long-term credit given to risky foreign (mainly LDC) customers. All British governments, like most OECD governments, have also been happy to provide cheap borrowing facilities to help finance the attractive credits which are offered to foreign buyers; these are known as 'soft loans'. Foreign buyers know about the British export-mania and exploit it. They need make only a small (and in extreme cases a zero) down- payment. Many of the repayments, which are rarely index- linked, are spread over 20–30 years at relatively low interest rates. It is a good business for the buyers and the only reason why it is also profitable for the patriotic exporters is that the government provides enough subventions to make it worthwhile. But above all, the UK exporters cannot go bankrupt. If the foreign buyer reneges on the interest or capital payments, the

ECGD bails out the British exporter though (like his confreres in other countries) does not automatically declare the guilty buyer to be in default. They may transform the amounts owed into another long-term credit with, say, no interest payment due for five years. The ECGD has over the years made losses of billions of pounds — in 1989 alone this amounted to £440m — because so many buyers, including foreign governments, have not honoured their agreements.

In 2004 the ECGD was owed more than £10b in deals which it had backed. Most of it will probably never be repaid and the Treasury will then belatedly acknowledge this by writing off the debt. It is of great political significance that only after many years, often decades, does it become an incontrovertible fact that the pertinent export had not benefited the UK economy. The time factor is decisively important. It is not possible to say with absolute certainty, at the time when the export project is submitted to the ECGD, whether the government is well advised to risk providing the hazardous insurance. When events finally prove that the decision had been a foolish one, the guilty politicians, who at one time basked in the glory of helping British workers to keep their jobs (through unrequited exports), are no longer ministers.

At the 1977 Labour Party conference Prime Minister James Callaghan was cheered when he told the delegates that thanks to his intervention thousands of shipbuilding jobs would be saved because he had arranged an export deal with communist Poland. The once famous British shipbuilding industry had become highly inefficient and foreign buyers knew it. But like the NCB, the industry became a sacred cow; in the then prevailing ethos, it merited being sustained from the public purse. The Labour government could of course have paid the redundant workers lavish bonuses not to work but to sit at home and watch TV. Presumably one would then have learnt of the cost involved from reading the budget documents. Alternatively, the authorities could have provided overtly a 60% subsidy for each ship ordered from abroad. This would have set dangerous precedents and would probably have led to retaliation from other shipbuilding countries. The astute Poles were happy to suggest a hare-brained scheme to their beleaguered socialist comrades in Britain. They were ready to buy at a bargain price of £125m 24 vessels. The government offered to offset the high production costs against this relatively low price: it said that this amounted to a subsidy of £15–20 m. In 1980 a parliamentary committee investigated the extravagant affair and found that the subventions had exceeded £70 m. But this was not enough to pay the wages because the astute communist Poles were not prepared to pay even a deposit, not a single penny would they remit to Britain, until the ships were in service and earned foreign currency. Though international agreements forbade 100% export financing, the government waived this rule and provided the Poles with 100% credit to be repaid only after seven years. The prime Minister and his advisers had no plausible grounds for believing that Poland, known to be approaching insolvency, would ever honour the credit arrangements. By 1981 the vessels were earning good money for the Poles but they defaulted formally, not having paid even the current interest due on the various loans. This is a significant instance when the leader of a political party used the export-mania as a means to sustain a domestic industry which was on the rocks. The Polish owners of the UK-constructed vessels were now in a position to undercut the prices of British shipping companies, especially those that were plying for trade in the UK. By 1982 some British seamen had lost their jobs because cargoes, traditionally carried in British bottoms, were now transported in the unpaid Polish vessels.

One Plus One Is Not Always Two

Juggling with figures is of course not the same as lying by inventing figures. While even illiterate voters realise that you cannot compare apples with pears, the public at large rarely discovers the incongruity of arbitrary changes in the *base* of statistical presentations. The president of the Royal Statistical Society described in the *British Medical Journal*[6] the potential confusion which is engendered when 'statisticians are trying to communicate without an agreed vocabulary'. For politicians this is a relished opportunity to deceive the ignorant electorate. The November 1974 general election was dominated by the issue of inflation. Had Labour's perfor-

---

[6] Adrian Smith, 'The Need for Independent Statistics', *British Medical Journal*, London, February 2 1997.

mance been better than the record of the Conservatives? Chancellor of the Exchequer Denis Healey made a sensational announcement that in the month of August the RPI had gone up by a mere 0.1% over July, thanks to the wise stewardship of the Labour government. The August RPI was a contrived fluke and Healey knew this. It was a month in which there were seasonal drops in food prices and VAT reductions, *planned* to take effect just before the general election. On the hustings the chancellor sinned by comparing annual inflation percentages with an unrepresentative three-months period. Healey's unsavoury PR tactics bore fruit at the polling booths. In 1975, the first year after the polls, RPI was up by 24.2% over 1974. In 1977, when it no longer mattered, Healey confessed that his use of misleading percentages had been his 'most culpable mistake' as chancellor. He maintained correctly that the figures per se were accurate 'but I think I made a mistake in saying it because it gave the impression [that] the rate of inflation would go down and down when in fact I didn't think that'. Just so! Edward Heath, the aggrieved leader of the Conservatives, described Healey's pre-election trump card as a fake: 'It was deceit by the chancellor — statistical deceit.' Nobody told Heath about people who live in glasshouses.

Changing goalposts while the players are still on the field can be very rewarding for opportunistic politicians. The humanitarian-minded Blair government stated at the beginning of its rule that by 2004 it will have reduced child poverty by 25% and by 2020 will have wiped it out altogether. This heralded announcement failed however to define how child poverty would be measured. In 2004 a parliamentary committee (with a majority of Labour MPs) was able to expose a statistical trickery. 900,000 children had been removed from poverty by the government's expedient decision to exclude housing costs — an important item in the budget of poorer families — from the official child poverty indicators. An opposition spokesman praised this report because it had demonstrated that the government was 'caught red-handed trying to change its figures'.

Quality changes can obscure the honesty of a variety of numerate data. When, for example, the state-owned Royal Mail is in financial difficulties and therefore raises its prices, most electors comprehend that they have thereby become worse off. Dishonest politicians therefore show an interest in alternative schemes which also help the Royal Mail financially. By paring down the frequency of deliveries and collections, cost reductions are considerable. But, as the deterioration in the value of the postal service is not clearly visible and quantifiable, the distress suffered by the public is less painful than a straight increase in the postal rates and of course the quality changes are not reflected in the official price indexes.

Manipulating meaningful averages is a fruitful, but not an edifying, pastime of unscrupulous politicians. Such deceitful behaviour was practised widely by the protagonists of the Blair government who wanted to convince the public how much better the Labour Party was managing the NHS than its predecessors. A large number of staff were recruited to measure periodically the performance of the NHS in general and of single hospitals in particular. The tables they produced were supposed to indicate the excellence of the NHS over time and the superior achievement of hospital A compared with that of hospital B. As the NHS and almost all hospitals are multi-product institutions, the (comparative) overall worthiness can only be judged by their *average* performances. For PR reasons, the Blair government wanted especially to highlight the rising *number* of operations carried out and the shrinkage of waiting lists. The administrative manager of each hospital was charged with recording improvements in accordance with these two statistical criteria. To put it crudely, this meant that hospital treatments, examinations and in particular operations for difficult cases, which were time-protracted and called for the more intensive attention of the medical personnel, were given a lower priority. Cases which were relatively simple were attended to more quickly. The noted statistical *average* improvements were thus often largely due to the priority accorded to the latter. In some places this produced clashes between the administrators and the medical specialists. The latter protested against the policy of aiming at a high average which lumped together indiscriminately all kinds of operations (and other treatments), irrespective of the medical complexities involved. There were also many reports about juggling with waiting lists.

The National Accounts

The national accounts are prepared by professional statisticians. The politicians do what is in their power to make them look as palatable as possible, with special reference to three features: the GDP should be as big as possible while the National Debt and the proportion of the public sector within the GDP should appear to be as small as possible. If the country has a predominantly free market economy, the value of the national output is largely determined by the prices at which producers actually sell their wares. However, the value of the output of the public sector monopolies is not always represented accurately in the National Accounts because its prices and costs can and are manipulated by the government. A very substantive share of the GDP has artificial price tags though I doubt whether more than a tiny minority of the public have the slightest idea that this is so. While the statistical size of the shoe-manufacturing sector is determined by a free market valuation, this technique cannot be applied to the output of millions of individuals in the public sector whose 'products' are not sold in the open market. The output of the NHS personnel, teaching profession, the judiciary, police and army and the rapidly growing number of state-employed administrators, managers and civil servants is measured arbitrarily by one factor: the costs of their emoluments and fringe benefits. It is assumed that these equal the arithmetic value of their activities and are recorded as such in the National Accounts. This perhaps understates the true contribution to the GDP made by some of them. On the other hand the capriciously calculated GDP output by the majority of the mentioned individuals may well constitute a crude statistical exaggeration.

Politicians do not hesitate to alter the definitions governing the National Accounts when it suits them and they have reason to believe that they will not be punished by the electorate for statistical sleight-of-hand. For years the Italian government refused to acknowledge the numerate significance of the country's black market economy; it did not acknowledge it as a part of the officially defined GDP. One day the Italian politicians decided to incorporate this vast illegal output. Consequently, the authorities in Rome were able to boast at home and abroad of their sudden economic successes; they could point to the fast growth of the Italian GDP from one year to the next.

Harold Lever has been dead for some time but leverettes are still appreciated in 10, Downing street. In the twenty-first century the PFI, launched by the Conservative chancellor Norman Lamont in 1992, is in full swing. Private contractors build, finance and own (state-controlled) schools, hospitals and other capital projects by entering into leasing agreements for up to 60 years. As private sector contractors find it more expensive to procure finance than does the government, the overall PFI costs to the taxpayers are ultimately greater than they would have been if the government had continued to provide directly the financial wherewithal for public sector capital investments. From the standpoint of PR, however, British politicians, guilty of the PFI trickery, have thus been able to halt the growth of the (nominal) National Debt. In addition, they have implicitly reduced the statistical size of the public sector.

Tax Exemptions a Duplicitous Machination

Tax exemptions are a duplicitous machination by which governmental extra-budgetary financial awards are channelled to corporate bodies and individuals, engaged on what the politicians in office regard as meritorious activities. All over the world a variety of dispensations relating to income, inheritance, sales and municipal taxes are in place; these make some mockery of the putative accountability to parliament by ministers of finance with regard to all state expenditure and revenues. In the UK we have had since WWII exemptions, the beneficiaries of which have been the private company sector, charities, export salesmen, senior citizens, religious institutions, political parties, 'deserving individuals' and those carrying on 'desirable pursuits'. The Inland Revenue publishes regularly a brochure, listing a large number of these extra-statutory tax exemptions. When the Treasury pays out subventions overtly, these are often announced in speeches by the chancellor of the exchequer and always recorded in the budget papers. Politicians, bestowing non-budgetary tax privileges, are usually not in a position to inform the public how much these cost. In some cases the rich were by far the largest beneficiaries. At one time Britain's most weighty tax exemption was accorded to owner-occupiers of dwellings who could write off the money they spent on servicing their mortgages. The very poor who paid no income tax lost out altogether while the very wealthy who were subject to a 98% top marginal tax rate could write off almost all their mortgage liabilities. If tax exemptions were abandoned, the government could commensurately reduce the existing tax rates. Alternatively, if the tax abatements were replaced by overt subsidies, the public would at least know the size and character of the state munificence.

Scheming politicians — many countries have a far worse record than the UK — find the status quo to their liking. A remarkable illustration, which dates from the days when the public regarded the British coal miners as saintly individuals on a par with the nurses, is still extant in the twenty-first century though, quantitatively, no longer the weighty political factor that it once was. As already mentioned, the operations of the state-owned National Coal Board were heavily subsidized overtly and covertly. The relatively high wages were supplemented by several fringe benefits, one of which was the right of each miner to receive annually five tonnes of coal. This applied not only to active miners but also to their widows and all retirees. The Inland Revenue would ordinarily have taxed this emolument but, on political orders, allowed the concessionary coal to be tax-exempt provided it was used in the homes of the miners or ex-miners. Five tonnes were such a large quantity that a portion was sold on the black market by many of the recipients. As years went by, environmental prohibitions increasingly prohibited the burning of coal in many areas of the UK. In any case the well-off miners found it more convenient to heat their homes with gas and electric fires. The diminishing demand for illicit coal and the lessening of opportunities to dispose of it progressively reduced the value of this fringe benefit. Hence, the robust miners' unions demanded that the employers (mainly the NCB) should henceforth, on request, pay in cash the value of the five tonnes. There was no question that this payment was equivalent to a money wage and income tax was due on it. Various British governments twisted the arms of the Inland Revenue which had to agree, under protest, that the tax exemption of coal would apply also to its monetary equivalent. By 1993, when the NCB was being privatized, only 30,000 miners were still working but more than 200,000 retired miners remained entitled to the tax-exempt cash payments, awarded in lieu of concessionary coal.

Dubious Loans

Politicians are sometimes in a position to camouflage deviously the extent of their subsidization policies. We have already referred to the 'clever' Callaghan tactic of supplementing export subsidies to Polish buyers of UK-built vessels with loans that had no reasonable chance of being repaid. There are occasions on which it is politically desirable to limit the *visible* amount of assistance that is being extended to a given LDC economy. This can be arranged by splitting the proffered aid into two parts: an outright non-repayable grant and a long-term ostensible loan, the interest payments on which need start only after some years. In the absence of a formal provision, there is an implied, non-publicized understanding between the donors and the recipients that if the latter do not repay the loans or not even defray the interest thereon, the default will be condoned.

British governments were too ashamed to let it be known that several of its state-owned enterprises were so inefficient that they could exist only by means of continuous lavish subventions, the real magnitude of which was initially concealed. The overt subsidies were accompanied by state loans, which the political manipulators and the recipients knew a priori would never be repaid. When, for example, after several such loans, i.e. disguised subventions, the debts of the NCB reached onerous dimensions, the Treasury used to announce that the loans are being written off.

A National Lottery

Many countries have a national lottery of one kind or another. It is an efficient contrivance to furnish the governing body of a country, region or municipality with tax revenues that are duly noted in the budget. Alas, it has not always proved politically possible to institute a monopolistic government-licensed and controlled lottery. Some politicians act in a hypocritical manner appertaining to gambling when powerful domestic voices condemn it on moral grounds and, in particular, denounce gambling ventures backed by the authority of the state. In the ethos of several countries it is considered obscene for the state to promote tax-raising lotteries while gambling ventures organized by the private sector for corporate gains are viewed with less abhorrence. Cowardly British politicians once arrived at a workable compromise: they blessed the flotation of state bonds, only the interest on which funded lottery prizes. This, they maintained, was a modest immoral arrangement which was therefore less sinful than full-scale lotteries. *The Times* described it as 'half a gamble'. They were called Premium Bonds and the innovation was launched by Harold Macmillan; it was probably the most remarkable accomplishment of his during his unremarkable short tenure as chancellor of the exchequer. The promoters were given strict orders to deny that this was in any way a state lottery; to protect the buyers of the Premium Bonds from the charge that they were gamblers, they were denoted 'investors'. The unfortunate Macmillan was nevertheless denounced by the leader of the Labour Party for giving the world the impression that the country's solvency 'depended on the proceeds of a squalid raffle'. Other critics in the HoC were outraged by this 'entirely anti-Christian and anti-socialist appeal to . . . lower instincts'. The Archbishop of Canterbury described Premium Bonds as an 'undignified and unedifying adulteration of public duty'. No wonder that the UK had to wait till the last decade of the twentieth century before a fully-fledged National Lottery was allowed to come into being. But even then its mammoth fiscal contribution to the British Treasury was cloaked in deceptive garbs.

The buyers of lottery tickets were put at ease by the politicians of all the national parties who assured them that they had no reason to feel guilty about gambling — the British Lottery was merely a conduit for transferring the money of altruistic citizens to charitable objectives.[7] For years I have spoken and written in favour of a national lottery but I never contemplated that the resultant gambling revenues taxes — an alternative to a further increase in the conventional taxes

---

[7] When I won a tiny prize, I received a letter from the promoters congratulating me on being a National Lottery Winner. There was not so much as a hint in the long letter to indicate that I had gambled and thereby helped my government to collect billions which were, however, not called 'taxes'. The promoters wanted me to feel good and explained that 'every time you play a National Lottery game, you help a Good Cause'. I assure my readers that I was not motivated by this noble notion.

— would be cleverly disguised in humbug by politicians who lied shamelessly. If it was moral to tax brothels, the sale of tobacco and the consumption of alcohol, why should not the country benefit from the taxation of lottery tickets? Admittedly, 10 Downing Street borrowed the sanctimonious publicity from foreign countries, where the politicians were also bashful about gathering revenues in a depraved fashion, but this did not make the UK government's apologia less mendacious.

The Japanese regarded it as obscene that the state budget should be bolstered by unclean revenues. It was forbidden to describe the state's profits from the lotteries as taxes because they 'are used for the development of educational equipment, road construction or repair, construction of dwellings, expenses for public prosperity and welfare'. This of course was pure double-talk. In other countries the alibis appealed to the moral sentiments of the gambling sinners. In Greece it had at first also been difficult to set up state-controlled lotteries but, thanks to the blessing by the Archaeological Society, Greek politicians were able to welcome two state lotteries without pangs of conscience: the profits were to be dedicated to the 'high purpose of financing excavations as might prove necessary in connection with the Acropolis'. After some time the profits were diverted to other purposes. The Greek government still asserted that its gambling ventures were cultural institutions that had a 'purely social character' and were conducted 'in the spirit of the highest modern criteria of public integrity'. Dublin pioneered its, morally ambivalent, national lottery several decades before the opposition of the moralists in its neighbouring country had finally been overcome. Very astutely, it was not called a lottery but a sweepstake, run by a Hospitals Trust. All the profits, except for a small stamp duty, were sent to Irish hospitals. Who would have dared to suggest that it is immoral to buy lottery tickets to help finance research into the causes of cancer? The double-tongued officials in Dublin went out of their way to boast that 'the proceeds of the Irish sweepstakes do not appear in our government's budget'. In a way the Irish politicians did not lie for it was certainly true that the sweepstake was run by a non-government agency. But this was a legal fiction because the draws were held under the protection of the police and the proceeds were paid into a fund, administered by trustees who were appointees of the government. The Irish claimed — as do the political tricksters in other countries where the revenues of the national lotteries are also handed over to charities — that the financial gambling awards to their hospitals do not influence the budgetary allocations to hospitals by the Irish state. This is a moral fig leaf. In the absence of the 'private' money from the sweepstake, the Irish government would have had to increase taxes to furnish additional finance for its hospitals.

The same political expediency has determined the manner in which the National Lottery is sponsored in the UK. The publicity does not highlight the direct and indirect benefits accruing to the Treasury. Instead there is the boast that 'over 140, 000 Good Causes have benefited from National Lottery funding including the Central Beacons Mountain Rescue Team'. The National Lottery operates entirely according to the dictates of the government and the trustees administering the Good Causes funds are also state appointees. Sometimes the cat is let out of the bag. Thus, when the Treasury is asked to finance a desirable enterprise for which it prefers not to make an allocation from the state budget, it has been known to tell the applicants that it will see to it that a Good Causes fund of the National Lottery provides the money. An act of parliament has laid down how the money, gathered from the sale of tickets, is to be spent. After deducting a prescribed percentage for expenses and managerial profits, 55.5% of all the revenue is allocated to finance the prizes; 31.1 % goes to Good Causes; only 13.3% is officially a tax accruing to the Treasury. If the Good Causes funds did not exist, the finance for many projects, now funded by the National Lottery, would have to be raised through the state budget. It is unadulterated bunkum to assert that the majority of the British public, who buy lottery tickets, do so because it makes them feel good to know that they are contributing to charities. They spend their money because they crave for the high prizes. Of course, if public opinion pollsters would ask them why they buy the tickets, many — perhaps most — would reply sanctimoniously that they are doing it for altruistic reasons.

The Lacunae of the National Debt

When approached for a loan, banks investigate not only the prospective borrower's certain financial liabilities but also his contingent ones. Those who are found to be solvent on the first count may nevertheless be treated as risky borrowers if they have heavy commitments on the second count. Governments, however, like to be judged solely on account of the certain liabilities which are incorporated in the National Debt, though implicitly and explicitly they also guarantee borrowings, pledges and undertakings by state agencies, nationalized corporations and government departments. (The ECGD is a good example.) There are good reasons why all contingent liabilities ought definitely be disclosed in the National Accounts. Private Sector companies are obliged to state, according to prescribed calculation methods, the pension liabilities for which they are responsible. If these exceed the assets of their pension funds, the deficits are an important element determining the financial worthiness of a corporation. The British state does not fund the index-linked, final salary, pension liabilities relating to millions of individuals, such as civil servants, MPs, policemen, judges, NHS personnel, teachers, soldiers; the pensions are paid from departmental budgets if and when they are due. The government provides periodically estimates of the total volume of these liabilities though critics would have it that they underestimate the likely cost. What is not done is to house these pending, but certain, commitments within the National Debt — and for good PR reasons. In April 2004 Watson Wyatt, an actuarial firm, released its estimate of the UK state pension liability. It amounted to nearly £600b. The size of the official National Debt was £400b.

Chapter VII

Two Vague Conclusions

> If the source of the problem is democracy, how can it be solved democratically? D. Marquand

With some lapses I have steered clear of homiletic exhortations in my analytical presentation of the book's two subject matters, the nature of truth and modern representative democracy. I did, however, attempt to pierce the veils of hypocrisy. My aim was to set out relevant descriptions but avoid displaying prescriptive messages. In this, the last chapter, I am straying from my precepts. Unfortunately, I have found it beyond the bounds of possibility to arrive at definite, comprehensive conclusions. Only to a limited extent was this feasible when comparing representative democracy with alternative systems. But my findings appertaining to truth and lying have also not lent themselves to being measured and evaluated to enable one to reach meaningful, firm and all-embracing conclusions. It can only be said that the merits of most cases must be judged individually in accordance with the moral criteria of each examiner. Intellectually, this is an impotent and cowardly culmination. But, unlike in the exact sciences, such an indeterminate verdict is not uncommonly the fate of many subjects of contention in the social sciences.

Democratic Governance

The size of the population of a country, aspiring to be a relatively independent political force on the world scene, is of great relevance — irrespective of whether the rulers are dictators or have democratic inclinations. Lichtenstein, Wales, Estonia are too small to be equipped with the expensive paraphernalia which a viable modern state must possess. The People's Republic of China is definitely too colossal and this will increasingly become apparent as its inhabitants are now beginning to taste the fruits of democracy and will want in future to influence directly the way they are governed. The same probably applies to India. The political structure of the United States is somewhat too cumbersome to allow all its citizens to feel that they are determining in a meaningful manner their own political fortunes: thus, many residents of Miami and Seattle feel politically remote from the powerhouse of Washington; there are, however, as yet no important secessionist forces and the English language is a powerful bonding element. The EU's attempts to become the United State of Europe may be thwarted by the historical, cultural, economic and linguistic features of the memberstates which are scheduled to be deprived of their sovereignty. The larger the population of a country, the less pronounced is the identification of its citizens with the state; the less does it matter to many of them whether they carry a passport of country A or country B. This is accentuated when nation-states are geographically vast and diverse in the make-up of their electorate. The USSR was one of the 20th century's superstates which was torn asunder. Its demise was due to religious oppression, tyrannical curbs on personal liberties and, above all, the pursuit of socialist policies which proved economically disastrous. But a vital element was also the simmering consciousness, felt by tens of million in the non-Russian regions, that it was preferable to belong to a medium-sized nation-state, with which one could more readily identify, than to remain a subject of the heterogeneous conglomerate administered from Moscow.

    Democratic governance does not depend only on the 'right size' of the country but also on the manner in which the voters can express their preferences. Our late friend Pericles ruled not only over a small area and population, which nowadays would rule out Athens as a viable state, but he also governed with direct democracy which is today seen to be inimical to efficient government. Switzerland's system of frequent national referenda has not been emulated by any large state in the twenty-first century; in any case it makes a mockery of parliament. The election of representatives, middlemen between the population at large and the government, is with us to stay. Neither the government nor elected presidents but the MPs are the main cornerstones of democracy. Universal suffrage and an electoral system, which the population believes to be confidential so that their own voting records cannot be discovered, are barriers foiling extra-parliamentary violent actions; they are safety valves, perhaps even antidotes to revolutions. This is on the whole a valid appraisal but, as Germany in 1933 and the experience of some other countries have shown, it is not an impregnable guarantee.

Today's parliamentary representatives face challenges that were not boldly apparent in the world before 1951. As previous chapters have exemplified, the voters are no longer obedient. They no longer recognize that the MPs they select are wiser and more proficient to judge what is good for the people than they are. Nowadays they tell their elected representatives how they should behave and vote in parliament. It is no comfort to the MPs that this unwarranted conduct and the concomitant relinquishment of the electorate's deferential stance are not confined uniquely to politics. Alvin Toffler reports that 'American doctors are under siege. Patients talk back'. The fact that most voters are stupid and their judgements about political affairs illogical, derisorily selfish and mostly superficial is not a novelty and the persons who seek a political career should surely be aware of this. If they feel they cannot live with this reality, they ought to seek an occupation where they do not depend on the approbation of ignoramuses. Michael Dukakis, who was defeated in the 1988 presidential contest, had been a governor of Massachusetts for one term and expected to win again but, to his dismay, the voters abandoned him at the polls in favour of an ex-football player. He was disgusted with the populace's rejection which, in his view, demonstrated that they were incapable of recognizing what really matters. Gary Wills relates that Dukakis asked himself if there is any reason 'to want the people's esteem' when they were capable of repudiating a person like him who was so much more knowledgeable than the 'clownish' candidate who replaced him: 'They are clearly not qualified to judge excellence.' I am sure that Dukakis was intellectually and perhaps also in other respects well equipped to serve the people superbly. But he has also proved that in our democratic age he, who stressed rationality and rejected the partialities of the Great Unwashed, was not an individual who was suited to represent an ungrateful and non-obsequious electorate.

Well-informed and sincere reasoning is not the hallmark of democracy in the twenty-first century. Opinions are not necessarily moulded by evidence that has established which are facts and which are delusions and fables: instead, it matters greatly what people believe to be true, which is why perceptions now rule supreme in politics as in other fields. In the past the views of the uneducated masses were also often founded on unproven, unreliable and irrational thinking but this did not cause so much harm for the political decision-makers, the parliamentary representatives, were of a kind who could afford to shrug this off and exercise their judgements in a cerebrally sound manner. Keith Davey, a Canadian senator, summed up succinctly today's environment: 'In politics, perception is reality.'

As the masses are today in a position to compel MPs to act in accordance with unproven assertions and reckless notions, politics has become a different ball game. But a dangerous pitfall awaits the representatives who feel obliged, in their own interest, to take account of a given policy supported by the majority of the electorate. Sometimes, many who belong to this majority are merely lukewarm supporters of the opinion which they profess; a few only are passionately concerned to see the policy implemented. On the other hand certain minority views, held by protagonists of fanatical causes, are buttressed by vehement fervour. The intensity with which certain minorities propagate their views can be a more potent factor than the dissemination of the views held by the less clamorous majority. MPs may be cajoled, pressured, and become subject to strident denunciations by the minorities that will be highlighted as newsworthy by the media while the contrary views of the majority are treated as blasé and consequently receive less publicity.

One may safely concede that representative democracy produces inefficient governance. In so far as economics is concerned, the GDP and the material well-being of the country are affected adversely. Denis Healey, an experienced chancellor of the exchequer, on whose competence to manipulate I have already commented, summed up his views on democracy when he was in retirement: 'It is much easier to manage an economy if you can use electrodes on the most sensitive parts of those who refuse to cooperate.' If one ignores this recipe, there is an alternative. A host of commentators have said, some glibly and sometimes seriously, that without lies humanity would perish of despair and boredom. Others have expounded that lying is an indispensable part of making life tolerable. These are far-reaching generalizations to which I do not subscribe. The half-hearted modest conclusion I have arrived at, reluctantly and somewhat shamefully, is that representative democracy can, at present, be best sustained if we tolerate it that altruistic MPs lie and deceive their voters.

There were and are people in the West who reject this reasoning and opt for a more definite panacea, i.e. dictatorships of one kind or another. Because I regard democracy as prone to bring about inefficient and weak systems of governance which, inter alia, are impediments to a faster growth in the material living standards, I am prepared to justify dictatorships in certain LDCs and in extreme circumstances even in Western countries on a temporary basis, if security considerations demand it. In theory at least there is much to be said for benevolent dictatorships (with or without servile parliaments). They can do much good provided the rulers do not exploit the situation to enrich themselves. The altruistically-minded Lee Kuan Yew, Singapore's founding father, instituted an authoritarian rule, directed by himself in person. He was not satisfied with parliamentary resolutions about the desirability to ensure clean public places — he draconically forbade the consumption of chewing gum. He thought it was in the interest of Singapore to discourage uneducated families from bringing too many children into being — he punished those who did not act in accordance with his edict by means that most of us in the West, including those who may agree with his aim, would not have endorsed. He did not want the youth of his country to emulate the, as he saw it, degenerate customs of the young people in the West — he restricted the visits of foreign pop stars and government posters proclaimed explicitly that any citizen with long hair, as defined by exhibited pictures, was automatically relegated to the end of the queues in post offices. Lee Kuan Yew's unorthodox rule made Singapore the envy of its Asian neighbours in so far as the growth of its GDP was concerned.

There are two reasons why, despite the flaws of our Western democracies, I find the case for dictatorships unpalatable. Even if the rulers are honest men and do more good for the material well-being of their citizens than would otherwise have been the case, the governance of benevolent and efficient dictators is fraught with danger. Their appetite might grow in the course of time and they, or their successors, could finish up as bloodthirsty rulers. The only way then to get rid of them is to topple the regime by assassinations or rebellions with all the ensuing bad consequences. But more importantly — to me at least — is the reflection that, despite all the drawbacks of the democratic governance prevailing in OECD countries, we have many civil rights, freedoms of expression, more or less independent judiciaries and the opportunities to replace an incumbent political party at a general election. Being as materially wealthy as we are, we can afford to be ruled by politicians who dare not introduce unpopular measures that would raise even further our material living standards. For the sake of our liberties, I reject authoritarian regimes first and foremost on the ground that I would rather enjoy our non-material freedoms at the expense of seeing our GDP grow faster. I am not very happy about my choice but the balance, however slim, is surely in favour of representative democracy and the concomitant right of MPs to utter, expediently, things they know to be untrue.

The Truth About Lying

Before my final thoughts on truth and lying are exemplified, some principled approaches that govern my thinking on the subject must be laid out. (a) Having already made crystal clear my rejection of perfectionism I am taking my opposition a step further. There are a host of semi-perfectionists who join the 100% perfectionists in rejecting any telling of lies but merely concede that in certain circumstances one may withhold telling the truth. To me this is intellectual cowardice which I scorn outright. I maintain that there are occasions on which one has even a duty to lie. (b) In the chapters in which lying was defined and described, I did not differentiate between morally good and bad liars. Whoever uttered or wrote things he knew to be untrue (and intended to deceive others) was connoted a liar. That was a clear, unadulterated semantic tenet. What I am attempting now is to advance beyond this formal definition to depict situations in which, by subjective criteria, some lies can and should be classified as good and others as bad. (c) Mahatma Gandhi has asserted that 'truth never damages a cause that is just'. This is factually not the case. Truth can and does often cause serious damage. (d) The truth is sometimes multifaceted. The British army was decisively beaten by the German army in May 1940 and had to retreat ignominiously; all the military transport and some 1,000 guns were lost. Germany's history books rightly portray this as a glorious victory. The successful evacuation of some 340,000 British and Allied troops from Dunkirk is recorded in Britain's history books as a heroic victory. It is indeed truthful to boast of a great achievement that, thanks to 200 British naval vessels and many civilian-manned small boats, such a large number of soldiers were successfully transported to England and thus escaped being incarcerated in German prisoner-of-war camps.

When the Truth is not Necessarily Virtuous or Efficacious

According to Michael Rubinstein, the dissemination even of true happenings which a person did not want disclosed was originally regarded as criminal libel. Modern libel laws find an individual guilty only when a false accusation is made.[1]

Individuals, who have confessed or been convicted of telling one substantive lie, are sometimes doomed never to be trusted even when they tell the truth. The Texan billionaire Ross Perot — once a presidential candidate — had a policy of not employing persons who had committed adultery on the ground that 'anyone who lies to his wife will lie to me'. Some thought it rash while others applauded the prominent Conservative John Redwood when he commented acerbically on the sexual involvement — exposed by the tabloids — of David Mellor, a former colleague in a Conservative government: 'Anyone who can betray his wife can betray his country.' Chancellor of the Exchequer Callaghan not only lied when he carried out a sterling devaluation but prided himself on being a good patriot who misled others in order to

---

[1] 'The worst libel can be the truth.' This pearl of wisdom was coined by an anonymous philosopher.

serve his country's national interests. He regarded his lying as necessary and virtuous. Yet, he demanded of the prime minister that he be given another important cabinet position when he resigned as chancellor. Why? He maintained that having once lied about an important economic issue, his credibility had been eroded in this field.

Under certain conditions telling-the-truth is not appreciated. This is so when people are made happy by being told a lie: they do not to wish to know the truth, they want to be lied to. Wise individuals may choose not to give true testimonies if they are aware that their stories will not be believed and perhaps thought to be 'the truth of a madman' — if the truth is not plausible, it tends to be rejected. When Kissinger planned a secret visit to China in July 1971, he first flew to Pakistan and this was well known to the world's press. When he clandestinely flew off to China from Pakistan, the ploy caught everyone — with one exception — by surprise. The *Daily Telegraph's* local correspondent, Mohammad Beg, discovered the truth and filed this world scoop to London. The editor, who did not accept its validity and even considered that their man might have been drunk, reckoned that if the story were true, the accompanying US press corps would already have reported it. The unique dispatch was spiked. Not much harm was done by ignoring this truthful story that was soon officially confirmed. But there are many occasions, on which news is cold-shouldered because it does not appear plausible; often the repercussions prove to be calamitous.

The intelligence services of important states are known to have disregarded vital information when they doubted its veracity on the ground that it went against the grain and conflicted with their expectation on how the country's adversary would operate. Before the outbreak of the Yom Kippur war, General Dayan had received information from Israel's agents about the impending attacks by Syria and Egypt. He ignored it because he thought that it was disinformation for, in his view, Israel's enemies would not be acting as the news suggested. His failure to recognize the truth had serious consequences. In January 1940 a German aircraft crashed in Belgium; it contained the complete operation plan relating to the invasion of France. When it become known that attempts by the pilot to burn the papers had failed, and consequently the Allies were now in possession of these top secrets, the

German army felt compelled to change radically their strategic plan. They need not have bothered for the Allies treated the genuine secrets with disdain because they believed 'that the captured plan was a deliberate deception'. Richard Sorge, who many years after his death was rehabilitated and made a Hero of the Soviet Union, sent from Tokyo exact information about Germany's plans to invade the USSR; he was also in a position to assure his spy masters in Moscow that Japan would not attack Russia simultaneously. This long-standing communist spy sent these truthful messages but they were scorned because Stalin would not hear of any suggestion that the Germans might be ready to renege on the treaty which he had signed with the USSR. Stalin denounced Sorge as a 'shit who set himself up with brothels in Tokyo' and the Russian intelligence service therefore obediently informed him that they now doubted his credibility. Stalin refused to exchange him for a Japanese prisoner as the Tokyo authorities proposed. Sorge was executed by the Japanese to the delight of Stalin; he paid with his life for telling the truth.

An even more brutal story emanates from the civil war in which the Bolsheviks defended the newly established communist state against the remnants of the Czarist army who were supported by foreign governments. Leon Trotsky was the minister of war who expediently recruited officers from the Czarist army for service in the Red Army. The soldiers were largely illiterate and did not trust the officers, almost all of whom had a non-proletarian background. Trotsky promised that anybody, soldier or officer, who deserted to the enemy and was later captured would be shot. One of the officers went missing and it was rumoured that he had absconded to the enemy. He had in fact been taken prisoner and only after some time managed to escape and return to his unit. It transpired that he had been ordered by the military intelligence service to reconnoitre the enemy's positions. The soldiers, however, did not believe this explanation; they were convinced that, because of his social origin, he would be treated leniently and not shot. Trotsky himself is said to have dealt with this affair. He was satisfied that the accused officer had carried out heroically the orders which he had received. But Trotsky was also certain that the rank-and-file soldiers could not be persuaded that this was the truth. If the officer was not seen to be punished, they would be demoralized. Trotsky, for the greater good, ordered that he be shot.

From an ethical standpoint it is highly pertinent whether a benevolent liar, who actively disseminates an untruth, genuinely believes that the ensuing consequences he *intends* to bring about are virtuous. In my view good intentions by themselves do not suffice. The liar must be also in a position where he can foresee with reasonable certainty that his meritorious intention will materialize the way he had planned it. If his lies do not bear fruit as he predicted, he can no longer claim to have been a benevolent liar. The obverse also applies. When a person tells the truth, he cannot rest on his laurels just because he was not guilty of lying. He is responsible for the bad consequences which flow from his telling-the-truth. Philip Agee volunteered for the CIA in 1956. In 1968, following an affair with an American lady in Mexico who was a pronounced leftist, he resigned. In 1970 he began the writing of *Inside the Company* though he was warned that he was subject to a secrecy undertaking that was binding on all ex-CIA employees. The book was completed in 1975 when he also published an article wherein he released a global list, containing the names and locations of numerous CIA agents. Very soon thereafter, the chief of a CIA station, whom he had identified, was murdered by an anti-American group. Later, another CIA station chief, exposed by him, was attacked. Agee did not do it for money but with the aim of harming his former employer, an ambition that was consonant with his new political convictions. This evil-minded man defended what he had done by asserting correctly that nothing he had written was mendacious; it was all true — as indeed it was.

Greater than the Truth

'Not even Marx is more precious to us than the truth.' Thus wrote the French philosopher Simone Weil in 1933 when she was still a revolutionary socialist and we conjecture that this impiety must have been anathema to her comrades. After converting to Catholicism in 1938, she did not change the wording of her aphorism by substituting 'God' or 'His Holiness, the Pope' for 'Marx' — and rightly so. Most Catholic theologians do not regard the truth as a pre-eminent virtue. Human beings can be guilty of greater wickedness than uttering falsehoods. It is indeed meritorious to tell the truth but not always. There are features of good, decent conduct which eclipse the virtue of telling-the-truth. Altruism is thought to be more ennobling than selfishness, but love of God takes precedence over everything. The Archbishop of Westminster, Cardinal John C. Heenan entitled the first volume of his autobiography '*Not The Whole Truth*' (with reference to the fact that 'ministers of Christ must keep confidences'). In his second volume he reported that some readers had been shocked by the declaration that he did not intend to tell the whole truth: 'My motive, of course, was to reassure former practitioners and other friends . . . '.

Secular-minded persons too regard certain touchstones of integrity and noble behaviour as being more meritorious than uttering the truth: love, charity, beauty, honour, compassion, kindness, global benevolence. The Hippocratic Oath, setting out moral guidelines for medical practitioners, is noteworthy as doctors can enhance life and bring nearer death. The list of moral injunctions in the Oath is significant per se but also because of what it does not contain. The offence of lying is never mentioned. Thus the Oath implies that there are ethical admonitions which transcend the morality of telling-the-truth.

How far should patriotism take precedence over the truth? In the Japanese ethos the answer is unequivocal. The Japanese education ministry has censored history textbooks which contain 'negative judgements' about the historic role of the Japanese army in the 1930s and during WWII. Factually accurate accounts of past Japanese aggressive and brutal conduct are not deemed to be truths which, in official thinking, ought to be communicated to Japanese children as the ensuing adoration of their own country might thus be undermined. The governments of the coalition, led by the United States, which destroyed Sadam Hussein's regime, initially believed that their adversary had massive weapons of mass destruction. Much of this false and grossly exaggerated 'intelligence' was supplied by Iraqi exiles and in particular by Ahmad Chalabi who headed the Iraqi National Congress. Even after it was established that his information had been designedly mendacious, Chalabi did not deny this charge but shrugged it off. He described himself as a 'hero in error'. In his view, it does not matter now whether he told the truth or not. He claimed that his aim to induce the US to invade

Iraq had, as a result, been 'entirely successful'. Because he told lies, Sadam Hussein was toppled and an American-led coalition was now in Iraq.

The Germans have two tendentious words for benevolent lies, to wit 'Notluege' and 'Lebensluege', which may be employed to save human lives. Helmut Schmidt, a former German chancellor, has expounded on when one should make use of them. He wants us to believe that politicians who are wedded absolutely to only telling the truth are irresponsible creatures. Politicians are accountable not only to their own conscience but also to their party, the electorate and the public at large. Lying may therefore take precedence over telling-the-truth. He relates with pride how his government deceived the kidnappers of a prominent industrialist, Herr Schleyer. This led Schmidt to enunciate that the lies he then told deserved to be not just applauded or tolerated: 'a politician is not only allowed to lie but actually has a duty to employ a Notluege'.

An 'historical truth' is essentially an untruth. It refers to a long-established, deep belief by the public that a certain event took place — which did not. Sticklers for the truth may of course feel obliged to debunk such beliefs. But is this always meritorious? If 'historical truths' cause no harm, while disclaimers may cause unhappiness, why not leave them undisturbed? The Church of the Holy Sepulchre, in an old part of Jerusalem, has been a holy shrine visited over many centuries by millions of devout Christians who fervently think that it contains the tomb of Christ. It is well nigh impossible to prove, after more than two thousand years, that this is indeed so. Many cognoscenti point to enough factual indicators to argue that it is highly unlikely to be the designated location which the faithful believe it is. Notwithstanding the strong case made out by experts, I, for one, would prefer not to impair this 'historical truth' and many others.

The Hazards of Telling the Truth

The HoC has an obsessively restricted view about lying. Punctiliously, it is not attached to truth in general but only to a particular truth, one which is uttered within its precincts. The Speaker cannot and does not castigate MPs who pronounce falsehoods outside the Palace of Westminster.

Not-telling-the-truth is regarded as a really heinous offence only when perpetrated within the Chamber and especially when addressing other MPs. In the past only active lying was taboo but for some years now passive lying is denounced with equal vehemence. Students of political science are taught that the 1963 downfall of the Secretary of State for War, John Profumo, did not come about because of his sexual relationship with Christine Keeler nor on account of his being guilty of a security lapse. (He had shared the favours of the young lady with a Russian diplomat.) His crime was not even that he had lied. His political demise was caused because he lied to the House. This surely is a mild caricature of morality. A heavy penalty is imposed by the HoC upon members who deceive other members — and are caught out. It does not appear to matter greatly what kind of lies are told for there is a principle at stake. In the absence of a scale of punishments, liars are not always penalized commensurately with the benevolence or malevolence of their mendacity. Unanswered remains the question: What if an MP embezzles money in his constituency or beats his mistress? An irreverent MP told me that there are occasions when a member of the HoC ought to be denounced for not telling a lie but for insisting upon telling-the-truth. MPs ought to be praised when events and morality dictate that lying is sometimes a more honourable course than the declamation of a conventional truth.

Despite his illustrious aristocratic background and his outstanding attainments at Eton, Harvard and Oxford — none of them nowadays ideal qualifications for a budding politicians in the UK's representative democracy — Arthur Waldegrave became a junior member of Major's cabinet. In March 1994 he found himself in deep trouble and, while until then probably fewer than 5% of the electorate had ever heard of him, he became a national celebrity. He stated in the HoC that 'in very exceptional cases it is necessary to say something in the House of Commons that is untrue'. Waldegrave made things even worse for himself by alleging that the HoC 'understands and accepts' this. When challenged, he elaborated on this theme. He insisted that in the past ministers, though loath to mislead parliament, nevertheless did 'not display everything they knew about the subject and [yet] answered the question accurately'. He admitted that he himself had given 'blocking' answers to MPs. In an interview he posed a rhetorical question: if we are going to have open government, 'do we maintain the benign myth that a minister never tells a lie?' This sanctimonious ruction made James Callaghan, a former chancellor of the exchequer, very cross. Waldegrave, when pressed, had mentioned explicitly that Cripps and Callaghan had lied about the devaluations which they had engineered. Callaghan screamed: 'Clear my name.' Waldegrave did not apologize and remained adamant that the two ex-chancellors had not told the truth. Far from disparaging Callaghan for deceiving the HoC, he praised him warmly: 'I have repeatedly referred to you as a statesman who did his duty in the national interest . . . your answers were justified . . . you were right to say what you said.'

Waldegrave was not denounced so bitterly because he pointed out that UK politicians had occasionally told untruths or avoided telling the truth. This was not news because some of the guilty ones have actually admitted what they had done. Waldegrave's sin was to have mentioned this parliamentary practice as something that might well be praiseworthy. One of his detractors said that he had 'impaled himself upon the cause of strict truth'. This was not meant as a compliment but as a subtle reprimand: a politician should not volunteer to tell the truth when this might blemish the public image of the government. In the most savage accusation which he had to suffer, he was told off for speaking honestly and thus appearing to be legitimatizing lying. Why, when he was interrogated in the HoC, did he not give a circumspect reply? An anonymous academic philosopher told a Sunday paper: 'I thought it rich that he failed to apply his own dictum when facing the committee of the House of Commons. If he had lied, none of this would have happened.' Journalists surrounded his home for they expected him to be thrown out of the cabinet. One of them managed to ask him what the British public was then eager to know: 'Are you going to resign?' His response was succinct: 'Why?' The journalist yelled back: 'For telling the truth.'

Bibliography of Sources

J. Alt, *The Politics of Economic Decline*, Cambridge, 1979.
D. Akenson, *Conor*, McGill University Press, Montreal, 1994.
B. Anderson, *John Major*, Fourth Estate, London, 1991.
H. Ansari, *The Infidel Within*, Hurst, London, 2001.
J.C. Ash & D.J. Smyth, *Forecasting the UK Economy*, Saxon House, London, 1973.
W. Bagehot, *The English Constitution*, King, London, 1872.
K. Baker, *The Turbulent Years*, Faber, London, 1993.
J. Barnett, *Inside the Treasury*, Deutsch, London, 1982.
T. Benn, *Diaries 1963-2001*, Hutchinson, London. 1987–2002.
J. Bentham, *An Introduction to the Principle of Morals and Legislation*, Pickering, London, 1828.
S. Blackburn & K. Simmons (editors), *Truth*, OUP, Oxford, 1999.
S. Bok, *Lying*, Harvester Press, Hassocks, 1978.
J. Boswell, *The Life of Samuel Johnson*, Dent, London, 1978.
S. Brittan, *Steering the Economy*, Secker & Warburg, London, 1969.
W. Broad & N. Wade, *Betrayers of the Truth*, Simon & Schuster, New York, 1982.
J. Brodrick, *Galileo*, Chapman, London, 1964.
A. Bouhdiba, *Sexuality in Islam*, Routledge, London, 1985.
G. Brook-Shepherd, *The Austrians*, HarperCollins, London, 1996.
J. Bruce-Gardyne & N. Lawson, *The Power Game*, Macmillan, London 1976.
J. Buchanan & G. Tullock, *The Calculus of Consent*, University of Michigan Press, Ann Arbor, 1962.
J. Calder, *Pursuit*, Calder Publications, London, 2001.
J. Callaghan, *Time and Chance*, Collins, London, 1987.
B. Castle, *The Diaries 1974-76*, Weidenfeld & Nicolson, London, 1980.
D. Caute, *The Fellow-Travellers*, Weidenfeld & Nicolson, London 1973.

A. Chiang, Economic Forecasting where the Subject of the Forecast is Influenced by the Forecast, *American Economic Review*, Evanston, September 1963.
C. Clark, *Australian Hopes and Fears*, Hollis & Carter, London, 1958.
R. Conquest, *Reflections on a Ravaged Country*, John Murray, London, 1999.
B. Cooper, *Sins of Omission*, University of Toronto Press, Toronto, 1994.
F.M. Cornford, *The Republic of Plato*, OUP, London, 1941.
E. Craun, *Lies, Slander and Obscenity in Medieval English Literature*, CUP, Cambridge, 1997.
A. Crawley, *Leap Before You Look*, Collins, London, 1988.
R. Crossman, *The Diaries 1951-70*, Hamish Hamilton, London, 1975–81.
H. Dalton, *High Tide and After*, Frederick Muller, London, 1962.
R. Davenport-Hines, *The Macmillans*, Heinemann, London, 1992.
R. Deacon, *The Truth Twisters*, Macdonald, London, 1986.
A.M. Dershowitz, *Chutzpah*, Little Brown, London, 1991.
N. Dixon, *On the Psychology of Military Incompetence*, Pimlico, London, 1994.
B. Donoughue, *Prime Minister*, Cape, London, 1987.
A. Downs, *An Economic Theory of Democracy*, Harper, New York, 1957.
M. Eck, *Mensonge et Verite*, Casterman, Paris, 1965.
R.D. Edwards, *Victor Gollancz*, Gollancz, London, 1987.
E. Ehrlich, *Nil Desperandum*, Hale, London, 1986.
Encyclopedia of Religious Quotations, F. Mead (editor), Peter Davies, London.
N. Etcoff, *Survival of the Prettiest*, Little Brown, London, 1999.
A, Etzioni, *The Moral Dimension*, Free Press, New York, 1988.
H. Evans, *Downing Street Diary*, Hodder & Stoughton, London, 1981.
H. Eysenck, *The Psychology of Politics*, Temple Smith, 1983.
L. Fisher, *Men and Politics*, Duell, Sloan & Pearce, New York, 1941.
A. Flew, *The Politics of Procustes*, Temple Smith, London, 1981.
M. Foot, *Aneurin Bevan II*, Davis-Poynter, London, 1973.
J. Fuegi, *The Life and Lies of Bertolt Brecht*, HarperCollins, London, 1994.
E. Giannetti, *Lies We Live By*, Bloomsbury, London, 1997.
L. Ginzberg, *Legends of the Bible*, Robson, London 2001.
I. Gilmour, *The Body Politic*, Hutchinson, London, 1969.
V. Gollancz, *The Betrayal of the Left*, Gollancz, London 1941.

S. J. Gould, *The Lying Stones of Marrakech,* Jonathan Cape, London, 2000.
Jonathon Green, *The Cynic's Lexicon,* Routledge, London, 1984.
B. Griffith, *Inflation,* Weidenfeld & Nicolson, London, 1976.
[Lord] Hailsham, *The Dilemma of Democracy,* Collins, London, 1978.
R. Harrod, *The Life of John Maynard Keynes,* Macmillan, London 1951.
F. Hayek, *Law, Legislation and Liberty,* Routledge, London, 1982.
D. Healey, *The Time Of My Life,* Michael Joseph, London 1989.
Hearings of the Preliminary Commission of Inquiry into the Charges made against Leon Trotsky, Secker & Warburg, London, 1937.
John C. Heenan, *Not The Whole Truth,* Hodder & Stoughton, London, 1971.
John C. Heenan, *A Crown of Thorns,* Hodder & Stoughton, London, 1974.
E. Heaton, *The Old Testament Prophets,* Darton, Longman & Todd, London, 1977.
H. Himmelweit & P. Humphreys & M. Jaeger, *How Voters Decide,* Open University Press, Milton Keynes, 1981.
P. Hollander, *Political Pilgrims,* OUP, New York, 1981.
A. Horne, *Macmillan,* Macmillan, London, 1989.
L. Houseman, *The Burden of Nineve,* [Old Testament Plays], Cape, London, 1950.
D. Hurd, *An End to Promises,* Collins, London, 1979.
W. Hutt, *Politically Impossible?* Institute of Economic Affairs, London, 1971.
Inflation, Institute of Economic Affairs, London, 1974.
A. Jaffe & H. Spirer, *Misused Statistics,* Decker, New York, 1987.
D. Jay, *Change and Fortune,* Hutchinson, London, 1980.
P. Jay & M. Stewart, *Apocalypse 2000,* Sidgwick & Jackson, London, 1987.
R. Jenkins, *A Life At The Centre,* Macmillan, London, 1991.
P. Johnson, *Intellectuals,* Weidenfeld & Nicolson, London, 1988.
P. Jungk, *A Life Torn by History,* Weidenfeld & Nicolson, London, 1990.
D. Kagan, *Pericles of Athens and the Birth of Democracy,* Secker & Warburg, London, 1990.
B. Kanner, *Lies My Parents Told Me,* Simon & Schuster, London, 1990.
W. Keegan, *Mr Lawson's Gamble,* Hodder & Stoughton, 1989.
J.F. Kennedy, *Profiles in Courage,* Harper, New York, 1956.
P. Kerr (editor), *The Penguin Book of Lies,* Viking, London, 1990.

C. Kersch, *A Few Gross Words*, Simon & Schuster, London, 1990.
V. O. Key, *The Responsible Electorate*, Harvard University Press, Cambridge, 1966.
A. Koestler, *Darkness at Noon*, Penguin Books, London, 1946.
A. Kohn, *False Prophets*, Blackwell, Oxford, 1988.
M. Kuehn, *Kant*, CUP, Cambridge, 1981.
N. Lawson, *The View from No 11*, Bantam Press, London, 1991.
S. Lipsett & W. Schneider, *The Confidence Gap*, The Free Press, New York, 1983.
J.R. Lloyd George, *Lloyd George*, Muller, London, 1960.
D. Macdougall, *Don and Mandarin*, John Murray, London, 1987.
N. Machiavelli, *The Prince*, Alexander Moring, London, 1929.
H. Macmillan, *Tides of Fortune*, Macmillan, London, 1969.
D.J. Manning, *The Mind of Jeremy Bentham*, Longman, London, 1968.
D. Marquand, *The Unprincipled Society*, Cape, London, 1988.
J. Masson, *The Assault on Truth*, Harper, New York, 1984.
J. Mayer & D. McManus, *Landslide*, Collins, London, 1988.
R. Maudling, *Memoirs*, Sidgwick & Jackson, London, 1978.
R. Melson, *False Papers*, University of Illinois Press, Urbana, 2000.
H. Mencken, *A Carnival of Buncombe*, University of Chicago Press, Chicago, 1980.
I. Mikardo, *Backbencher*, Weidenfeld & Nicolson, 1988.
J.S. Mill, *Utilitarianism, On Liberty And Considerations on Representative Government*, Dent, London, 1972.
K. Monroe, *Presidential Popularity and the Economy*, Praeger, New York, 1984.
D. Morgan, *Over-Taxation by Inflation*, Institute of Economic Affairs, London, 1977.
O. Morgenstern, *On the Accuracy of Economic Observations*, Princeton University Press, Princeton, 1963.
G. Myrdal, *Economic Theory*, Duckworth, London, 1957.
D. Murphy, S. Kondrashev, G. Bailey, *Battleground Berlin*, Yale University Press, New Haven, 1997.
New Catholic Encyclopedia, McGraw-Hill, New York, 1967.
F. Nietsche, *Twilight of the Idols*, OUP, Oxford, 1998.
E. Nolle-Neuman, *Die Schweigespiralle*, Piper, Munich, 1980.
E. Nolle-Neumann (editor) *Jahrbuch der Oeffentlichen Meinung*, Verlag fuer Demoskopie, Allensbach, 1968.
D. Owen, *Time to Declare*, Michael Joseph, 1991.
V. Packard, *The Hidden Persuaders*, Pocket Books, New York, 1958.
M. Parris, *Parliamentary Scandals*, Robson, London, 1995.

Bibliography of Sources 285

M. Parris, *Scorn*, Penguin Books, London, 1996.
M. Parris & P. Mason, *Read My Lips*, Penguin Books, London, 1997.
J. Paxman, *The Political Animal*, Michael Joseph, London, 2002.
E. Phelps, *Altruism, Morality and Economic Theory*, Sage, New York, 1975.
L. Pliatzky, *Getting and Spending*, Blackwell, Oxford, 1982.
K.R. Popper, *The Open Society and its Enemies*, Routledge, London, 1952.
W. Poundstone, *Prisoner Dilemma*, OUP, London, 1993.
E. Powell, *Freedom and Reality*, Batsford, London, 1969.
E. Powell, *The Evolution of the Gospel*, Yale University Press, New Haven, 1994.
J. Ranelagh, *Thatcher's People*, HarperCollins, London, 1991.
J. Rees, *Looking for a Mr Nobody*, Phoenix, London, 1997.
N. Ridley, *My Style of Government*, Hutchinson, London, 1991.
B.M. Rigg, *Hitler's Jewish Soldiers*, University Press of Kansas, 2002.
J.M. Rist, *Augustine*, CUP, Cambridge, 1994.
A. Roberts, *Hitler and Churchill*, Weidenfeld & Nicolson, London, 2003.
M. Rosenbaum, *From Soapbox to Soundbite*, Macmillan, London, 1997.
N. Rosenblum, *Bentham's Theory of the Modern State*, Harvard University Press, Cambridge, 1978.
B. Rowley (editor), *Democracy and Public Choice*, Blackwell, Oxford, 1987.
M. Rubinstein, *Wicked, Wicked Libels*, Routledge, London, 1972.
A. Rubner, *The Ensnared Shareholder*, Macmillan, London, 1965.
A. Rubner, *The Might of the Multinationals*, Praeger, New York, 1990.
S. Sayers, *Plato's Republic*, Edinburgh University Press, Edinburgh, 1999.
J. Schumpeter, *Capitalism, Socialism and Democracy*, Allen & Unwin, London, 1976.
E. Short, *Whip to Wilson*, Macdonald, London, 1989.
H. Sidgwick, *The Methods of Ethics*, Macmillan, London, 1877.
R. Skidelsky, *John Maynard Keynes*, Macmillan, London, 1982 and 1983.
A. Smith, *The Wealth of Nations*, Pelican, London, 1970.
G.C. Smith, *The American Statistician*, Washington, 1964.
E. Stourton, *Absolute Truth*, Viking, London, 1998.
C. Stockman, *The Triumph of Politics*, Bodley Head, London, 1985.
A. Teale, *Kantian Ethics*, OUP, London, 1951.

M. Thatcher, *The Downing Street Years*, HarperCollins, London, 1983.
R. Titmuss, *The Gift Relationship*, Allen & Unwin, London 1970.
A. Trollope, *Can You Forgive Her?*, OUP, London, 1982.
G. Tullock, *The Vote Motive*, Institute of Economic Affairs, London 1976.
G. Walden, *The New Elites*, Allen Lane, London, 2000.
N. West, *Counterfeit Spies*, St Ermins Press, London, 2000.
R. Whymant, *Stalin's Spy: Richard Sorge*, Tauris, London, 1996.
O. Wilde, *Intentions*, Methuen, London, 1908.
G. Wills, *Under God*, Simon & Schuster, New York, 1990.
H. Wilson, *The Labour Government 1964-70*, Weidenfeld & Nicolson, London,1971.
H. Wilson, *Final Term 1974-76*, Weidenfeld & Nicolson, London 1979.
P. Wyden, *The Unknown Iacocca*, Sidgwick & Jackson, London, 1988.

Index

Aborigines, 48
Acropolis, 264
Adam, 122
Adler, Alfred, 29
AFL-CIO federation (US), 225
Africa, 110
Agamemnon, 78
Agee, Philip, 276
AIDS, 109
Air France, 197
Al-Qaradawi, Yusuf, 94
Albania, 16, 17, 65
Alexanderplatz, 118
Allies (WWII), 52, 274, 275
Alt, J., 217
American Economic Review, 79
American Journal of Political Science, 170
Amery, Julian, 195, 196
Amsterdam, 254
Anglo-French Suez Expedition, 199
Anderson, Bruce, 152
Apartheid, 79
Apocalypse 2000, 185
Apollo, 78
Aquinas, Thomas, 30
Archaeological Society (Greece), 264
Archbishop of Canterbury, 263
Archbishop of Westminster, 277
Aristotle, 150
Armenians, 14
Armstrong, Robert, 22, 23
Aryan, 91
Ash, J., 83, 84
Ashfield constituency, 158
Asia, 18, 162, 218, 221, 238, 271
Asquith, 172
Athens, 132, 268
Atlantic Ocean, 33, 39, 80
Attlee,, Clement, 181, 203, 218
Augustine, Saint, 1, 7, 8, 9, 11, 34, 91

Australia, 22, 47, 49, 194, 225
Austria, 16
Ayres, C.E., 36

Babbage, Charles, 51
Baghdad, 15, 16
Bagehot, Walter, 133, 152, 158, 183
Baker, Kenneth, 215
Baldwin, Stanley, 120
Balfour, Arthur, 156
Ball, R.J., 82
Balogh, Thomas, 115
Bangladesh, 103
Bank of England, 57, 62, 107, 184, 190, 192, 194, 199, 252
Barber, Tony, 228
Barnett, Joel, 22, 198, 199, 231-3, 236-9, 248
BBC, 31, 112, 152, 155, 181, 187, 249
Beaverbrook, Lord, 120
Becher, Kurt, 116, 117
Beg, Mohammed, 274
Behrend, Hilde, 166
Belgium, 274
Benn, Tony, 196, 197, 206
Bentham, Jeremy, 100, 101, 102, 103
Beringer, Johann, 50, 51
Berlin, 44, 107, 114, 118
Berlin Wall, 118
Bevan, Aneurin, 160, 213, 214
Bible, 14, 22, 92, 122, 123, 124, 125, 126, 171, 173
Birch, Nigel, 187
Birmingham, 48
Blair, Jayson, 49
Blair, Tony, 131, 143, 153, 169, 182, 192, 194, 223, 257, 258
Blow, Simon, 46
Blunt, Anthony, 71
Boer War, 172
Bolshevik(s), 92, 275
Bombach, G., 82

Booth, Alan, 218
Boswell, James, 9
Bouhdiba, 93
Brazil, 219
Brecht, Bertolt, 50, 69
Bretton Woods, 192
Britain, 23, 57, 58, 61, 67, 68, 72, 82, 111, 121, 136, 137, 143, 146, 149, 157, 163, 166, 174, 181, 182, 185, 188, 215, 255, 261, 273
British Aircraft Corporation 197
British Airways, 197
British democracy, 179, 180, 184, 185, 189
British government, 38, 57, 99, 100, 106, 110, 112, 120, 138, 140, 145, 149, 162, 184, 191, 194, 226, 254
British Market Research Bureau, 165
British Medical Journal, 166, 256
British people, 106, 107, 111, 120, 145, 150, 169, 171, 172, 174, 175, 182, 194, 207, 216, 240, 248, 265, 280
British Psychological Society, 150
British Rail, 247
Brittan, Samuel, 61, 80, 133, 181-4, 230
Brixton, 152
Broad, William, 51
Brodrick, James, 43
Brook-Shepherd, Gordon, 16
Brown George, 80, 227
Brown, Gordon, 153, 169, 189, 192, 223
Bruce-Gardyne, Jock, 177, 228
Brussels, 58, 117, 189-93, 251
Buchanan, James 144, 145
Bulgarian horrors, The 171
Bulgarians 171, 172
Bundesbank 111, 112, 193, 209
Burgess,, 70
Burke, Edmund, 134, 150, 157, 201
Burns, T., 82
Burt, Cyril, 51

Cadillacs, 149
Cairncross, Alec, 79, 82
Calcott, Mary, 67

Calder, John, 29
Callaghan, James, 34, 58, 59, 106, 107, 113, 181, 198, 199, 201, 203, 211, 218, 227, 255, 262, 273, 280
Cambridge, 119
Cambridge spies, 70
Canada, 159
Canterbury, Dean of, 64,
Capitol Hill, 23
Carcassonne, Guy, 153
Carter, Jimmy, 164, 165, 228
Cassandra, 78
Castle, Barbara, 113, 160, 203
Castro, Fidel, 65
Catholicism, 276
Catholics, 141, 173
Cat on a hot tin roof, 46
Caute, David, 63, 64
Ceausescu, President, 31
Center for the Study of Public Choice, 144
CGT (France), 224
Chalabi, Ahmad, 277
Chan, An-Wen, 51
Chernobyl, 110
Chiang, Alpha, 21, 81,
Chicago Tribune, 154,
China, 20, 55, 63, 64, 65, 70, 122, 268, 274
Chirac, Jacques, 153
Christian Democrats, 191
Christians, 91, 171, 173, 278
Christianity, 11, 63, 64, 92
Chrysler, 160, 251
Church of England, 173
Church of the Holy Sepulchre, 278
Churchill, Winston, 23, 137, 171, 212
CIA, 44, 276
City of London, 189, 193, 205, 241, 245
City (Stock Exchange), 30, 76, 203
Clark, Alan, 22, 23
Clark, Colin, 225, 226
Clark, William, 234
Clifford, Max, 34
Clinton, President, 39
Cold War, 44, 53
Collard, Dudley, 69

Index

Coming of age in Samoa, 50
Common Market, 117, 162, 163, 174, 183, 190, 200, 201, 254
Commonwealth, 119, 120
Communist International, 65, 68, 73
Communist Party, 2, 71, 72, 73, 74
Concorde, 195-7
Confederation of British Industry, 190, 236, 239
Congress, US, 19, 23, 131, 148
Conservative Central Office, 179
Conservative Government, 206, 215, 226, 227, 243, 245, 257, 260, 273
Conservative Party, 147, 151, 186, 200, 201, 212, 214
Conservatives, 100, 140, 143, 147, 149-152, 155, 169, 170, 177, 180, 185, 193, 194, 202, 212-5, 229, 234
Conservatism, 212
Cooke, Gresham, 75
Cooke, Janet, 49
Cooper, Barry, 33
Corriere della Sera, 49, 50
Costain, 77
Cot, Pierre, 110
Court of Appeal, 105
Crawley, Aidan, 36
Cripps, Stafford, 203-5, 280
Cromer, Earl of, 57
Crossman, Richard, 106, 107, 119, 195, 215, 226, 227
Cuba, 65
Currency Commission, 184
Czarist army, 275

Daily Telegraph, 49, 274
Daily Worker, The, 63, 120
Dalton, Hugh, 214
Darville, Helen, 47
Davenport-Hines, R., 12
Davey, Keith, 270
David, King, 122
Davies, Howard, 180, 190
Davis, Jerome, 69
Dawson, Christopher, 7
Dayan, General, 274
DDR, 50, 118
Deedes, W.F., 185

De Gaulle, Charles, 148
Delilah, 1
Democratic Party, 140
Demoskopie-Demokratie, 142
Denmark, 163, 164
Deuteronomy, 124
Devil's Island, 42
Dieppe, 90
Disraeli, Benjamin, 172
Dollar (US), 222
Donoughue, Bernard, 198, 199, 228
Doomsday agenda, 198
Downing Street, 112, 121, 153, 196, 200, 202, 227, 228, 241, 252, 260, 264
Downs, Anthony, 144, 177
Dreadnought, 172
Dresden, 118
Dreyfus, Alfred, 42
Driberg, Tom, 120
Dublin, 264
Dukakis, Michael, 269
Dumas, Alexandre, 96
Dunkirk, 273

East Berlin, 118
ECGD, 254, 255, 266
Eck, Marcel, 109
Economic contradictions of democracy, The 183
Economic Journal, 79, 83
Economic Service, 79
Economist, The, 14, 61, 80, 203-5
Eden, Anthony, 100, 199, 200
Edwards, George, 197
Edwards, Ruth, 71, 74
Egypt, 200, 274
Ehrlich, E., 200
Eichmann,, 116
Elizabeth II, 31, 120, 253
Eltis, Walter, 241
EMNID, 175
England, 72, 145, 158, 163, 225, 273
Ensnared shareholder, The 239
Epping Forest, 163
ERNIE, 162
Essex University, 169
Estonia, 267
Etcoff, Nancy, 150

Ethiopia, 55, 56
Eton, 152, 279
Euro, 193, 194
Europe, 18, 121, 217
European Community, 142, 163, 190
European Union, 174, 175, 180, 183, 187, 189-94, 251, 253, 254, 268
Eve, 122
Exchange Rate Mechanism, 58, 59, 188, 192, 193
Express Group, 120
Eysenck, Hans, 13
Ezekiel, 123

Feuchtwanger, Lion, 65, 69
Fildes, Christopher, 179
Financial Services Authority, 190
Financial Times, The, 61, 181, 199, 230
Fisher, Louis, 66
Fletcher-Cooke, Charles, 234
Fliess, Dr Wilhelm, 114
Foot, Michael, 160
Ford Corporation, 141, 222, 251
Forward, Rev Toby, 48
FORWARD BOOK, 62, 63
France, 15, 42, 52, 100, 153, 194-7, 199, 200, 224, 229, 250, 253, 274
France, Anatole, 40
Francis of Assisi, Saint, 12
Franco, General, 73, 137, 223
Frankel, Professor, 34
Freud, Anna, 115
Freud, Sigmund, 114, 115
Friedman, Milton, 184, 219
Fuchs, Klaus, 99, 100
Fuegi, John, 50
Full Democracy, 135

Gaitskell, Hugh, 230
Galatin, Malcolm, 83
Galbraith, John, 80
Galileo, 42, 43
Gallup Polls, 102, 163, 167, 169, 170
Gandhi, Mahatma, 7, 273
Gaza, 1
GDP, 37, 39, 55, 82, 85, 166, 181, 218, 231-3, 259, 260, 270-2

General Motors, 102, 251
Gentiles, 91, 126
George, Lloyd, 1, 114, 156, 171
George, Maggie, 114
German measles, 109
German Society for the Prevention of Suicide, 118
Germany, 13, 16, 20, 32, 45, 52, 53, 59, 70, 73, 88, 91, 111, 116-8, 121, 142, 163, 164, 165, 169, 172, 191, 194, 210, 211, 213, 221, 223, 254, 269, 273-5, 278
GESTAPO, 68, 69, 91
Giannetti, E., 12, 17
Gilmour, Ian, 140, 170
Giscard d'Estaing, Valery, 229
Gladstone, William, 146, 171, 172
Glenamara, Baron, 157
GNP, 83, 237
God, 7, 8, 41, 42, 50, 94, 122-7, 133, 276, 277
Goering, Herman, 16
Goldwater, Barry, 54
Gollancz, Victor, 2, 63, 71, 72, 73, 74
Gorbachev, Mikhail, 33, 57
Gould, Stephen Jay, 50
Greater London Council, 215
Greece, 192, 264
Gross, B., 54
Guatemala, 49
Guildhall, London, 153, 154
Gulag, 44
Gulf War, First, 15
Gulf War, Second, 17

Hailsham, Lord, 134, 135, 146
Hall, Peter, 46
Hamburg, 91, 116
Handelsblatt, The, 121
Hansard, 228
Harland and Wolff, 149
Harrod, Roy, 35, 159, 160
Harvard, 7, 279
Hauptmann, Elisabeth 50
Hayek, F.A. von, 134, 144, 179-81, 192
H-Bomb, 99, 100
Healey, Denis, 2, 7, 81, 113, 114, 153, 160, 197-9, 202, 203, 227, 230-6, 257, 270

Heath, Edward, 117, 118, 120, 121, 140, 174, 196, 201, 226, 228, 234, 243, 248, 257
Heenan, Cardinal John, 277
Henderson, Sir Neville, 16
Heseltine, Michael, 151
Himmler, Heinrich, 91
Hinduism, 92, 93
Hindus, Maurice, 68
Hippocratic Oath, 277
Hirohito, Emperor, 20
Hitler, Adolf, 16, 18, 20, 33, 44, 50, 70, 71, 73, 116, 132, 133, 137
Hitlerjugend, 91
Hitler-Stain pact, 66, 70, 71
Hoechst, 76
Hollander, Paul, 63
Hollywood, 47
Holocaust, 91, 115, 116
Holy Office, 42
Hospitals Trust (Ireland), 264
House of Commons, 3, 15, 23, 35, 58, 77, 106, 107, 111, 135, 136, 138, 146, 149, 152, 157, 158, 173, 174, 179-82, 186, 189-91, 193, 199, 202, 203, 205, 235, 236, 241, 243, 245, 263, 278-80
House of Lords, 157, 199, 228
Housing, Ministry of, 212, 213
Housman, L, 126
Howe, Geoffrey, 196
Hoxha, Enver, 65
Hungary, 116, 133
Hurd, Douglas, 151, 152
Hussein, Saddam, 15, 17, 277, 278
Hutt, William, 20
Huxley, Julian, 67
ICI, 77
IMF, 54, 188, 198, 199

India, 39, 238, 268
Inland Revenue, 109, 201, 207, 212, 221, 235, 260, 261
Inside the company, 276
Iraq, 15, 17, 170-2, 277, 278
Iraqi National Congress, 277
Ireland, 173
Ireland, Home Rule, 172
Ireland, Republic of, 172, 200, 254, 265
Irish Labour Party, 201

Irish Sweepstake, 264, 265
Islam, 92, 93, 94, 171
Israel, 1, 116, 117, 124, 200, 274
Italy, 19, 55, 66, 110, 141, 259, 260

Jacob, 122
Jacob's Ladder, 93
Japan, 19, 20, 39, 54, 55, 162, 251, 264, 275, 277
Jay, Douglas, 14, 58, 181
Jay, Peter, 181-5
Jenkins, Roy, 77, 153, 204-8
Jeremiah, 123, 124
Jerusalem, 278
Jesus Christ, 14, 22, 64, 92, 277, 278
Jews, 91, 93, 116, 117, 173
John Paul I, 44
Johnson, Colin, 48
Johnson, Hewlett, 63
Johnson, Lyndon, 53, 54, 155, 219
Johnson, Paul, 63
Johnson, Samuel, 9
Jonah, 2, 124-7
Journal of the American Medical Association, 51
Judah, 124
Judaism, 92

Kadar, Janos, 132, 133
Kahn, Rahila, 48
Kaldor, Nicholas, 119
Kanner, Bernice, 15
Kant, Immanuel, 7, 9, 10
Kastner, Israel, 116, 117
Katyn massacre, 53
Kaufman, Henry, 180
Keeler, Christine, 279
Kelley, Jack, 49
Kemp, Murray, 78, 79, 82
Kennedy, John F., 112, 148, 155
Kentucky, 49
Kersh, Cyril, 31
Keynes, J.M., 20, 21, 35, 84, 87, 136, 145, 189, 192, 194, 217, 218, 239, 246
KGB, 44, 66, 71
Khrushchev, Nikita, 162
King, Anthony, 169
King James Bible, 173
Kinnock, Neil, 142, 143, 153, 202

Kirkland, Lane, 225
Kissinger, Henry, 274
Klagenfurt, 91
Klein, Richard, 141
Koestler, Arthur, 70, 92
Kohl, Helmut, 13, 191
Kohn, Alexander, 51, 52
Kondratiev, Nikolai, 57, 58
Konigsberger, H., 65
Koran, 171
Korea, 20
Kroll, Jules, 35
Kurds, 87
Kurz, Diane, 100
Kyslant, Lord, 104, 105

Laban, 122
Labour Government, 66, 107, 113, 119, 158, 195, 196, 198, 199, 202, 203, 205, 206, 211, 212, 215, 234-6, 245, 255, 257
Labour Party, 33, 59, 63, 115, 119, 142, 143, 147, 148, 151, 153, 158, 160, 168, 169, 189, 198, 202, 204, 206, 213, 214, 218, 229, 233-5, 238, 255, 258, 263
Lamont, Norman, 58, 180, 260
Laski, Harold, 33, 34, 45, 68, 72
Latin America, 218, 221, 250
Lawrence, Larry, 39, 40
Lawson, Dominic, 230
Lawson, Nigel, 59, 62, 81, 133, 155, 156, 177, 191-3, 202, 223, 242, 243, 245
LDC countries, 54, 55, 56, 103, 121, 249, 253, 254, 262, 271
Lee, John, 205, 235
Left Book Club, 71, 72, 73, 74
Legislative Commission on Jails in Connecticut, 69
Lenin, 20, 217, 218
Lever, Harold, 203, 211, 231, 232, 236, 260
Liberal Party, 169, 171, 172, 206
Liberals, 172, 234
Lichtenstein, 267
Lincoln, Abraham, 131
Lippmann, Walter, 148
Liverpool, 115
Llewellyn, Richard, 48
Lloyd, Richard, 48

Lloyds Bank, 241
Lockheed, 19
London, 52, 74, 121, 155, 163, 174, 180, 184, 191,197, 215, 274
London School of Economics, 60, 96, 190
Luegensteine, 50
Luke, Saint, 22

McCarthy era, 47
McManus, Doyle, 23
MacFadzean, F., 37, 38
Machiavelli, Niccolo, 134
Maclean, Donald, 70
Macdonald, Ramsey, 156
Macdougall, Donald, 236, 248
Macmillan, Dorothy, 12
Macmillan, Harold, 12, 100, 149, 150, 186, 187, 200, 201, 212-8, 244, 263
Magee, John, 44, 45
Major, John, 58, 59, 143, 151, 152, 182, 188, 193, 242, 279
Manchester, 155
Marquand, David, 3, 158, 159, 267
Marshall Plan, 54
Marx, Karl, 13, 276
Marxism, 64, 72, 73, 87
Massachusetts, 269
Masson, Jeffrey, 115
Matisse, Henry, 39
Matthew (Gospel of), 92, 123
Maudling, Reginald, 79, 81
Mayer, Jane, 23
Mead, Margaret, 50
Meade, James, 170
Mellor, David, 273
Melson, Robert, 114
Members of Parliament, 113, 135, 136, 138, 140, 146, 148, 150-2, 154, 157, 168, 171, 173, 181, 185, 186, 191, 199, 200, 203, 205, 232, 234, 235, 266, 269-72, 278-80
Menchu, Rigoberto, 48
Mencken, H.L., 144
Meteorological Office, 75
Mexico, 41, 276
Miami, 268
Michalos, Christina, 12
Mikardo, Ian, 168

Milch, Oskar, 91
Mill, John Stuart, 132, 133, 135
Miller, Warren, 65
Minister of Health , 113
Ministry of Defence, 2, 110
Mitterand, President, 15
Molotov, V.M., 44
Montaigne, Michel de, 150
Moore, Charles, 182
Morgenthau, Henry, 219
Moscow, 2, 34, 63, 66, 67, 69, 70, 71, 73, 74, 110, 268, 275
Moscow Trials, 92
Moscow-Volga Canal, 67
Moser, Claus, 119
Moses, 14, 124
Moslems, 47, 171, 172
Mount Sinai, 14
Mudrooroo, 48
Musa Dagh, 14
Mussolini, Benito, 50, 55, 137
Myrdal, G., 237
Myrdal, Jan, 65

Napoleon, 53
National Accounts, 259, 266
National Cash Register, 40
National Chamber of Trade, 75
National Committee for the Abolition of the Death Penalty, 74
National Debt, 220, 227, 259, 260, 266
National Enterprise Board, 238, 239
National Health Service, 113, 151, 152, 166, 249, 258, 259, 266
National Insurance, 248, 249
National Lotteries, 262-5
National Opinion Polls, 163
National Plan, 80
National Statistical Institute (Spain), 224
Nature, 162
Navy League, The, 172
Nazis, 53, 68, 116
Nazism, 45, 91
NCB, 252-5, 261, 262
Neale, John Mason, 92
New Deal, 83
New English Bible, 173

New Labour, 169
Newman, Cardinal, 209
New York Times, 49
New Zealand, 65
News of the World, 31
Newton, Isaac, 51
Niebuhr, Reinhold, 185
Nietzsche, 16
Nineveh, 2, 124-7
Nixon, President, 41
Nobel Peace Prize, 49
Nolle-Neumann, Elisabeth, 32, 169
North America, 69
North Carolina, 48
North Sea oil, 174
Northern Ireland, 149, 172, 201, 254
Not the whole truth, 277
Nottingham, 165
Nuremberg, 117

O'Brien, Conor Cruise, 200, 201
Observer, The, 60
October Revolution, 68, 70
OECD, 120, 121, 251, 254, 272
Office for National Statistics, 223
Oh, S., 81
OGPU, 66
Old Testament, 122
Open Government, 231, 280
Orwell, George, 73
Oxbridge Universities, 173
Oxford, 60, 241, 279
Oxford Dictionary, 33
Oxford University, 51
Oxford University Press, 173

Pakistan, 274
Palace of Westminster, 278
Palliser, G. Plantagenet, 149, 152
Palmerston, Henry, 156
Pareto, 100
Paris, 47, 65, 90, 110, 190, 197
Paris Match, 50
Parkinson, C. Northcote 134
Parliaments, 23, 180, 182, 189, 193, 194
Parris, Matthew, 23
Paxman, Jeremy, 146
Peloponnesian War, 132

People, The, 114
Pepsico, 41
Pericles, 131, 132, 134, 268
Perot, Ross, 273
Perth, 48
Peru, 55
Peter, Saint, 22
PFI, 260
Philby, Kim, 70
Philippines, 41
Philistines, 1
Pigou, 159
Pilkington, Lord Harry, 239-41
Plaid Cymru, 138
Plato, 52, 132, 133, 186
Pliatsky, Leo, 231, 232, 236-8
Poehl, Otto, 112
Poindexter, John, 23
Poland, 53, 139, 255, 256
Pollitt, Harry, 71, 72, 73, 74
Pontifical College, 43
Pope, His Holiness the, 141, 276
Poundstone, W., 99
Powell, Enoch, 42, 119, 149, 187
Premium Bonds, 162, 263
Prest, A.R., 190
Pritt, Denis N., 67, 69
Profumo, John, 279
Protestants, 173
Proverbs, Book of, 122
PSBR, 248
Public Accounts Committee, 228
Pulitzer Prize, 49

Quarterly Journal of Economics, 81
Queensland, 225

Reagan, Ronald, 33, 155, 164, 165, 229
Rebecca, 122
Red Army, 68, 275
Red Cross, 122
Red Dean, 64
Red Flag, The, 154
Redwood, John, 273
Reisman, David, 96
Renault, 224
Republic (Athenian), 132
Republican Party, 140, 229

Retail Prices Index, 18, 162, 163, 220-3, 225-9, 257
Revised English Bible, 173
Richtigkeit, 82
Rigg, B.M., 91
Riyadh, 47
Roberts, Andrew, 146
Robin Hood, 15, 107
Rogers, William, 40
Rolls-Royce, 197
Roman Catholic Church, 43
Rome, 43, 260
Rome, Treaty of, 117
Roosevelt, Theodore, 53, 155
Roper surveys, 164
Rosenbaum, Martin, 153
Rousseau, J.J., 97, 108
Rowley, Charles, 170
Royal Dutch Shell, 37, 38, 254
Royal Economic Society, 79
Royal Mail, 257, 258,
Royal Mail Packet Company, 104
Royal Navy, 2, 110
Royal Statistical Service, 228
Royal Statistical Society, 223, 256
RPI, 18, 162, 163, 220-3, 225-9, 257
Rubashov, 70, 92
Rubinstein, Michael, 273
Russia, 35, 58, 64, 65, 67, 68, 70, 72, 74, 79, 99, 100, 218
Russians, 53, 71
Russian Revolution, 33

Sacher, Harry, 34
Sacred Hunger, 46
Sahib (Royal Navy submarine), 110
Salisbury, Lord, 172
Salvation Army, 172
Samson, 1
Sandys, Duncan, 23
SARS, 55
Sartre, Jean-Paul, 65
Saturday Evening Post, 31
Saudi Arabia, 47
Schadenfreude, 165
Schleyer, Herr, 278
Schmidt, Helmut, 278
Schumpeter, Joseph, 179-81
Scotland, 173, 174, 245
Scottish National Party, 174

Index

Scottish Parliament, 245
Seattle, 268
Shaw, George B., 67
Shell, 37, 38, 76
Shore, Peter, 77, 226
Short, Edward, 158
Siberia, 20, 71
Sicily, 110
Sidgwick, H., 92
Sikhs, 136
Singapore, 19, 271
Smith, Adrian, 256
Smith, George Cline, 84
Smith, John, 143
Smith, Dr Tony, 166
Smyth, D., 83, 84
Socialism, 212
Solicitor General, 196
Somme, 36
Sony, 76
Sorge, Richard, 275
South Africa, 79, 253
Soviet Union, 14, 65, 66, 68, 72, 99, 275
Spain, 38, 39, 73, 224
Spanish Inquisition, 41
Speaker, The, 278
Spectator, The , 35, 62, 100, 143, 180
Spiral of silence, The, 169
SPOT BOOK, 62
Sri Lanka, 119
SS, 116, 117
Stacey, Kim, 49
Stalin, Joseph, 33, 34, 44, 57, 58, 63, 67, 68, 69, 71, 72, 118, 137, 275
Stalinism, 2, 35, 45, 57, 64, 65, 66, 71, 73, 74, 110
State Pensions, 248
Sterling, 194, 198, 200, 211
Stern, 50
Stockholm, 250
Stourton, Edward, 45
Strachey, John, 72
Strong, Anna Louise, 68
Sudan, 56
Suez, 100, 199
Sunday Times, 49, 50, 83
Survival of the prettiest, 150
Sweden, 65, 250, 251

Switzerland, 122, 268
Syria, 274

Taft, Robert A., 148
Taiwan, 121, 122
Talmud, 93, 94
Taylor, A.J.P., 34, 45
Tebbit, Norman, 183
Teheran, 15
Tennyson, Alfred, 18
Texas, University of, 48
Thalheimer, August, 73
Thatcher, Margaret, 14, 59, 62, 63, 133, 138, 143, 151, 153, 155, 156, 174, 179, 182, 183, 188, 191-3, 202, 227, 228, 241, 242, 245, 252
Theodoracopulos, Taki, 35
Third World, 168, 238
Thorneycroft, Peter, 187
Thoughts from a dangerous man, 180
Times, The, 121, 181, 184, 263
Titmuss, Richard, 96
Toffler, Alvin, 269
Tokyo, 275
Tories, 172
Torron, Ricardo, 224
Tory Party, 149, 171
Trade Unions, 96
Transport Committee, House of Commons, 241
Treasury, 77, 80, 81, 82, 85, 107, 172, 174, 181, 190, 198-200, 203, 211, 218, 221, 227, 228, 231-3, 237, 244, 246-8, 253, 255, 260, 262, 263, 265
Trefgarne, Lord, 111
Trollope, Anthony, 146, 149, 152
Trotsky, Leon, 68, 71, 101, 275, 276
Troy, 78
Trudeau, Pierre, 159
Tullock, Gordon, 144, 170
Turkey, 38, 54, 171
Turks, 14

UK, 2, 32, 53, 59, 96, 100, 107, 109, 112, 117, 119, 121, 138, 140, 145, 158, 162, 163, 166, 170-2, 174, 175, 177, 180, 183, 184,

188-90, 193, 194, 198, 207, 213, 218, 222, 223, 232, 233, 240, 242, 254, 260, 264
Ukraine, 47, 54, 67
Unionist Party, 149
United Nations, 121, 122, 188
United States of Europe, 117, 174, 192, 193, 268
Unsworth, Barry, 46
US Today, 49
USA, 33, 46, 49, 50, 54, 67, 81, 83, 84, 96, 99, 111, 112, 131, 140, 144, 146, 150, 154, 164, 165, 170, 181, 184, 194, 200, 207, 219, 224, 229, 251, 268, 269, 277
USSR, 20, 44, 45, 50, 52, 57, 58, 63, 64, 65, 66, 67, 68, 70, 79, 100, 110, 118, 175, 268, 275
Utilitarians, 92, 100
Utopia, 34

Value Added Tax, 227-9
Vatican, 44
Vauzelle, Michel, 15
Vegetarian Party, 138
Venice, 55
Victoria, Queen, 162, 172
Vietnam, 54, 170, 219
Virginia, 144, 145, 170
Vishynski, 72
Voltaire, 11
Von Hayek, Friedrich, 134, 144, 179-81, 192

Wade, Nicholas, 51
Waldegrave, Arthur, 279, 280
Walden, George, 148
Waldman, M., 81
Wales, 48, 138, 173, 267
Walker, Peter, 215
Wall Street, 30, 180
Wall Street Journal, 112
Waller, Robert, 168
Washington, 23, 40, 54, 82, 131, 155, 200, 224, 251, 268
Washington, George, 1, 10, 11,
Washington Post, 49
Watson Wyatt, 266
Webb, Beatrice, 65, 66, 68
Webb, Sidney, 65, 66, 68
Weber, Max, 93, 131

Weil, Simone, 276
Weizsaecker, Richard von, 142
Werfel, Franz, 14, 15
Werth, Alexander, 66, 67
Wesley, John, 1, 7, 171
West, Nigel, 45
Wessex, Earl of, 12
Westminster, 183
Whitehall, 196
White House, The, 131, 165
WHO, 56
Wilde, Oscar, 13, 34, 87
William, Prince, 12
Wills, Gary, 269
Wilson, A.N., 133
Wilson, Harold, 37, 57, 58, 59, 60, 61, 62, 80, 106, 113, 115, 119, 120, 142, 155, 157, 158, 160, 163, 181, 195, 196, 198, 201, 203, 204, 211, 215, 226, 227, 229, 234, 238, 242, 252
Windscale, 110
World Cup, 163
World Health Organisation, 122
World War I, 221
World War II, 42, 45, 47, 52, 70, 91, 99, 110, 112, 139, 172, 175, 203, 211, 218, 221, 225, 238, 248, 260, 273, 274, 277
Worsthorne, Peregrine, 209
Wright, Mr Justice, 104, 105
Wyatt, Petronella, 34

Yew, Lee Kuan, 271
Yom Kippur, 274
Young, Lord, 156
Yugoslavia, 19

Zangwill, Israel, 93
Zola, Emile, 42
Zorin, V.A., 44